CREATE YOUR OWN FAMILY HISTORY COOKBOOK

Dear Reader,

For the first time there is a book that will help you create your own Family History Cookbook. The easy-to-use templates on my Web site at www.NancyMilesInGoodTaste.com will get you started on your own family heirloom.

—Nancy J. Miles

1. Click on the "Contact Me" tab on the menu bar. Fill out the template with all of your contact information, including your e-mail address. Under "Additional questions and comments," type in "Request access codes." You will then be e-mailed the codes to access the templates.

2. Once you receive your access codes, return to the web site and click on "Templates" in the menu bar. Enter your codes and you will be able to download the templates to personalize your own cookbook cover as well as a template for your family history recipes.

3. Open the Microsoft Word document for the Cover Template, highlight the name in the title with your cursor and type in your own family name. Print this full size on your printer and insert it into your own three-ring binder with a clear plastic window.

4. Next download the Recipe Template which is also a Microsoft Word document.

5. With your cursor, highlight RECIPE TITLE and type in the title of your own recipe.

6. Next highlight the HISTORY OF ANCESTOR copy and type in your ancestor's name from whom the recipe has come and a little bit of information about them and about the recipe.

7. Proceed and highlight the INSERT PHOTO HERE, then go to INSERT on the tool bar above, click on PICTURE and locate the photo you want to use where you have saved it on your computer. Do not drag and drop. It will not work.

8. And finally, highlight the INGREDIENTS AND INSTRUCT-IONS and type in your recipe.

9. Print it, punch it and add it to your binder!

Note: If you have a handwritten recipe from your grandmother, your mother, etc., scan the recipe and save it as a JPG in the same folder where you are saving your photos for the recipes and just insert it in the INGREDIENTS AND INSTRUCTIONS box.

Create Your Own Personalized Cover

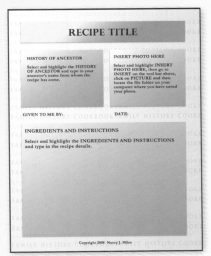
Recipe Template

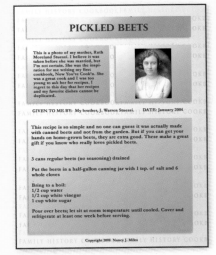
Example of Finished Recipe Page

Some of our happiest memories are of when we spent time at the Miles' home. We love going for dinner and enjoying Nancy's creative flair with food! She is always coming up with new ideas and recipes. Her home has been a haven for young and old alike. She really knows how to entertain and make people feel warm and welcome. I am so excited about this new cookbook!

—*Leslie Tall*

What a special treasure to have all your recipes in one terrific book like *In Good Taste*. How many times have I looked through shelves of recipe books trying to find a certain recipe? Now it's goodbye to all the old recipe books.

—*Joan R. Thomsen*

Nancy Miles is the best cook we know. Our copy of her *Now You're Cook'n* cookbook is hardly legible from using the recipes so often. Growing up, my little brother would ask Nancy to make her famous pickled beets for his birthday and Christmas. Potato Cheese Soup is a staple around our home. Her Texas Sheet Cake is so easy and delicious, people always ask us for the recipe when we make it. However, our all-time favorite recipe is her Licorice Creams. They taste like a little bite of heaven.

—*Emily and Russ Carlson*

Every cook should have a copy of *In Good Taste*. It is the final word on cooking. Whenever I use Nancy's recipes, people tell me I'm the world's greatest cook. Little do they know I just use the world's greatest cookbook.

—*Lana F. Richardson*

As far as I know, my mom, Nancy Miles, has always loved to cook. Her real joy of cooking comes from feeding others good food. Countless times she has created special dishes to accommodate my vegetarian eating habits, experimenting with tofu and organic vegetables. She always goes out of her way to make great food that everyone will love and she certainly has succeeded with me.

—*Lori Miles*

I have known Nancy all of her life. I'm her sister, Carol. She has always been involved with the art of cooking. I have never seen anyone who enjoys cooking and entertaining more than she does. She has a talent for bringing people and good food together. Nothing makes her happier than seeing friends and family enjoying her good recipes and the time they spend together. Everyone looks forward to being invited to her home and enjoying something new that she has created. Nancy is the best cook I know.

—*Carol Dyson*

There is always something wonderful cooking at Nancy's house . . . and here are all her recipes—all in one place. Thanks, Nancy, for *In Good Taste*. My old *Now You're Cook'n* is worn out!

—*Gayle Thacker*

Nancy's recipes are as fun and as full of personality as she is.

—*Lory Erickson*

Nancy is a wild woman. She can make even a sandwich exciting!

—*Sue Holmes*

I have attended dinners at Nancy's and participated in cooking classes with her. I loved the food and learned valuable cooking tips that I didn't know. This cookbook is a fantastic addition to any kitchen.

—*Janna Ormond*

I spent many days and nights in Nancy's home and a good part of that time lingering in her kitchen. For Nancy, cooking was not a production out of the ordinary. Frequently I would visit to find Nancy bringing a pot of soup or chili to a simmer. My mouth is watering just thinking of her chili—one bowl was never enough. At Christmas I expected to find a variety of chocolates and treats ready for assembly—gifts for family and friends. I loved being an "official" taster. I am anxious to open her new book of secrets and try to duplicate the flavors I enjoyed as a youth.

—*Toni Baker*

I always remembered hanging out in Nancy's kitchen. She made us amazing cabbage rolls on request one time. Haven't had those in forever—sounds really good right now. With *In Good Taste*, I can have the recipe and try to make them myself.

—*Dale Rogers*

I'm absolutely thrilled with Nancy's success! Congratulations! She is an amazing woman and I'm so delighted with the new cookbook!

—*Paula Fellingham*

During a recent kitchen renovation, I found myself needing to pack away my cookbooks. With upcoming family functions, I had to have access to basic recipes. The only cookbook I didn't pack so I could refer to it was Nancy's first cookbook, *Now You're Cook'n*. It truly was an invaluable book. Now I have *In Good Taste* to complement it!

—*Linda Sue Forrister*

Nancy's original thinking and home-spun techniques produce sensational menus and meals. Everyone should have the good fortune to share in Nancy's cooking talents. Now they can with *In Good Taste*.

—*Bob and Donna Knowlton*

How wonderful that Nancy is sharing her amazing recipes with the world. I am so excited to have *In Good Taste* in my kitchen.

—*Erica Williams*

Nancy makes the most unbelievable chocolates. During the holidays she has a table full of homemade goodies hidden away for presents. Whenever I am in the house, I make sure to sneak away and snatch as many treats as possible!

—*Chris Walsh, Australia*

Nancy and I have been cooking for years, in fact we have even collaborated on a cookbook of our own. But she has beaten me to it yet again with this fantastic new cookbook. Congratulations, Nancy!

—*Sandi Anderson*

Nancy is one of my dearest friends and so when I learned that she was writing a new cookbook, I was so excited I couldn't stand it! *In Good Taste* is everything I had hoped it would be!

—*April Carter*

BookWise Publishing
65 E. Wadsworth Park Drive
Suite 110
Salt Lake City, Utah 84020
801 676-2420
www.bookwisewritewise.com

To contact Nancy Miles:
In Good Taste
P. O. Box 95347
South Jordan, UT 84095-0347
www.NancyMilesInGoodTaste.com
njmiles@mac.com

Book Design by Paul Killpack, Highland, Utah

Library of Congress Cataloging-in-Publication Data: Pending

LCN #2008928039

In Good Taste / Nancy Miles

ISBN 978-1-60645-001-7

First Printing

10 9 8 7 6 5 4 3 2 1

Printed in China

In Good Taste

Nancy J. Miles

TABLE OF CONTENTS

In Good Taste

Let me introduce Nancy Miles. She is an inventor, an artist, a business woman; she sings, she teaches, and above all else, she loves to cook!

Growing up in a household replete with German and Swiss heritage, wholesome, soul-satisfying food was abundant in her childhood home. For decades Nancy collected favorite recipes from good cooks in her family. As she grew up and left home, she met even more amazing cooks who shared their favorite coveted dishes with her. With years of recipe compilation and cooking experience behind her, Nancy made many of these recipes into her own original recipes. Her passion for good food and love for people snowballed into an amazing recipe collection from around the world.

When Nancy's daughter, Lori Jane, was born, priorities shifted somewhat but she knew that she didn't want these recipes that had become so special to her to fall by the wayside and be lost. So she started writing them down. Nancy conjectured that if Lori would enjoy the recipe collection, so would some of her closest friends, family members and work acquaintances. That is how Nancy's first book, *Now You're Cook'n*, was born. After it was published, she gave a lot of the books away as gifts and all of a sudden, the book was in demand!

Since then as years have passed, Nancy has continued to collect more wonderful recipes. The result is a revised, and perfected collection of all of her best recipes for everyone to enjoy—*In Good Taste* is the only cookbook you will ever need.

With the support of John, Nancy's dear husband of 30 years, she now is ready to share her love of cooking with family, friends—old and new— and the rest of the world.

In Good Taste will be the best cooking investment you will make, eliminating frustration at cooking time and garnering amazing praise at meal time.

—Gregg Stuessi, Executive Chef

Appetizers

DEVILED EGGS

These delicious deviled eggs make a great appetizer to take to a family party or get-together.

8 hard boiled eggs
1/8 tsp dry mustard
1/2 tsp prepared mustard
1 Tbsp sweet pickle relish
1 Tbsp rice vinegar
1 tsp sugar
Salt and pepper to taste
Enough salad dressing (not mayonnaise) to make a good mixture

- *Peel the eggs, cut them in half and separate the yolks from the whites; save the egg whites.*
- *Lightly mash the yolks with a fork and add the next ingredients.*
- *Fill whites with a heaping amount of yolk mixture.*
- *Sprinkle with paprika and refrigerate.*
- *Makes 16 individual eggs.*

MEXICAN APPETIZER

This great appetizer comes from Gayle Thacker of Bluffdale, Utah.

1 regular can of white albacore tuna
1 jalapeño pepper chopped very fine with seeds removed
Enough mayonnaise to hold mixture together

- *Place in a small baking dish and top with cheddar cheese.*
- *Bake at 350° until the cheese bubbles.*
- *Remove from the oven and top with salsa.*
- *Serve with chips.*

LETTUCE WRAPS

This is a wonderful buffet party dish.

4 precooked Mesquite-flavored chicken breasts, cut into 1/2 inch cubes
1 cup diced carrots
1/2 cup green onions, sliced
1/4 cup chopped slivered almonds, toasted
1 Tbsp fresh cilantro, minced
1 head butter lettuce

Combine the following in a bowl:

3 Tbsp soy sauce
1 Tbsp Hoisin Sauce (found in the Oriental food section of your grocer)
5 tsp cornstarch
3 tsp minced garlic
3/4 tsp sugar

- *Mix with chicken and let stand for 15 minutes.*

Then combine:

1 Tbsp soy sauce
1 tsp cornstarch
1/2 cup water

- *Heat 1 Tbsp oil in a hot skillet.*
- *Add chicken and stir-fry for 4 minutes; remove from heat.*
- *Add 1 Tbsp oil to skillet and stir-fry carrots and 1 tsp garlic for another minute.*
- *Add green onions and continue cooking for another minute.*
- *Add soy sauce mixture and chicken.*
- *Stir-fry until mixture thickens.*
- *Stir in almonds and cilantro.*
- *Fill each lettuce leaf with chicken mixture; wrap lettuce around filling and eat by hand.*

NOTE

Substitute ground beef for chicken sometimes or, as an option, add additional sauce to the chicken mixture and serve over rice.

10

CHEESE LOG

Two 8 oz packages of cream cheese, softened
2 Tbsp Worcestershire Sauce
2 Tbsp minced onion
1 Package Deli ham or lunch meat, chopped finely

- *Mix ingredients in a bowl and form into a log.*
- *Wrap in plastic wrap.*
- *Chill overnight.*
- *Serve with your choice of crackers.*

DILL PICKLES — SWEET & HOT

This recipe is from my good friend, Josette Rogers Davis. These pickles are hot and crisp. I don't think I have ever met anyone who enjoyed these pickles more than Dawn Adams, one of my fellow-workers, in Chico, California.

1 gallon of whole dill pickles, any brand

Brine:

4 cups sugar
1/2 oz garlic juice
One 20 oz bottle of Tabasco Sauce
1/2 cup tarragon vinegar
1½ tsp alum

- *Remove pickles from the jar, saving the juice.*
- *Slice pickles into spears and return to the jar.*
- *Warm brine until the sugar is melted and pour it over pickles.*
- *Fill the jar with left over juice you saved.*
- *Let it sit overnight on counter, then refrigerate for one week.*

> ### NOTE
>
> These pickles need to cure for at least one week.
>
> Pickling is a way to preserve foods for out-of-season but is now widely used mainly because of the variety of flavors. With pickles themselves, you'll find them sweet or sour, hot or mild, salty, garlicky, and lots of other flavors in between. Try them all.

GLAZED NUTS

1 cup nuts, any kind
1/4 cup sugar

- *In a small skillet, sprinkle nuts with sugar and cook over medium heat until they are coated and the sugar is dissolved.*
- *Use these in green salads or in vegetables.*

LINDA SUE'S SMOKY CHEESE BALL

From Linda Sue Forrister of Chico, California, this has become a tradition at holiday times. Start making your own traditions; use the Family History Cookbook Template on my website.

11

Two 8 oz packages of cream cheese, softened
2 cups, shredded smoky cheddar cheese
1/2 cup butter, softened
2 Tbsp milk
2 tsp steak sauce
1 cup of finely chopped nuts

- *Put in mixer and beat until fluffy.*
- *Chill slightly and shape into balls.*
- *Roll in finely chopped nuts.*
- *Makes 2 to 3 cheese balls.*

SWEET & HOT RELISH DIP

One 8 oz package of cream cheese, softened
1/2 jar Harry and David's Sweet 'n' Hot Pepper & Onion Relish

- *Mix relish and cream until smooth.*
- *For a variety, add drained, crushed pineapple to the mixture.*
- *Serve with chips and crackers.*

TOMATO SANDWICHES

These make a great party sandwich.

- *Pick tomatoes that are large enough to fit on round slices of bread.*
- *Peel tomatoes by dropping them in boiling water for just long enough to have skins split. Remove the skin and put the tomato in ice water.*
- *Slice the tomatoes and place them on a paper towel to drain a bit.*
- *Sprinkle with seasoning salt.*
- *Using a round biscuit cutter, cut rounds from white and brown bread.*

Topping Mixture:

Mayonnaise
Salt
Fresh ground pepper
Fresh, finely grated onion or a thin slice of red onion

- *Spread mixture on a slice of bread, add a slice of tomato, and cover with opposite color of bread.*
- *Put a dollop of mayonnaise on top of each slice of bread and a tiny piece of parsley.*
- *Serve immediately.*

CORN DIP

This is wonderful with tortilla chips or as an appetizer. It comes from Taralee Enger.

1 can of Green Giant Mexican Corn
1 can regular corn, drained
1/2 cup mayonnaise
1/2 cup sour cream
1 jalapeño pepper, seeded and chopped
One 4 oz can green chopped chili peppers, drained
1 cup cheddar or Jack cheese
Dash of garlic salt
2/3 cup green onions, chopped

- *Mix all ingredients together and chill before serving.*
- *Serve with tortilla chips, crackers or appetizer breads.*
- *Or spread on crackers or breads and broil until the cheese melts.*

OYSTER CRACKER SNACKS

These are great with chili and soup.

Two 12 oz packages of Oyster crackers
1 cup canola oil
2 tsp dill weed
1½ tsp garlic salt
2 packages of Original Ranch Dressing, use the dry mix only (the one that uses buttermilk)

- *Mix all but the crackers in a large zip-lock bag and shake well.*
- *Add crackers and shake bag until all crackers are well coated.*
- *Transfer to a clean bag and store.*

TWO-INGREDIENT CHEESE BALL

It's faster to make this cheese ball than to get in the car, drive to the store, decide which cheese ball to get, go through the line, pay, get back in the car—you get the idea.

Two 8 oz packages of cream cheese at room temperature
1 package of Hidden Valley Ranch Dressing mix (dry)
Pecans or walnuts

- *Mix all ingredients together and from into a ball.*
- *Roll cheese ball in chopped nuts.*
- *Wrap in plastic wrap until ready to serve.*
- *Serve with a variety of crackers on a serving plate or platter.*

SMOKIE LINK APPETIZERS

3 packages of small Smokie Links
1½ cups real maple syrup
4 Tbsp brown sugar
2 tsp prepared mustard

- *Mix together the syrup, brown sugar and mustard.*
- *Cook on medium heat until sugar has dissolved.*
- *Add links and cook an additional 30 minutes.*
- *Keep warm in a crock pot.*
- *Serve with toothpicks.*

12

Mexican Chip Dip

This is always the most popular item on the party tray.

1 large can of jalapeño bean dip
3/4 cup sour cream
4 Tbsp salsa
2 tomatoes, diced
Cheddar cheese, shredded
Avocado, chopped (put in a small amount of
   lemon juice to keep its color)
1 small can of black olives, chopped or sliced
Tortilla chips

- *On a large platter, spread the dip, leaving room around the edge to put tortilla chips.*

Layer as follows:

Salsa
Sour cream
Tomatoes
Cheese
Avocado
Olives

- *Finish top with dollops of salsa and sour cream*
- *Place tortilla chips around edges.*

Party Cheese Balls

12 oz cream cheese, softened
1/2 tsp Worcestershire Sauce
4 green onions, finely chopped
1 to 1½ package of dried pressed beef, chopped
Parsley, chopped

- *Mix all but the parsley together to form a ball.*
- *Roll in chopped parsley, wrap in plastic wrap.*
- *Refrigerate at least overnight.*

Party Nuts

4 cups almonds, walnuts, peanuts, pecans, etc.
2 eggs, whites only
1 cup sugar
Dash of salt
1/2 cup butter, melted

- *Toast nuts at 350° for 10 to 12 minutes or until lightly brown.*
- *Whisk egg whites, sugar and salt by hand until stiff.*
- *Fold mixture into the nuts.*
- *Put the melted butter in a jelly roll pan.*
- *Spread whipped mixture over nuts.*
- *Bake at 325° for 30 minutes, stirring every 10 minutes until butter is gone.*

Sheepherder's Dip

13

This dish has been around and should stay around. The bread bowl can be eaten when the dip is finished.

1 large round of Sheepherder's bread (from a
   bakery or use Brown and Serve loaves)
Fresh spinach, chopped in food processor
1½ cups sour cream
1 cup mayonnaise (do not use salad dressing)
1 package of dry Knorr Vegetable Soup/Recipe Mix
3 green onions, chopped
Garlic salt to taste

- *Cut the top off the bread and remove the insides making it look like a bowl.*
- *Cut the insides from the bread bowl into bite-size pieces.*
- *Blend remaining ingredients together and chill.*
- *When ready to serve, fill the bread bowl and serve with the cut-up pieces of bread.*

APPETIZERS

What is a party without an appetizer? You can never go wrong taking an appetizer to a get-together of any kind. The sky is the limit and you will always be a welcome guest!

NOTES

Beverages

NANCY'S LEMONADE

This is the best lemonade ever.

1 cup freshly squeezed lemon juice
1 cup sugar
5 cups water

- *Mix well with ice.*

LEMONADE

1 large lemon sliced thinly
1½ cups sugar
7 cups cold water
2 cups fresh lemon juice (from about 12 lemons)
Ice (for serving)

16

- *Using a potato masher, mash the lemon slices and sugar in deep bowl until the slices release their juice and the sugar begins to dissolve.*
- *Stir in water and lemon juice until the sugar completely dissolves.*
- *Strain out lemon slices and chill or pour over ice before serving.*
- *Refrigerate for up to 3 days.*
- *This is best served with crushed ice.*

OPTION

This makes the best, refreshing fruit drink. To a quart of this lemonade, add one container of Crystal Light Raspberry Ice soft drink mix. Do not add any additional sugar or water.

HOT CHOCOLATE MIX

This makes enough for seventeen servings and is great for gift jars.

One 25.6 oz package instant nonfat dry milk
   (measures 10 2/3 cups)
One 6 oz jar powdered non dairy creamer
2 cups powdered sugar
One 16 oz can of instant chocolate drink mix,
   Nestle Quick works well

- *Mix ingredients well in a large bowl.*
- *Put in an airtight container. Quart jars work well.*
- *Be sure and put the directions on the container, especially if you're using it for a gift.*
- *Directions: Add 3 heaping Tbsp to 8 oz hot water.*

HOT CHOCOLATE

One 14 oz can Sweetened condensed milk
1/2 cup cocoa powder
Pinch of salt
6½ cups boiling water
1½ tsp vanilla

- *Heat ingredients together and slowly add boiling water.*
- *Remove from heat and add vanilla.*
- *Serve with real whipped cream.*
- *Serves 6.*

LEMON PARTY PUNCH

6 cups cold water
1 container Crystal Light Pink Lemonade
1 cup ice cubes
1 cup ginger ale
1 cup orange juice

- *Mix water and Crystal Light in pitcher and stir until dissolved.*
- *Add ice, ginger ale and orange juice.*

PARTY PUNCH

2 small bottles of Hawaiian Punch concentrate
Two 2 liter bottles of cold 7-Up
2 pints pineapple sherbet
Two 10 oz packages of frozen strawberries, crushed
4 ripe bananas, mashed

- *Mix all ingredients together and serve immediately.*

SHERBET PUNCH

Two 2 liter bottles of cold strawberry soda
1/2 gallon pineapple sherbet

- *Mix together and serve immediately.*

SLUSH PUNCH

This is ranked #1 by our family. Make it a day or so ahead of time to allow for freezing.

7 cups water
4 cups sugar
One 6 oz package of Banana/Strawberry Jell-O
One 20 oz can crushed pineapple
Two 10 oz packages of frozen strawberries
1 tsp of grated lemon rind
Three 2 liter bottles of cold 7-Up

- *Boil the water and sugar together in a large pot.*
- *Add the Jell-O, stir and let cool.*
- *Add pineapple, strawberries and lemon rind and mix well.*
- *Put in freezer container until ready to serve.*
- *When ready to serve, remove from freezer and let sit at room temperature for one hour.*
- *Mix 1/3 of the frozen mix to three 2 liter bottles of cold 7-Up.*

NOTE

If you don't chill 7-Up before you mix it into a frozen mixture, it has a tendency to go flat. This is true any time you use the bubbly stuff. It should be very cold.

FROSTED PUNCH

2 small cans of frozen limeade concentrate
3 cups water
Two 2 liters lemon-lime soda, chilled
1 cup lime sherbet

- *Mix limeade, water and soda in a large punch bowl.*
- *Spoon sherbet into mixture.*
- *Serve immediately.*
- *Serves 12 to 18.*

MULLED CIDER

This hot cider is a must for Halloween parties or just on a cold winter night.

12 cups apple cider
2 cups orange juice
3/4 cup light brown sugar, firmly packed
1½ tsp whole allspice
1½ tsp whole cloves
10 to 15 sticks of cinnamon, for garnish

- *Combine cider, orange juice and brown sugar in a large pot.*
- *Wrap the allspice and cloves in a piece of cheesecloth; tie at the top with string.*
- *Drop spice pack into the cider and bring to a boil.*
- *Reduce heat and simmer covered for 15 minutes.*
- *Remove spice bag and discard it.*
- *Serve in mugs with cinnamon sticks in each cup.*
- *Serves about 15.*

17

NOTES

Breakfast

BAKED PANCAKES

These are also known as German pancakes.

- *Melt 4 Tbsp butter on bottom of a 9 x 13 baking pan in a warm oven.*

Combine in blender:

6 eggs
1 cup flour
1 cup milk
1/4 cup orange juice
1/4 tsp salt
1/2 cup sugar

- *Fold in fresh or frozen raspberries, cranberries, blueberries, etc.*
- *Pour into the buttered pan and bake for 30 minutes at 350° or until brown.*
- *Serve with syrup or powdered sugar.*

20

BLUEBERRY PANCAKES

1 cup milk
4 Tbsp butter
2 large eggs
1¼ cups flour
1½ Tbsp sugar
4 tsp baking powder
Pinch of salt
2½ cups fresh or frozen blueberries

- *Heat milk and butter just until the butter melts.*
- *Stir and set aside until cool.*
- *In a large bowl, beat eggs with a fork.*
- *Add the cooled milk mixture and beat well.*
- *In another bowl, combine flour, sugar, baking powder and salt.*
- *Mix while gradually adding the milk and eggs, stirring with a spoon just until batter is combined. Do not over mix.*
- *Gently stir in berries.*
- *Spray griddle with vegetable oil.*
- *Ladle batter onto the griddle and cook on one side until the berries split open.*
- *Turn and cook for 20 to 30 seconds longer.*
- *Serve with Blueberry-Maple Syrup (next page).*

STRAWBERRY BUTTER

One 10 oz package of frozen or fresh strawberries
1 cup butter, softened
1 cup powdered sugar, sifted

- *Blend all ingredients on high speed until smooth.*
- *Refrigerate until ready to use.*
- *Makes 2½ cups.*

GRANOLA

This is a recipe shared by a Bed and Breakfast in St. George, Utah. They named it "P. F." Granola.

8 to 9 cups of oats (not quick oats)
1½ cup light brown sugar, packed
1 cup whole almonds, raw
1 cup pecans, raw
1 cup hazel nuts, raw
1 cup cashews or pine nuts
1 to 2 cups ribbon coconut
1/2 cup sunflower seeds
White raisins

In a large pan, heat the following:

1/2 cup water
1/2 cup olive oil
1/2 cup honey
1/2 cup chunky peanut butter

- *Add 2½ tsp vanilla.*
- *Spread on cookie sheets in a single layer.*
- *Bake at 200° for 2 to 3 hours, stirring several times.*
- *Remove from heat and add white raisins.*

APRICOT-PINEAPPLE JAM

This jam comes from my niece, Carrie Severn, now living in Illinois.

5 cups of fresh apricots
5 cups sugar
One 3 oz package of pineapple or apricot Jell-O
1/2 cup crushed pineapple

- *Put apricots, sugar and pineapple in a large pot.*
- *Bring to a boil and cook for 20 minutes.*
- *Turn burner off and add Jell-O.*
- *Mix well and put into canning jars and seal.*

SAUSAGE & EGG BREAKFAST CASSEROLE

Leslie Tall prepares this recipe when we get together in Island Park, Idaho. Make it the night before.

6 slices of bread (any kind), cubed
1½ lbs ground sausage, browned and drained
1 lb mild cheddar or a combination of cheddar and Jack cheese, shredded
8 eggs, beaten
2 cups whole milk
1 tsp salt
Pepper to taste
Canned, chopped Jalapenos, optional
Sliced mushrooms, optional
Chopped onion, optional

- *Spray a 9 x 13 inch baking dish with vegetable spray.*
- *Cover the bottom of the dish with cubed bread.*
- *Mix the eggs, milk, salt, and pepper together.*
- *Add any optional ingredients.*
- *Cover with cooked sausage.*
- *Sprinkle with cheese.*
- *Pour egg mixture on top.*
- *Bake 45 minutes at 325°.*
- *Let sit for 5 minutes.*
- *Cut in squares.*
- *Serves 8 to 10 people.*

HONEY BUTTER

Everyone can find a use for honey butter—homemade bread, rolls, toast with peanut butter, pancakes or waffles. Put some in little plastic cups that have lids and give them with bread as gifts.

1 cup butter, softened
1 cup honey
1/2 tsp vanilla

- *Beat ingredients in an electric mixer for 2 to 3 minutes.*
- *Spoon into small containers with lids or into a plastic container with a lid.*
- *This keeps well in the refrigerator for 3 to 4 weeks.*

BLUEBERRY-MAPLE SYRUP

1 cup blueberries, fresh or frozen
½ cup maple syrup
1 tsp lemon juice

- *Heat 1 cup fresh or frozen blueberries and ½ cup pure maple syrup.*
- *Heat for a few minutes until berries split.*
- *Strain through cheesecloth.*
- *Add 1 tsp lemon juice to the strained juice.*
- *Serve warm.*

STRAWBERRY JAM

This is the recipe I use to triple a batch of jam. Do not follow the recipe that comes with the box of pectin. This is a technique I learned from a very old woman. You have to watch it to know how to tell when the jam is jelled. It will save you preparing, cleaning up and cooking the jam three times.

15 cups of crushed fresh strawberries
2 cups water
1/4 cup lemon juice
15 cups sugar (pre-measure so it's ready to use)
3 boxes pectin

- *Put strawberries, water and lemon juice in a very large kettle, such as a canning kettle.*
- *Add pectin one package at a time, mixing well after each package. Do not turn the heat on until this process is done, making sure there are no lumps of pectin.*
- *Cook over medium high heat until it comes to an rolling boil (a boil that cannot be stirred down). This may take up to 30 minutes.*
- *Quickly add the sugar, stirring fast and mixing well.*
- *Bring to another boil.*
- *Cook until the jam sheets off a large metal spoon. When two separate drops come together as one big drop, it is ready to bottle. This could take an additional 30 minutes.*
- *Bottle while the jam is still very hot in hot sterile bottles.*
- *Makes about 15 pints.*

STUFFED FRENCH TOAST

1 loaf of French bread sliced into one inch thick slices, 2 slices per serving

Mix together:

One 8 oz package of cream cheese at room temperature
1 pint of fresh strawberries, chopped small and sweetened with sugar

- *Spread a good amount of cream cheese mixture on a slice of the bread and top with another piece of bread.*
- *Place them on a cookie sheet.*

Beat together:

4 eggs
1 cup half & half
1/2 tsp vanilla
1/4 tsp nutmeg

- *Melt butter on a griddle or in a large skillet.*
- *Dip both sides of bread in the egg mixture.*
- *Grill on both sides until nicely browned.*
- *Remove and put in a baking dish in a 250° oven until ready to serve.*

Topping:

One 12 oz jar of apricot preserves
1/2 cup orange juice

- *Heat ingredients together and put in serving pitcher*
- *Dust each serving with powdered sugar.*

22

COOKED WHEAT

This is also known as bulgur and is a "super food." It is 100% wheat. The recipe calls for a pressure cooker.

2 cups of wheat kernels or "berries"
4 cups water
2 Tbsp salt

- *Put all ingredients in a 5 quart pressure cooker.*
- *Bring to high heat then reduce to low.*
- *Cook for 55 minutes.*
- *Let cool naturally (a natural release).*

> **NOTE**
>
> Ways to use bulgur: as a base for a salad such as Tabouli, as a substitute for couscous, as a hot cereal, as a replacement for rice or stuffing, even as an additive for meat, such as meatloaf. See more recipes in the index.

PERFECT SCRAMBLED EGGS

This recipe is perfect for young people just leaving home for the first time who may not know how to do some basic cooking. My brother, Richard, taught me how to cook them when I was in my twenties. One of the best vacations I ever had was visiting him in Kansas City.

6 eggs
3 Tbsp water (this is the secret to light eggs)
2 Tbsp melted butter
3 drops of Tabasco sauce
Dash of onion salt (my addition)
Salt and pepper to taste

- *Whisk all ingredients together with a fork and pour into a non-stick skillet sprayed with vegetable oil.*
- *Cook over medium heat; with a heat-resistant spatula, gently lift the eggs as they cook, letting the uncooked egg fill the open space.*

  Do not overcook as the eggs will get too dry.

Breads

CREAM CHEESE ROLLS

These are very quick and easy.

2 packages refrigerator Crescent Rolls
**Two 8 oz packages cream cheese at room
    temperature**
2 Tbsp sugar
I tsp lemon juice
I cup powdered sugar
2 Tbsp milk
I tsp vanilla

- *Preheat oven to 375°.*
- *Separate each portion of dough to form 8 rectangles.*

Mix together:

Cream cheese
Sugar
Lemon juice

- *Spread mixture on one side of each dough rectangle.*
- *Roll up jellyroll-style starting with long end.*
- *Cut each roll into six 1 inch thick slices.*
- *Place on a greased 9 x 13 pan.*
- *Bake at 375° for 15 minutes until lightly browned.*
- *In the meantime mix powdered sugar, milk and vanilla.*
- *Drizzle over hot rolls.*

24

> ### NOTE
> How many times have you had your bananas turn black and thrown them in the garbage? Too many, right? Well, 15 minutes is all it takes to mix up a couple of loaves of banana bread that the whole family will love, not to mention the wonderful aroma of it baking. Your banana bread fans will come running!

BANANA BREAD

1¾ cups all purpose flour
2/3 cup sugar
2 tsp baking powder
1/2 tsp baking soda
1/4 tsp salt
3 ripe medium bananas, mashed
1/3 cup butter or margarine
2 Tbsp milk
2 eggs
1/4 to 1/2 cup chopped nuts

- *Mix together half of the flour, all of the sugar, baking powder, baking soda and salt.*
- *Add the mashed bananas, butter and milk.*
- *Beat in electric mixer on high for 2 minutes.*
- *Add eggs and remaining flour and blend together.*
- *Add nuts.*
- *Put in 3 greased mini loaf pans—5¾ inches x 3¼ inches—at 350° for 35 to 45 minutes.*
- *Cool on a wire rack.*
- *As an option add chopped cherries*

BLUEBERRY MUFFINS WITH TOPPING

3/4 cup sugar
1/4 cup margarine
1/2 tsp salt
I egg
1/2 cup milk
1½ cups flour
2 tsp baking powder
I cup well drained blueberries

- *Mix all ingredients together in the order listed until just blended.*

Topping:

1/2 cup sugar
1/2 tsp cinnamon
1/4 cup butter
1/2 cup flour

- *Mix until texture is like course cornmeal.*
- *Fill muffin tins ¾ full; sprinkle with topping.*
- *Bake 400° for 25 to 30 minutes.*

In Good Taste

BANANA CHERRY NUT BREAD

This was my Aunt Evelyn's recipe. She was from the German side of my family and was a great cook. Several of her recipes are in this book.

1 cup shortening
1 cup sugar
2 eggs, beaten
1/4 cup nuts, chopped (walnut or pecan)
2 large, very ripe bananas, mashed
2 to 2½ cups flour (watch as you mix it; not too moist or too dry)
1/4 tsp salt
1 tsp baking soda
1 tsp cinnamon
Maraschino cherries, chopped and well drained (as many as you would want and optional)

- Cream shortening and sugar, add beaten eggs.
- Add flour and baking soda, mashed bananas, nuts and cherries.
- Put in small loaf pans.
- Bake at 350° for 35 to 45 minutes.
- Makes 3 small loaves.

CORNBREAD

Normally I'm not a fan of cornbread, but this is excellent because it has more of a cake texture. So if you like cake, you should like this.

2 eggs, beaten
1 cup milk
1/2 cup butter or margarine
2 cups Bisquick
1/2 cup cornmeal
1/2 cup sugar
1/2 tsp baking powder

- Mix all together; do not beat or over mix; the texture will be lumpy.
- Pour into a 9 x 9 inch greased baking dish.
- Bake at 350° for 30 to 35 minutes.

PUMPKIN CHOCOLATE CHIP MUFFINS

Mix together:

4 eggs
2 cups sugar
One 16 oz can pumpkin
1½ cups vegetable oil

Combine:

3 cups all-purpose flour
2 tsp baking soda
2 tsp baking powder
1 tsp ground cinnamon
1 tsp salt

Add:

2 cups, or 12 oz, semi-sweet chocolate chips

- In a large mixing bowl, beat eggs, sugar, pumpkin and oil until smooth.
- Fill greased or paper-lined muffin cups ¾ full.
- Bake at 400° for 16 to 20 minutes or until muffins test done.
- Cool in pan 10 minutes.

SEASONED DINNER ROLLS

1/2 cup butter, melted
1 package Chili Seasoning Mix
Brown and Serve dinner rolls
- Brush butter and chili seasoning mixture on top of Brown and Serve dinner rolls.
- Bake as instructed on package.

Cinnamon Rolls Made Easy

You may think this is cheating, but when you eat them, who cares?

1 loaf of frozen white or wheat bread, thawed
Cinnamon
Butter at room temperature
Granulated sugar
Raisins (optional)
Nuts, chopped (optional)

- *Preheat oven to 250°.*
- *Roll out bread in a strip approximately 15 inches long and 9 inches wide.*
- *Spread soft butter on top.*
- *Sprinkle with cinnamon, sugar, nuts and raisins.*
- *Roll up lengthwise and cut into 2 inch pieces.*
- *Put 7 rolls in each round pie tin sprayed with vegetable spray.*
- *Turn off oven and place rolls in oven.*
- *Let rise for 25 minutes or intil one inch over the top of the pan.*
- *Turn oven to 375° and bake 25 minutes.*
- *Top with glaze while rolls are still hot.*

Glaze:

1/2 cup powdered sugar
1/2 tsp vanilla
1 Tbsp butter, room temperature
Just enough milk to make the icing pourable

- *Mix until smooth and pourable.*
- *Drizzle over top of hot rolls.*
- *Makes approximately 12 to 14 rolls.*

Onion Cheese Bread

This is excellent with chili or stew.

1½ cups buttermilk
1 egg
3 cups Bisquick
1/2 envelope of dry onion soup mix
1 cup cheddar cheese, shredded

- *Combine buttermilk and egg in a bowl.*
- *Stir in Bisquick, soup mix, cheese and mix well.*
- *Pour into an 8 x 5 loaf pan.*
- *Bake at 350° for 45 to 50 minutes.*
- *Remove and place on a cooling rack.*

Monkey Bread

This is a great birthday gift for friends or neighbors. Deliver it first thing in the morning.

3 containers of refrigerator biscuits
2 tsp cinnamon
1 cup sugar

- *Mix the cinnamon and sugar together in a large zip-lock bag.*
- *Cut each biscuit into 4 pieces and place in the bag.*
- *Butter a Bundt pan and sprinkle the bottom with chopped nuts.*
- *Place half of the biscuit pieces in the bottom of the pan.*
- *Sprinkle half of the remaining sugar mix over biscuits and repeat.*

Topping:

1/4 cup butter or margarine
1 tsp cinnamon
1 cup light brown sugar

- *Mix all ingredients in a saucepan over low heat, until dissolved. Do not overheat.*
- *Pour over biscuits.*
- *Bake at 350° for 30 to 40 minutes.*
- *Cool 10 minutes and turn upside down on a plate.*
- *Serve warm, if possible.*

BANANA-NUT BREAD

Everyone needs a good banana-nut bread recipe.

1/2 cup shortening (use the convenient sticks of shortening)
1½ cups sugar
2 eggs, well beaten
4 Tbsp buttermilk or white vinegar
2 cups cake flour (this helps make the bread less heavy and more like a light cake
1/2 tsp baking soda
1 tsp vanilla
1 cup chopped nuts, optional
1 to 1½ cups (it depends on how large they are) ripe bananas, mashed

- *Mix shortening, sugar, eggs and buttermilk or vinegar by hand.*
- *Put in greased bread pans.*
- *Bake at 350° for 45 to 60 minutes.*
- *Makes 2 medium loaves.*

CARAMEL PECAN PULL-A-PARTS

Prepare these the night before. They're a perfect gift to take to a neighbor.

24 pieces of frozen dinner rolls
3/4 cup light brown sugar
One 3.5 oz package of Jell-O Cook & Serve Butterscotch Pudding (don't use instant and use the dry mix only)
1 tsp cinnamon
1/2 cup chopped pecans or walnuts (optional)
Squeeze butter

- *Place frozen dinner rolls in a well-greased Bundt pan.*
- *Sprinkle with the brown sugar, dry pudding mix, cinnamon and nuts.*
- *Drizzle butter over the top.*
- *Cover with a clean towel and let rise overnight.*
- *In the morning, bake at 350° for 30 minutes.*
- *Cool slightly and turn onto a serving plate.*

FRENCH BREAD BROIL

1 loaf of fresh French bread
1/3 cup Parmesan cheese
3/4 cup mayonnaise
1/2 cup onions, finely chopped
Dash of Worcestershire sauce
Salt and pepper to taste (optional)

- *Combine cheese, mayonnaise, onions, Worcestershire sauce, salt and pepper and mix well.*
- *Cut bread lengthwise.*
- *Spread mixture on each half.*
- *Broil until brown.*
- *Slice and serve.*

PARMESAN CHEESE ROLLS

27

This recipe makes a very large roll cut into eight pieces, so one usually is enough.

3 loaves of frozen bread
Butter at room temperature
Parmesan cheese, grated

- *Place the frozen bread on a greased cookie sheet and let thaw for one hour.*
- *Cut each loaf into eight pieces.*
- *Dip each slice in the soft butter and sprinkle with Parmesan cheese.*
- *Let rise for 3 hours.*
- *Bake at 350° for 20 to 25 minutes.*

PIZZA DOUGH

This is very quick in a food processor.

1½ cups flour
2 Tbsp instant yeast
1 tsp sugar
3/4 tsp salt
1/2 cup plus 2 Tbsp warm water
2 tsp olive oil

- *Put flour, yeast, sugar and salt in food processor using the steel blade and process for 5 seconds.*
- *While the machine is running, slowly pour water and oil through the feeding container.*
- *When the dough forms, process for 30 seconds.*
- *Continue to process dough for 45 seconds. This will knead the dough.*
- *Makes two 6 inch rounds or one 12 inch round for pizza.*

28

COCO MUFFINS

1/4 cup butter or margarine, melted
1/4 cup cocoa powder
3/4 cup applesauce
1¼ cups flour
1 cup sugar
3/4 tsp baking soda
1/2 tsp cinnamon
1/4 tsp nutmeg
1/4 tsp salt
1 egg, slightly beaten
1/2 cup raisins (optional)
1/2 cup nuts, chopped (optional)

- *Mix melted butter, cocoa powder, and applesauce and set aside.*
- *In a large bowl, combine flour, sugar, baking soda, cinnamon, nutmeg and salt.*
- *Add egg and cocoa to the mixture.*
- *Mix just until moistened, folding in raisins and nuts.*
- *Fill greased muffin tins 3/4 from top.*
- *Bake at 350° for 20 minutes.*
- *When cool, dust with powdered sugar.*

> **NOTE**
> These are best served warm and eaten the day you make them. But don't worry, they won't last the day!

WHEAT BREAD

I have fallen in love with my Bosch Mixer and homemade breads. This is a recipe I finally came up with that works well. I use what they call "white wheat" because the bread turns out lighter in color and texture. Even kids like this bread.

4 cups of very warm water (85 to 90°)
1 Tbsp sea salt
1/3 cup vegetable oil
1/2 to 3/4 cup honey, according to your taste
3 Tbsp wheat gluten
3 Tbsp dough enhancer
2 Tbsp Saf Instant Yeast (or use instant yeast)
7 cups wheat kernels, ground into flour (about 10 cups of wheat)

- *Four 4 x 8 loaf pans sprayed with vegetable spray.*
- *Preheat oven to 200°.*
- *Using your dough hook, put 4 cups warm water and 3 cups flour in large mixing bowl and mix on #1 speed until a paste texture.*
- *Add salt, oil, honey, gluten and yeast (the dough enhancer is added later) and mix briefly on low.*
- *While mixing on #1 speed, add more flour until the dough pulls away from the sides of the bowl. Don't measure the flour from this point, just keep slowly sprinkling additional flour until it pulls away from the sides. It is better to add too little flour than too much. The dough should be sticky and moist.*

- *On speed #2, knead the bread with the dough hook for 7 minutes, then add the dough enhancer. Continue kneading for 3 more minutes. Don't add any more flour after this point.*
- *Wet hands and work area with water to shape the dough. Remove dough and separate into four evenly measured pieces.*
- *Knead by hand to remove any air bubbles. Slam the dough down on the counter to release air.*
- *Form the dough into four loaves and put in pans and place in the oven.*
- *Turn off the oven and set the timer for 25 minutes or until the dough is double in size.*
- *Turn the oven to 350° and bake the loaves for an additional 30 minutes or until golden brown.*
- *The bread is done when the internal temperature reaches 190°. Brush the tops with melted butter.*
- *Remove from pans and put on cooling rack.*

29

NOTES

Cakes and Frostings

APPLE COFFEE CAKE

3 cups flour
2 Tbsp baking powder
1/3 cup dried egg powder
1½ cups water
1½ cups sugar
1/2 cup shortening
1½ Tbsp salt
1 cup dried apple slices, reconstituted and chopped

- *Blend all ingredients together and mix well.*
- *Pour into a greased baking dish.*
- *Sprinkle on top with topping mix.*

Topping Mix:

2/3 cup brown sugar
3/4 cup margarine powder
2 Tbsp water
1/2 cup flour
1 tsp cinnamon

- *Bake 45 minutes at 350°.*

APPLE HILL CAKE

2 cups sugar
1/2 cup vegetable oil
2 eggs
4 cups apples, chopped
2 cups flour
1 tsp salt
2 tsp cinnamon
1 tsp nutmeg
2 tsp baking soda
1/2 cup chopped nuts (walnuts or pecans, optional)

- *Combine sugar, oil and eggs.*
- *Add the apples.*
- *Stir in flour, salt, cinnamon, nutmeg, baking soda and nuts.*
- *Mix well and put into a 9 x 13 baking pan.*
- *Bake 45 to 50 minutes at 350°.*

APPLE HILL CAKE FROSTING

One 1 lb bag of powdered sugar, sifted
1/2 cup Crisco shortening
1/4 cup milk
1 tsp vanilla
1/4 tsp butter flavoring
1 Tbsp meringue powder
Pinch of salt

- *Mix all ingredients and beat until light and fluffy.*

CHOCOLATE SOUR CREAM FROSTING

2 cups semi-sweet chocolate chips
1/2 cup butter
8 oz sour cream
3 3/4 cups powdered sugar, sifted

- *In a large saucepan, heat the chocolate chips and butter until melted.*
- *Cool 5 minutes, then stir in the sour cream.*
- *Gradually add 1 bag (3¾ cups) sifted powdered sugar and beat on medium speed until smooth.*

FRUIT COCKTAIL CAKE

This is a very quick, easy and moist cake. It's best served with Hot Vanilla Sauce on it.

1¾ cups sugar
2½ cups flour
2 tsp baking soda
1 tsp salt
1/8 tsp nutmeg
1 tsp cinnamon
One 25 oz can of fruit cocktail, including the juice

- *Mix all ingredients except the vanilla in a medium bowl with a large spoon. Do not beat. Just mix well.*
- *Bake in a 9 x 13 baking dish for 50 to 60 minutes at 350°.*
- *Serve warm with Hot Vanilla Sauce (see recipe on page 33.*

COCONUT COFFEE CAKE

Sandy Carlsten, who use to work with me in Chico, California, always made a fuss when I brought this in to work for her birthday.

1 cup flour
1 tsp baking powder
1/4 tsp salt
1 cup sugar
2 eggs
1 tsp vanilla
1/2 cup whole milk
2 Tbsp butter

- *Sift flour, baking powder and salt.*
- *Beat eggs and sugar and add to flour mixture.*
- *Heat ½ cup milk and 2 Tbsp butter but do not boil.*
- *Add vanilla and stir well. Mixture will be runny.*
- *Pour into a greased and floured 9 x 9 pan.*
- *Bake at 350° for 25 to 30 minutes. Check after 20 minutes.*

Make the following Coconut Topping:

2 Tbsp butter, melted
5 Tbsp brown sugar, heaping
2 Tbsp milk
3/4 cup sweetened coconut flakes

- *While cake is still warm top with coconut mixture.*
- *Place under broiler until browned.*
- *Serves 9.*

HOT VANILLA SAUCE

Serve over Fruit Cocktail Cake (see page 32) or other desserts that would be appropriate.

1 cup butter (not margarine)
2 cups sugar
1 cup evaporated milk
1/2 tsp vanilla extract
1/8 tsp nutmeg

- *Mix all ingredients except the nutmeg in a medium saucepan.*
- *Heat over low heat. Do not let it boil but simmer on low for 15 to 20 minutes until thickened.*
- *Add the nutmeg just when you're ready to serve it.*

COFFEE CAKE

This is quick, easy and kid friendly—and there's no coffee in it.

1 cup pancake mix or **Bisquick**
1/3 cup sugar
1/3 cup milk
1 egg
1/4 cup butter, melted

- *Mix ingredients together and pour into a well greased 8 inch round pan.*
- *Mix ingredients for topping (below) until crumbly. You may need to mix more flour to the mix.*
- *Sprinkle the topping over the batter and bake at 375° for 20 minutes.*
- *Serves 6 to 8.*

Topping:

1/4 cup brown sugar
1/4 cup flour
1/4 tsp cinnamon
2 Tbsp melted butter

- *While still hot, drizzle with icing below.*

Icing:

1/4 cup powdered sugar
1 tsp soft butter
Touch of vanilla
Just enough milk to make a thin consistency

- *Drizzle with a spoon.*

NOTE

The Hot Vanilla Sauce is fantastic over a wide variety of desserts. Memorize the recipe as you will use it over and over again.

33

JOHNNY APPLESEED CAKE

1/2 cup margarine
One 15 oz can of applesauce
1 tsp vanilla
2 cups flour
1 cup sugar
1 tsp soda
1 tsp cinnamon
1/4 tsp nutmeg
1/4 tsp cloves

- *Melt margarine in a 4 cup microwave-safe bowl.*
- *Add remaining ingredients.*

Dredge the following in flour:

1 cup raisins
1 cup nuts

- *Mix all ingredients and pour into a 9 x 9 greased pan.*
- *Bake at 350° for 35 to 40 minutes.*

LAYERED ANGEL FOOD CAKE

This looks beautiful on a pedestal cake plate.

One large prepared angel food cake
One 20 oz can crushed pineapple, including juice
1 cup Cool Whip, thawed
One 3.4 oz package instant vanilla pudding and pie filling

- *Mix pineapple and juice with the dry pudding mix in a medium bowl.*
- *Carefully fold in the Cool Whip and set aside.*
- *Cut cake horizontally into 3 layers.*
- *Place the bottom of cake on a cake pedestal and spread a layer of pudding mixture on top.*
- *Place middle layer and repeat with a layer of pudding mixture.*
- *Top with final layer of cake and remaining pudding mixture.*
- *Have the pudding mixture drip over the outside edge but do not ice the sides.*
- *Refrigerate for at least 1 hour before serving.*
- *Just prior to serving, place fresh strawberries on top.*

LEMON BUNDT CAKE

Prepare the Bundt pan ahead of time.

- *Grease the Bundt pan with butter (not spray) and then powder with Baker's Sugar. This is the secret that makes the topping crisp. Baker's Sugar is an ultrafine, professional-grade sugar so the top of the cake is not gritty, but sugary.*

1 lemon cake mix (no pudding in the mix)
One 5.8 oz package of instant vanilla pudding
4 eggs
3/4 cup vegetable oil
1 cup water
1½ Tbsp lemon extract
Baker's Sugar

- *Beat all ingredients except the Baker's Sugar in an electric mixer for a full 4 minutes on medium.*
- *Pour into a greased and sugared Bundt pan.*
- *Bake at 350° for 45 to 50 minutes.*
- *Cool for 10 minutes in the pan then invert onto a cake plate.*

NOTE

Do not put frosting on this Lemon Bundt cake. The crispy top is what you want.

PINEAPPLE ANGEL FOOD CAKE

Easy on the waistline, this recipe is from Sandi Anderson of Paradise, California. Over the years we have made and shared a lot of recipes and meals together.

1 Angel food cake mix (a big name brand only)
1 20 oz can of crushed pineapple with heavy syrup, including the juice

- *Mix with whisk and pour into an angel food cake pan sprayed with vegetable spray.*
- *Bake according to the directions on the box.*
- *Let cool and serve with whipped cream.*

LEMON POPPY SEED CAKE

This is the best lemon poppy seed cake ever—from Lynsey Butler of South Jordan, Utah.

1 lemon cake mix (no pudding in the mix)
One 5.8 oz package of instant vanilla pudding
4 eggs
3/4 cup oil
1 cup water
2 tsp poppy seeds
1½ tsp lemon extract

- *Grease the Bundt pan with butter (not spray) and then powder with Baker's Sugar. This is the secret that makes the topping crisp. Baker's Sugar is an ultrafine, professional-grade sugar so the top of the cake is not gritty, but sugary.*
- *Beat all ingredients in an electric mixer for a full 4 minutes on medium speed.*
- *Pour into a greased and sugared Bundt pan.*
- *Bake at 350° for 45 to 50 minutes.*
- *Cool 10 minutes in the pan then invert onto a tray.*
- *Do not frost this cake ... it will ruin it.*

NOTE

You can leave the poppy seeds out and the cake will be like a lemon sponge cake or you can use different flavorings for totally different cakes.

YELLOW SUPREME CAKE

This is a most unusual and delicious cake.

1 yellow cake mix (No pudding in the mix)
3 eggs
1 package Dream Whip
1 cup water

- *Put all ingredients in a mixer bowl and beat on high until the batter is double in size.*
- *Bake according to the directions on the box.*

NOTE

This cake will rise very high so cut into layers and use different fillings.

PUMPKIN CHIFFON CAKE

1 yellow cake mix, any brand with or without pudding
1 egg
1/2 cup butter, melted

- *Mix by hand, until well blended.*
- *Press into a 9 x 13 dish and set aside*
- *Do not bake yet.*

In an electric mixer combine:

One 8 oz package of cream cheese at room temperature
One 15 oz can pumpkin pie filling
3 eggs
1 tsp vanilla
One 16 oz bag of powdered sugar
1/2 cup butter, melted

- *Beat cream cheese until smooth, then add the pumpkin pie filling, eggs, vanilla and powdered sugar and mix well.*
- *Slowly pour in melted butter.*
- *Pour on top of cake mixture.*
- *Bake 40 to 50 minutes at 350°.*
- *Remove from the oven and allow to cool completely before cutting into squares.*

35

NOTE

The center is supposed to be a little gooey so don't bake past 50 minutes.

SPICE CAKE FROSTING

1/2 cup shortening or 1 stick of shortening
1/2 cup butter, softened
1 tsp maple-flavored extract
4 cups powdered sugar, sifted
2 Tbsp milk

- *In a mixer bowl, cream butter and shortening.*
- *Add maple flavoring.*
- *Gradually add powdered sugar and milk.*
- *Continue to beat until light and airy.*
- *Add more milk if necessary.*
- *Color with maple coloring if desired.*

PUMPKIN PIE CAKE

Our family has been using this recipe at Thanksgiving instead of regular pumpkin pie. Many of our friends and family have joined in making this the dessert of choice.

1 large can of solid pack pumpkin
3 eggs, slightly beaten
1 large can of evaporated milk
1¼ cups sugar
1/2 tsp salt
1/2 tsp cinnamon (you may want more)
4 tsp pumpkin pie spice
1 yellow cake mix (less ¼ cup)
1 cup walnuts, chopped
1/2 cup butter or margarine, melted

- Whisk all but the cake mix, walnuts and butter.
- Pour in a 9 x 13 pan sprayed with vegetable spray.
- Sprinkle dry cake mix over the top and swirl knife gently through the mixture.
- Drizzle melted margarine over the top.
- Sprinkle with nuts.
- Bake at 350° for 50 to 60 minutes or until a knife inserted comes out clean.
- Top with whipped cream.

36

PINEAPPLE CAKE

2 cups sugar
2 tsp baking soda
Pinch of salt
2 eggs
1 tsp vanilla
One 20 oz can crushed pineapple, in sweetened juice, including juice
2 cups flour

- Mix all ingredients in an electric mixer and on medium speed for 2 minutes.
- Pour in a glass 9 x 13 pan sprayed with vegetable oil.
- Bake in 350° oven for 35 to 40 minutes.
- <u>Ice while the cake is still hot</u> using the following recipe for Coconut-Nut Frosting.

COCONUT-NUT FROSTING

1½ cups sugar
1 cup of evaporated milk
3/4 cup butter
1 cup coconut
1 cup nuts, any kind

- Bring sugar, evaporated milk and butter to a boil and boil for 2 minutes.
- Add coconut and nuts.
- Pour over hot cake.

DOUBLE CHOCOLATE CHIP CAKE

1¾ cup water (boiling)
1 cup oatmeal
1 cup light brown sugar
1 cup sugar
1/2 cup butter
2 eggs
1¾ cup flour
1 Tbsp baking soda
1 Tbsp cocoa powder
1/2 Tbsp salt
12 oz chocolate chips
¾ cup nuts, chopped

- Pour boiling water over oatmeal and let it stand for 10 minutes.
- Add brown sugar.
- Cream sugar, butter and eggs in another bowl.
- Add flour, baking soda, salt and cocoa.
- Fold in nuts.
- Add to the oatmeal mixture.
- Pour half of the mixture into a 9 x 13 pan sprayed with vegetable spray.
- Sprinkle with nuts and half of the chocolate chips.
- Repeat.
- Bake at 350° for 30 to 35 minutes.

> ### NOTE
> Holiday traditions begin in unusual ways, No one really sets out to create tradition. They just happen. The trick is to remember what works and then repeat it!

CHOCOLATE TURTLE CAKE

This cake is a specialty of Tova Wilson of Northern California.

1 box German chocolate cake mix
1 1/3 cups water
1/3 cup butter, melted
3 eggs
1 cup chocolate chips
1 cup nuts, chopped (optional)
1 lb package caramels
2/3 cup evaporated milk

- *Combine cake mix, water, and eggs.*
- *Put half of the mixture in a 9 x 13 glass baking dish.*
- *Bake for only 15 minutes at 350°.*
- *While the cake is baking, unwrap the caramels and put in a saucepan on low heat.*
- *Add evaporated milk and heat until caramels are melted.*
- *Take the cake out of oven and spread half of the caramel mix over the top.*
- *Sprinkle the chocolate chips and nuts over caramel.*
- *Cover with remaining cake batter.*
- *Bake 20 to 25 minutes longer.*

DUMP CAKE

It doesn't come any easier than this.

1 cup butter or margarine (2 sticks)
One 20 oz can pineapple chunks, including juice
1 box yellow cake mix (no pudding in the mix)
1 can cherry pie filling
1 cup nuts, optional

- *Spray a 9 x 13 cake pan with vegetable spray.*
- *Put fruit in pan.*
- *Sprinkle with dry cake mix.*
- *Add 1 cup nuts.*
- *Melt butter and pour over top.*
- *Bake at 350° for 1 hour.*

YELLOW PINEAPPLE COCONUT CAKE

This cake needs to be started the night before.

1 box yellow cake mix
One 20 oz can crushed pineapple, drain and save the juice
1 large box instant vanilla pudding
1½ cup whole milk
One 8 oz Cool Whip
Shredded, sweetened coconut flakes

The night before:

- *Make the yellow cake as directed on the box and bake in a 9 x 13 cake pan.*
- *Drain the pineapple and reserve the juice.*
- *While the cake is still hot puncture holes with a fork.*
- *Pour the pineapple juice over the cake.*

The next day:

- *Spread pineapple over the cake.*
- *Make vanilla pudding with 1 cup of the milk.*
- *Fold in Cool Whip.*
- *Spread mixture on the cake.*
- *Sprinkle with coconut.*
- *Cover and refrigerate until ready to serve.*

37

CRÈME DE MINT FUDGE CAKE

1 white cake mix
3 Tbsp crème de mint
1 can Hershey's Hot Fudge Topping
One 8 oz container of Cool Whip
Crème de mint or peppermint oil

- *Prepare cake as directed on box adding 3 Tbsp crème de mint.*
- *Bake in an oblong pan and slightly cool.*
- *Spread hot fudge topping over cooled cake.*
- *Fold 3 Tbsp crème de mint into the Cool Whip.*
- *Spread over the top of cake.*
- *Refrigerate until ready to serve.*

OPTION

Substitute 2 drops peppermint oil plus 3 Tbsp water when it calls for crème de mint.

TEXAS SHEET CAKE

This cake recipe has been around the country but I was making it before it was so well known. It's great for a crowd as it makes a large sheet cake.

1 cup butter
4 Tbsp cocoa powder
1 cup water

Melt in sauce pan and remove from heat and then add the following:

2 cups flour
2 cups sugar
1 tsp baking soda
1/2 tsp salt
1/2 tsp cinnamon
2 eggs
1 cup buttermilk
1 tsp vanilla

- *Combine all ingredients and pour into an 11 x13 x 1 jelly roll pan (or close to this size).*
- *Bake at 400° for 25 minutes.*
- *Frost while cake is still hot with the Frosting below.*

Frosting:

1/2 cup butter
4 Tbsp cocoa powder
6 Tbsp buttermilk

Heat until butter is melted and add:

One 1 lb box of powdered sugar, sifted
1 tsp vanilla
1 cup walnuts, chopped (optional)

- *Pour over hot cake.*

NOTE

Cakes delight everyone from little children at birthday parties and Halloween cakewalks, to grandmas and grandpas celebrating scores of special days. Make them with flour and sugar, cheese and ice cream, fruit and candy, frosting and flowers. They commemorate weddings and anniversaries and so many more special occasions too many to number. Enjoy!

MARBLE CAKE

This is a family recipe from generations back on my mother's side and is completely handmade. No mixes here. Don't ice this cake as it will ruin it. People will fight over the top crusty part.

5 egg whites
2 cups sugar
3/4 cup shortening (use the sticks)
1 1/4 cups water
1/4 tsp salt
2 Tbsp baking powder
3 cups flour
1 Tbsp vanilla

- *Mix all ingredients on high speed for 4 minutes.*
- *Separate half of the mix into another bowl.*

Add the following ingredients to the 2nd bowl:

2 Tbsp cinnamon
1/2 tsp nutmeg
1/8 tsp clove
4 Tbsp cocoa powder

- *Prepare an angel food cake pan with vegetable spray.*
- *Alternate large spoonfuls of each batter, being careful not to overlap the chocolate and the vanilla.*
- *When all the batter is used, drag a knife through the batter and swirl it around, just to barely blend the two colors.*
- *Let bake at 350° for 45 to 50 minutes. Then let cool for 10 minutes and remove from pan.*

39

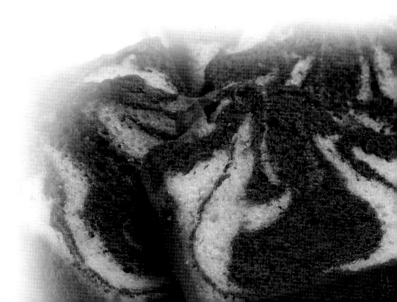

MISSISSIPPI RIVER MUD CAKE

I don't know where this name came from but wouldn't want to change it.

I cup margarine or butter
2 cups sugar
4 eggs
1/4 cup cocoa powder
1/2 tsp salt
1½ cups flour
I tsp vanilla
1½ cups flaked coconut
1½ cups chopped pecans
I jar marshmallow cream or miniature
   marshmallows

- *In an electric mixer, cream together the butter and sugar.*
- *Beat in eggs, one at a time, beating well after each egg.*
- *Sift cocoa and flour and add to egg mixture.*
- *Stir in vanilla, coconut and nuts.*
- *Pour into a greased and floured 9 x 13 x 2 pan.*
- *Bake at 350° for 35 to 40 minutes.*
- *Remove from oven and immediately top hot cake with either the creamed marshmallow or the miniature marshmallows.*
- *When marshmallow melts, spread with a knife and let cool.*
- *Frost with the chocolate frosting.*

Frosting for Mississippi River Mud Cake:

1/3 cup cocoa powder
1/2 cup butter
1/2 tsp vanilla
1/3 cup whole milk
I lb box of powdered sugar, sifted

- *Beat until light and fluffy.*

PIG-PICK'N CAKE

This recipe is from Deloris Kelly of Santa Ana, California. It's a great summer choice for a cool, pretty cake in spite of the name. I don't know where it got its name, but I am keeping it. No one forgets the name.

I yellow cake mix, with pudding in it
2/3 cup vegetable oil
4 eggs
I can mandarin oranges, including the juice

- *Mix all but the mandarin oranges in electric mixer for 2 minutes.*
- *Fold in the oranges including the juice.*
- *Bake in two 9 inch round pans at 350° for 30 to 40 minutes.*

Frosting for Pig-Pick'n Cake:

8 oz container of Cool Whip
One 3.4 oz package of instant vanilla pudding
One 3.4 oz can crushed pineapple, slightly drained

- *Mix well and frost cake.*
- *Refrigerate for several hours.*
- *Serve cold.*

CHOCOLATE-CHOCOLATE CAKE

I package of fudge cake mix with pudding
   (do not follow box directions)
1/2 cup vegetable oil
1/2 cup warm water
4 eggs
8 oz sour cream
One 12 oz package chocolate chips

- *Mix cake mix, oil and warm water.*
- *Add sour cream and eggs, one at a time, beating well after each egg.*
- *Fold in chocolate chips.*
- *Bake in greased Bundt pan at 350° for 45 minutes to one hour until cake springs back when touched.*
- *Let sit for 10 minutes and turn onto a serving plate.*
- *Sprinkle with powdered sugar, when cooled.*

STRAWBERRY CAKE

For years this was my nephew's favorite cake and was nicknamed Danny's Cake.

1 white cake mix
1/2 cup flour
One 3.4 oz strawberry Jell-O
1/2 cup water
2/3 cup vegetable oil
One 10 oz frozen strawberries, divided in half
4 eggs

- *Mix all ingredients (only half of the strawberries) in a large bowl.*
- *Beat on high for 4 minutes.*
- *Put in a 9 x 13 x 2 dish sprayed with vegetable spray.*
- *Bake at 350° for 45 minutes.*

Frosting for Strawberry Cake:

One 1 lb box powdered sugar, sifted
1 cup butter or margarine at room temperature

- *Using the remaining strawberries, blend together in mixer and beat until fluffy.*
- *You may want to add a few drops of red food coloring for more color.*
- *Ice cake and keep refrigerated.*

CHOCOLATE-LAYERED CREAM CHEESE CAKE

I have had this recipe for decades. When it was first created, it was called The Next Best Thing to Robert Redford. I still call it that but the younger generation asks me, "Who is Robert Redford?" So now I don't know what to call it other than delicious!

Crust:

1 cup flour
1/2 cup butter
1/2 cup nuts, chopped
1/4 cup powdered sugar

- *Mix together with a pastry blender or two knives.*
- *Pat mixture into the bottom of a 9 x 13 glass dish.*
- *Bake at 350° for 15 minutes then let cool.*

In the meantime mix together:

One 8 oz package of cream cheese at room temperature
1 cup powdered sugar, sifted

Beat on low speed and add:

One 8 oz container package Cool Whip
- *Spread on cooled crust.*

Beat together:

One 5.8 oz box instant chocolate pudding
2/3 cup whole milk

- *Beat on medium speed for 2 minutes.*
- *Pour on creamed mixture.*
- *Let sit for 5 minutes.*
- *Top with another 8 oz container of Cool Whip.*
- *Grate a milk chocolate candy bar over the top or sprinkle with chopped nuts.*
- *Chill several hours before serving.*

41

CARROT CAKE

This is my favorite. I usually don't order it at a restaurant because it is never this good.

2 cups flour
2 tsp baking powder
1½ tsp baking soda
2 tsp cinnamon
1/2 tsp nutmeg
1 tsp salt
2 cups sugar
4 eggs
1 cup vegetable oil
2 cups grated carrots
One 8.5 oz can crushed pineapple with juice
1½ cups chopped nuts
Raisins, optional

- *Sift dry ingredients except the sugar.*
- *Beat together the sugar, oil and eggs.*
- *Mix with dry ingredients.*
- *Fold in grated carrots, pineapple, nuts and raisins.*
- *Pour into three 9 inch greased cake rounds.*
- *Bake at 350° for 50 to 60 minutes. Check it as the optional ingredients you put in it will cause the cooking time to increase.*
- *Remove from pans and cool before icing the cake.*

Frosting for Carrot Cake:

1 cup butter, at room temperature
Two 8 oz packages of cream cheese at room temperature
One 2 lb bag of powdered sugar, sifted
2 tsp vanilla
One 8.5 oz can crushed pineapple, well drained

- *Beat the butter and sugar with electric mixer.*
- *Add the powdered sugar and vanilla.*
- *Add crushed pineapple.*
- *Add nuts and raisins, if desired.*
- *Ice cake and refrigerate until ready to serve.*

NOTE

Because this is a very large cake, don't put too much icing between the layers as it will cause the cake to slide.

MICROWAVE WHITE FROSTING

This is a five minute recipe. It's a bit like marshmallow topping.

1 cup sugar
1/2 cup water
1/4 tsp cream of tartar
Dash of salt
2 Tbsp light corn syrup
2 egg whites
1 tsp vanilla

- *Combine sugar, water, cream of tartar, salt and corn syrup in a 4 cup microwave-safe measuring cup.*
- *Cook on high for 4 to 5 minutes, stirring a few times, until it comes to a boil.*
- *Beat egg whites and vanilla in an electric mixer until it forms soft peaks.*
- *Very slowly add the syrup to the egg whites, beating on high speed.*
- *Beat for 5 minutes or until you have stiff peaks*

Note: This will ice a two-layered cake.

GLOSSY FROSTING

2 egg whites
1/4 tsp salt
1/4 cup sugar
3/4 cup Karo light corn syrup
1¼ tsp vanilla

- *Beat the egg whites and salt until foamy.*
- *Gradually beat in the sugar until mixture is smooth and glossy.*
- *Beat in the corn syrup a little at a time until it holds a firm peak.*
- *Fold in the vanilla and food coloring of your choice.*
- *Makes enough for two 9 inch cake layers.*

UNIVERSAL FROSTING

This is soft and fluffy icing and great for summer cakes.

One 8 oz container of Cool Whip
One 3.4 oz package of instant vanilla pudding
I small can crushed pineapple, well drained

- *Beat for several minutes until light and fluffy.*
- *This will frost two 9 inch cake layers.*

CHOCOLATE FROSTING

This is a good frosting for many kinds of cakes and is especially good on brownies—easy to make and it keeps well.

1/3 cup cocoa powder
1/2 cup of butter or margarine
1/2 tsp vanilla
1/3 cup milk
One Ilb box of powdered sugar, sifted

- *Mix well and beat until fluffy.*
- *Frosts one 9 inch two-layered cake, brownies or one 9 x 13 sheet cake.*

ORANGE FROSTING

You may substitute lemon for the orange.

1/2 cup butter (not margarine)
One 1 lb box of powdered sugar, sifted
Concentrated frozen orange juice
Orange zest

- *Beat butter and sugar on high speed until light and fluffy.*
- *Add just enough concentrated frozen orange juice until desired consistency.*
- *Add grated orange peel, to taste.*

PINEAPPLE FROSTING

One 8 oz container of Cool Whip
One 3.4 oz package instant vanilla pudding
One 8 oz can crushed pineapple, slightly drained

- *Mix well and ice a cake of your choice.*

VANILLA FROSTING

I cup shortening (stick type)
1/2 cup butter, room temperature
Pinch of salt
I tsp vanilla
2 boxes powdered sugar, sifted
1/4 cup light Karo syrup
1/2 cup milk

- *Put in electric mixer and mix for 10 minutes on high speed.*

WHITE FROSTING

Just like the bakers use.

1/2 cup margarine
1/2 cup shortening
1/8 tsp salt
1½ tsp clear vanilla extract
5 cups powdered sugar, sifted
1/4 cup whole milk

- *In a large bowl, cream margarine and shortening until light and fluffy.*
- *Add remaining ingredients and beat well.*

43

NOTE

Get clear vanilla from a candy supply store. It will keep the frosting white. Use clear vanilla whenever anything you are making needs to be white.

CREAM CHEESE FROSTING

One 8 oz package of cream cheese at room
   temperature
1/2 cup butter
One 1 lb box of powdered sugar
I tsp vanilla

- *Mix all ingredients well.*
- *Use chopped nuts on top if desired.*

NOTES

Candies

BAKED CARAMEL CORN

This is easy, easy, easy, but read the directions first as all of the ingredients are not listed at the top.

- *Preheat oven to 250°.*
- *Spray a large roasting pan, like a turkey roaster, with vegetable oil spray.*
- *Put 3 quarts of popped corn with the unpopped kernels removed.*
- *Keep in 250° oven while you bring to a boil in a 2 quart pan the following:*

I cup light brown sugar
1/2 cup of real butter
1/2 cup light corn syrup

Remove from stove and add:

46   **I tsp baking soda (this helps to coat the kernels evenly)**

- *Pour over corn and bake for 40 minutes, stirring well every 10 minutes.*
- *Pour onto waxed paper and spread out to cool.*

NOTE

Barrel O'Fun Corn Pops make great caramel corn as they are very puffy and have no hard kernels, if you can find them at your grocery.

CHOCOLATE TRUFFLES

1/2 pint whipping cream
I lb dipping chocolate
I lb dark chocolate, melted in microwave

- *Heat whipping cream on medium heat until it comes to a boil. Cool slightly.*
- *Add milk chocolate, cover and let melt.*
- *Pour into a mixer bowl and refrigerate for 1 hour.*
- *Beat on high speed until fluffy.*
- *Return to refrigerator until firm.*
- *Make into mounds and dip in dark chocolate.*
- *See right hand note for a variation on this recipe.*

CANDIED NUTS

Single Batch

One lb of nuts (your choice)
1/8 tsp salt
2 egg whites
I cup sugar
3/4 tsp cinnamon
I stick melted butter, cooled

Triple Batch

3 lbs nuts
1/2 tsp salt
6 egg whites
3 cups sugar
2¼ tsp cinnamon
3 sticks melted butter

- *Beat eggs whites and salt until stiff.*
- *Gradually add sugar and cinnamon.*
- *Pour over nuts.*
- *Pour melted butter over nuts.*
- *Bake at 250° for 45 minutes. Stir every 15 minutes; watch closely the last 15 minutes as they could scorch.*

CHOCOLATE PEPPERMINT CHIPS

I lb white dipping chocolate
Peppermint candy canes

- *Melt chocolate in the microwave at 50% power starting with 2 minutes. Stir and add 30 seconds at a time until almost melted. Stir until completely melted. The chocolate will continue to melt after you take it out of the microwave.*
- *Break peppermint candy canes into small pieces.*
- *Add candy chips to melted chocolate, pour onto a greased jelly roll pan and let set until firm.*
- *Break into pieces and store in an air-tight container.*

NOTE

Make Chocolate Cherry Truffles by adding 1/4 tsp cherry extract and 1/4 cup marashino cherries, chopped and well drained; 1/4 cup chopped nuts optional.

CHOCOLATE CHERRIES

My husband and I have been making hand-dipped chocolates for Christmas gifts for over 30 years.

60 Maraschino cherries with stems
6 Tbsp softened butter or margarine
6 tsp light corn syrup
1/4 tsp salt
One 1 lb box of powdered sugar

- *Drain cherries on a paper towel until completely dry This may take overnight.*
- *Combine butter, corn syrup and salt.*
- *Stir in powdered sugar and knead until mixture is smooth. Use plastic gloves to make it easier.*
- *Shape about 1 tsp of the mixture around the cherry, leaving the stems on but covering where the stem meets the cherry.*
- *Place on large cookie sheet covered with waxed paper and chill overnight.*
- *Dip in dipping chocolate and let stand on a clean sheet of waxed paper.*
- *Store in the refrigerator in a covered container for 1 to 2 weeks before serving. This allows the center to liquefy.*

CHOCOLATE CRISPY BARS

These are not too fattening and a good snack for kids.

2 Tbsp butter
1 oz unsweetened chocolate, finely chopped
1 tsp vanilla
6 cups Rice Krispies cereal
One 7 oz jar marshmallow cream

- *Melt butter and chocolate on low heat.*
- *Add remaining ingredients, stirring until smooth.*
- *Remove from heat and gently add cereal.*
- *Spread into a greased 9 x 13 pan.*
- *Cool 10 minutes.*

CARAMEL CORN

2½ quarts of popped corn
  (discard kernels that did not pop)
1 lb light brown sugar
1/2 cup corn syrup
1/2 cup water
1/2 cup butter
2 tsp salt
1 tsp vanilla
1 cup peanuts, almonds, pecans or mixed nuts
  (optional)

- *Prepare a large piece of foil with soft butter spread on it.*
- *Put popped corn in a large, well-buttered pan such as a turkey roaster.*
- *Keep it in a 200° oven until syrup is ready.*
- *Put the brown sugar, water, butter and salt in a large, heavy pot.*
- *Cook on medium high heat to a hard-crack stage— 300° on a candy thermometer.*
- *Remove from heat and add vanilla and peanuts.*
- *Pour over popped corn and mix well as fast as you can.*
- *Spread out on the large piece of buttered foil you prepared earlier.*

47

CREAM CENTERS FOR MAKING HANDMADE DIPPING CHOCOLATES

This recipe is from Becky Sandberg. We have gotten together often with the Sandberg's since we moved to Utah to share our Christmas chocolate candy-making. Thanks for this recipe, Becky.

3 cups sugar
I cup whipping cream
2 Tbsp butter
2 Tbsp corn starch

- Mix ingredients and bring to boiling point.
- After it comes to a boil, stir continuously.
- Slow cook until a soft ball stage—230° where a ball can be formed in a cup of cold water.
- Pour onto a marble or a stone slab and let cool until warm to touch.
- Hand-knead until it turns almost white and creamy which may take 5 to 10 minutes. It is handy to use a pastry scraper to move the mixture around.
- Separate into balls and flavor each ball with your choice of flavorings such as lemon or cherry. Also use the color of food coloring that you desire.
- Roll into bite-sized balls and put on a tray lined with waxed paper.
- Refrigerate until set and cold.
- Dip in dipping chocolate.
- Store in cool, dry place.

BUTTERSCOTCH FUDGE

You're looking at a five minute prep time. This fudge makes a nice gift. Just wrap it in cellophane with a bow.

- *In a heavy pan, melt on medium heat:*

2 cups of semi sweet chocolate chips
I cup butterscotch chips
I can sweetened condensed milk

Add:

I tsp vanilla
I cup chopped walnuts (optional)

- Pour fudge mixture into a 9 x 9 inch square pan.
- Refrigerate for 30 minutes.
- Cut into squares or wrap for a gift.

FUDGE

5 cups sugar
2 tsp margarine
I large can evaporated milk
2½ cups semi-sweet chocolate chips
2 cups of miniature marshmallows or 7 oz jar marshmallow cream
I cup chopped nuts, optional
I tsp vanilla

- Combine sugar, margarine, milk and bring to a rolling boil.
- Cook rapidly to the soft ball stage—240°—over medium heat, stirring constantly.
- Remove from heat.

Add:

Vanilla, chocolate chips, marshmallows and nuts

- Beat until smooth.
- Pour onto waxed paper or into a greased pan.
- Mark for cutting and let cool.

CHOCOLATE CHOPPED NUTS

This recipe is about as fast as you can get.

- Chop any type of nuts you like and as much as you like.
- Melt dipping chocolate in a microwave-safe bowl.
- Mix nuts with melted chocolate.
- Spoon onto foil sprayed with vegetable oil spray.

49

FUDGE FILLING FOR CHOCOLATES

This recipe is also used to make Easter eggs. Read the instructions and have the ingredients ready.

1/2 cup butter

- *In a 3 quart heavy saucepan, melt the butter.*

Add:

One 5.8 oz package chocolate Jell-O pudding and Pie Filling (not instant)

- *Blend until smooth.*

Add:

1/2 cup whole milk
One 1 lb box of powdered sugar, sifted

- *Cook until the filling is thick and leaves the sides of the pan when boiling.*
- *Remove from heat and stir in powdered sugar.*

Add:

1 tsp vanilla
1 cup nuts, optional

- *Shape into small balls or egg shapes.*
- *Dip into dipping chocolate and place on waxed paper.*

ORIENTAL CHOCOLATES

One 12 oz package of chocolate chips
One 12 oz package of butterscotch chips
1 regular size can of Spanish peanuts (salted)
1 can Chinese noodles

- *Melt chips in a 4 cup glass measuring cup in the microwave or in double boiler.*
- *Add enough peanuts and noodles to make an even mixture.*
- *Drop by tablespoon onto waxed paper.*

> ### NOTE
> Dipping chocolate works best. Substitute chocolate chips for one pound of dipping chocolate and add butterscotch chips to that.

PEANUT BRITTLE

This recipe comes from Lily Ann Peeler. Your friends and family will love this as a gift.

2 cups sugar
1 cup light corn syrup
1/4 cup water
1½ cups salted peanuts
3 Tbsp butter
1 tsp vanilla
2 tsp baking soda

- *Place two long strips of foil together and roll up the edges to make one large piece of foil, twice the normal width. Spray heavily with vegetable spray.*
- *Combine sugar, corn syrup and water in a heavy 3 quart saucepan.*
- *Cook over medium high heat, stirring until sugar dissolves.*
- *Using a candy thermometer, continue to cook until it reaches 285° which is the soft crack stage.*
- *Immediately remove from heat and stir in peanuts and butter.*
- *Return to the stove and cook to 295°.*
- *Remove from heat and add vanilla and soda.*
- *Stir quickly and spread on foil as quickly as possible as it will set up very fast.*
- *Let cool at room temperature and break into pieces.*
- *Package in gift bags or boxes, serve on a plate or store in an airtight container.*

PEANUT BUTTER BALLS

1½ cup peanut butter (creamy style)
1/4 cup margarine at room temperature
1 tsp vanilla
3 cups powdered sugar, sifted

- *Mix together and form into a long, skinny log and wrap in plastic wrap.*
- *Refrigerate for several hours.*
- *Cut into 3/4 inch pieces, roll into balls.*
- *Dip in dipping chocolate.*

> ### NOTE
> Sift the powdered sugar for these or pieces of the sugar will show in the candy.

In Good Taste

PEANUT CRACKLE

This is from my sister, Carol Dyson. It's easy and a great gift.

2 lbs white melting, dipping chocolate
3 cups Rice Krispies
I cup salted peanuts
2 cups miniature marshmallows
I cup creamy peanut butter

- *In an 8 cup measuring cup or a large microwave safe bowl, melt the white chocolate starting with 3 minutes and stirring, until melted. Do not overheat.*
- *Add peanut butter and stir until well mixed.*
- *Put the remaining ingredients in a very large bowl, fold chocolate mix into the remaining ingredients.*
- *Pour in a 10 x 15 pan that is sprayed with vegetable spray.*
- *After it sets awhile, cut into squares while it is still soft but leave in the pan.*
- *Let cool, then finish cutting into the squares you had marked off.*

PECAN TURTLES

Think Holiday treats and gifts.

- *Roast pecans for 15 minutes at 200°.*
- *Melt caramels with a small amount of water in the microwave.*
- *Place 4 pecans in position as 4 legs on a turtle on a piece of parchment paper sprayed with vegetable oil.*
- *Pour a small amount of caramel over pecans making sure you use enough to cover all the ends of the pecans.*
- *When cooled, using a spoon, cover the tops with dipping chocolate.*

NOTE

Figure on four pieces of pecans per turtle, then figure out how many turtles you want to make; then you will need one caramel per turtle.

PEPPERMINT BARK

This is a favorite at holiday time. You can put this in a nice decorative plastic bag and tie it with a bow.

I lb white dipping chocolate
6 to 8 crushed peppermint candy canes
    (leave some larger pieces)
¼ tsp peppermint flavor

- *Melt chocolate in microwave. Start with 1 minute on high. Stir well before adding any more as it needs time to melt.*
- *Mix in crushed peppermint and peppermint flavoring.*
- *Spread onto waxed paper.*
- *Chill in refrigerator and break into pieces.*

NOTE

You may want more or less candy in it. Check as you add it to the chocolate.

POPPYCOCK

This is a great popcorn treat. The recipe was given to me by Tiffany Nish. Another gift idea.

8 cups of air popped popcorn
    (remove un-popped kernels)
I cup pecans
I cup almonds
I tsp vanilla
I I/3 cups sugar
I/2 cup light Karo syrup
I cup butter

- *In a large, heavy saucepan combine Karo syrup and butter.*
- *Cook to softball stage—240°.*
- *Add vanilla and nuts.*
- *Pour over popcorn and mix well.*
- *Spread on waxed paper and cool.*

Nancy Miles

WHITE ALMOND FUDGE

This makes a very beautiful gift and will be a pleasant surprise to those to whom you give it. It freezes well, too.

20 oz white chocolate
1/4 tsp salt
1 can sweetened condensed milk
1 tsp vanilla
1 cup roasted almonds
Maraschino cherries, cut in half and well drained
   (optional)

- *Slowly melt chocolate in microwave. All ovens vary but it does not take long.*
- *Add milk, vanilla and salt.*
- *Stir very gently until blended.*
- *Add almonds and cherries.*
- *Pour onto a greased cookie sheet.*
- *When cooled, cut into squares.*

52

FUDGE EASTER EGGS

1/2 cup butter
One 5.8 oz package of Jell-O Pudding and Pie
   Filling (not instant)
1/2 cup whole milk
1 tsp vanilla
One 1 lb box of powdered sugar, sifted
1 cup nuts, chopped, optional

- *Melt butter in a heavy 3 quart saucepan.*
- *Add the Jell-O pudding mix and stir until smooth.*
- *Add ½ cup milk and bring to a low boil.*
- *Cook until thickened and it leaves the side of the pan.*
- *Remove from heat and stir in the powdered sugar.*
- *Add the vanilla.*
- *Add nuts.*
- *Shape into eggs and dip in dipping chocolate.*

MOLDED MARSHMALLOW EGGS

This is another long recipe, but I put it in because this candy will become a favorite for your family to make together. Adults as well as children love to make these eggs. I was taught how to make them by a friend in Anaheim, California—Marie Taylor. Have fun and make the Molded Marshmallow Eggs an annual event. They make wonderful, personalized gifts.

6 Tbsp cold water
2 envelopes of unflavored gelatin

- *Mix water and gelatin in a small bowl to soften the gelatin. This takes about 5 minutes.*
- *In the meantime prepare a 9 x 13 pan with 1½ inch flour.*
- *Using a large plastic Easter egg or a large serving spoon, make impressions with the plastic egg or spoon in the flour. Make them as deep as you can, keeping the egg shape and being careful not to touch each other, about about 1 inch apart.*
- *Makes about 24 eggs.*

1/2 cup water
1½ cup sugar
Dash of salt
1 tsp vanilla

- *In a medium saucepan, bring water, sugar and salt to a boil.*
- *Add gelatin mixture and stir well.*
- *Cool until warm.*
- *Beat on high speed for 5 minutes. It will look like whipping cream but do not over beat.*
- *Add vanilla.*
- *Spray a large spoon with vegetable spray and spoon marshmallow mixture into the impressions. It will start to set so move quickly.*
- *Refrigerate for 30 minutes.*
- *Now the fun begins.*
- *Let the kids get their hands into the eggs. Have them turn them over so the eggs are completely covered with flour. This allows you to handle them. Pat off the excess flour and set them aside.*
- *Dip them in dipping chocolate and decorate for Easter with pre-made flowers or individuals names.*

LICORICE CREAMS

For those who like black licorice, this is a real hit. It has become one of my signature candies. It was originally given to me by Gaylene Weaver. Read all the directions before starting this one.

1 can Sweetened condensed milk
2 cups sugar
1½ cups light corn syrup
1/2 cup real butter or 1/4 cup butter and 1/4 cup margarine

- *In a heavy saucepan, bring all ingredients to a boil, stirring constantly to avoid scorching.*
- *Using a candy thermometer, bring to 234°.*

Remove from heat and add:

3/4 tsp oil of licorice (it must be oil, not flavoring)
1 tsp (or more) black paste food coloring (found in candy supply store) it should be dark black, not gray in color

- *Pour into a well-greased large cookie sheet (vegetable spray will not work as well).*
- *Let sit on counter overnight.*
- *Cut into squares and wrap in waxed paper that has been cut into rectangles, leaving room to twist both ends.*

COCONUT EASTER EGGS

Here's some more fun with Easter eggs. These take no cooking and are really quick and easy.

2 lbs powdered sugar, sifted
1/2 cup butter, softened
1 can sweetened condensed milk
2 cups chopped nuts, optional
1 cup of sweetened coconut flakes

- *Mix all together and hand form into egg shapes.*
- *Dip in dipping chocolate.*
- *Decorate when chocolate has set.*

BUNNY CUTOUTS

These are made like the Marshmallow Eggs but cut with cookie cutters instead of formed eggs.

- *Line the bottom of a 9 x 13 inch pan with waxed paper and spray with vegetable spray.*

1/2 cup cold water
2 envelopes unflavored gelatin
1 cup light corn syrup
1½ tsp vanilla
Powdered sugar

- *In a 2 quart heavy saucepan, sprinkle the gelatin on top of the water and let sit for 5 minutes.*
- *Over low heat, stir until gelatin dissolves.*
- *Add sugar and corn syrup.*
- *Remove from heat and add vanilla.*
- *Beat on high speed until the mixture thickens and looks like marshmallow, about 5 minutes.*
- *Pour onto greased pan and spread flat with a buttered spatula.*
- *Let stand uncovered at room temperature for 8 to 12 hours.*
- *On the next day, cover a cutting board with powdered sugar and turn marshmallow upside down on powdered sugar.*
- *Peel off waxed paper and heavily dust top with more powdered sugar.*
- *Grease metal bunny or chick cookie cutter. Do not use plastic cutters as they won't work.*
- *Cut into shapes and completely dust with powdered sugar.*
- *Dip in dipping chocolate and decorate with frosting.*

53

TRUFFLES

Truffles are also known as Bavarian Mints

3/4 lb milk chocolate, melted
3/4 lb bittersweet chocolate, melted
1/2 pint whipping cream, scalded and cooled to lukewarm

- *In a medium heavy saucepan, melt butter, brown sugar and milk.*
- *Bring to a boil, stirring often.*
- *Cook exactly 3 minutes, wiping the sides of the pan with a wet pastry brush.*
- *Remove from heat and allow to cool for 2 minutes.*
- *Beat in sifted powdered sugar. If you do not sift, it will not melt.*
- *Beat until it is well blended and it gets glossy.*
- *Add vanilla and nuts.*
- *Spread onto a buttered pan.*
- *Mark for cutting and chill.*

54

FONDANT

This is best if made on a sunny day.

3 cups sugar
1/4 cup butter (do not use margarine)
1 cup heavy cream
1/4 cup whole milk
2 Tbsp light corn syrup
Maraschino cherries, chopped
**   (eye ball as much as you want)**
Nuts, chopped (as many as you want)

- *In a heavy saucepan, bring to a boil the sugar, butter, cream and milk.*
- *Add corn syrup.*
- *Cook to 228°.*
- *Add cherries and nuts.*
- *Continue cooking back to 232°.*
- *Remove from heat and drop by spoonfuls onto waxed paper.*

CARAMELS

From Gaylene Weaver of Salt Lake City, Utah.

1 cup sugar
1/4 tsp salt
1 cup light Karo syrup
1/4 cup sweetened condensed milk
1½ cups whipping cream
1½ tsp vanilla

- *Attach a candy thermometer to the side of a large, heavy saucepan.*
- *Bring the sugar, salt, Karo syrup and milk a boil.*
- *Cook to a temperature of 245°, stirring constantly. It will scorch if you do not stir it.*
- *Slowly add whipping cream.*
- *Continue to cook to 232° but don't cook past soft ball stage.*
- *Take off the stove and add vanilla.*
- *Pour onto a buttered cookie sheet.*
- *Cool and cut into squares.*
- *Wrap in waxed paper.*

COCONUT BON-BONS

I've been told that these are better than the commercial candy bar.

1 cup butter or margarine
2 boxes of powdered sugar
2 cans sweetened condensed milk
Two 14 oz packages of sweetened coconut flakes

- *Mix well and roll into small balls about the size of a quarter and freeze.*
- *Dip in dipping chocolate or a mixture of 2½ oz chocolate chips and ¼ lb paraffin melted in double boiler.*
- *Place on waxed paper after dipping.*

Cookies and Bars

CHOCOLATE BROWNIE CRACKLE COOKIES

These are pretty, quick and make a nice gift.

I Devil's food cake mix
2 eggs, slightly beaten
I Tbsp water
1/2 cup shortening
Powdered sugar

- *Combine all ingredients but the powdered sugar.*
- *Mix with a spoon. The batter will be very thick.*
- *Shape into balls about the size of a walnut and roll in powdered sugar.*
- *Place on greased cookie sheet.*
- *Bake at 375° for 8 to 10 minutes.*
- *Remove from the oven and sprinkle additional powdered sugar on tops, if needed.*
- *Makes about 4 dozen cookies.*

56

PEANUT BUTTER CHOCOLATE CHIP BARS

You can also make cookies with this recipe instead of bars.

I yellow cake mix
2 eggs
1/3 cup vegetable oil
1/2 cup chunky peanut butter
    (don't use creamy or you'll lose the nutty texture)
I cup chocolate chips

- *Preheat oven to 350°.*
- *Mix together the cake mix, eggs and oil.*
- *Mix in peanut butter.*
- *Stir in chocolate chips.*
- *Spread in a prepared 9 x 13 pan.*
- *Bake 15 to 20 minutes or until brown around edges.*
- *Cut into squares.*

PERSIMMON COOKIES

This recipe is from my daughter, Lori Miles, and is in demand during the Christmas holidays.

I cup Hachiya persimmon pulp
I cup sugar
1/2 cup butter
I egg, well beaten
1/2 cup prunes, chopped into small pieces
1/2 dried apricots, chopped into small pieces
I tsp vanilla
I tsp cinnamon
1/2 tsp salt
I tsp soda
I cup chopped nuts
2 cups flour
1/2 tsp nutmeg
1/2 tsp cloves

- *Cream the sugar and butter together.*
- *Add the egg.*
- *Sift dry ingredients and add to the butter mixture.*
- *Add prunes, apricots, nuts, and vanilla.*
- *As an option add chocolate chips to mix before cooking.*
- *Drop by tablespoons on a greased cookie sheet.*
- *Bake 15 to 20 minutes at 350°.*

NOTE

Hachiya has the shape of a Roma tomato and is sweet. These are not the ones you usually see on the tree in your neighbor's yard.

PUMPKIN SPICE COOKIES

I would pretty much consider this a diet cookie, keeping it to one or two cookies at a time.

I packaged spice cake mix
I small can of pumpkin
1/2 cup chocolate chips

- *Mix all together and drop by the spoonful onto a prepared cookie sheet.*
- *Bake at 375° for 10 to 12 minutes.*
- *Makes 4 dozen cookies.*
- *For a nice twist, use mint chocolate chips.*

APPLE-GRAPE NUTS COOKIES

1¾ cups flour
1/2 tsp baking powder
1/2 tsp baking soda
1/2 tsp salt
1 tsp cinnamon
1/2 tsp cloves
1/2 tsp nutmeg
3/4 cup shortening (use pre-packaged shortening in sticks)
1 cup sugar
1 egg
1 cup sweetened applesauce
1/2 cup raisins
1 cup **Grape Nuts**

- *Mix all dry ingredients.*
- *In an electric mixer, cream shortening, add sugar and egg and beat well.*
- *Add dry ingredients alternating with the applesauce.*
- *Add raisins and Grape Nuts.*
- *Drop by teaspoons on a prepared cookie sheet.*
- *Bake at 375° for 15 minutes.*

LEMON BARS

2/3 cup butter or margarine at room temperature
1/2 cup powdered sugar
1½ cups flour

- *Mix together with a pastry blender or knife.*
- *Press into a 9 x 13 greased pan.*
- *Bake at 350° for 20 to 25 minutes, remove and cool.*

For the filling combine the following:

4 eggs
4 Tbsp flour
6 Tbsp lemon juice
1/2 tsp baking powder
2 cups sugar
1/2 tsp salt

- *Beat eggs until fluffy and add sugar, salt, flour, baking powder and lemon juice.*
- *Mix and pour on top of the baked crust.*
- *Bake again at 350° for 20 to 25 minutes.*
- *When almost cool, sprinkle with powdered sugar.*
- *Cut into 30 two-inch squares.*

LILY ANN'S SUGAR COOKIES

This recipe is from Lily Ann Peeler who shared many good recipes with me over the years. These are the best cut-out cookies I have ever eaten.

1/2 cup butter
1 cup sugar
1 egg
1/2 tsp vanilla
2 Tbsp milk
1/2 tsp each salt and nutmeg
2 Tbsp baking powder
2½ cups flour

- *In a mixer bowl, mix butter, sugar, egg and vanilla together on low speed.*
- *Combine the remaining dry ingredients and add to other mixture, mixing well.*
- *Cover with plastic wrap and refrigerate for 1 to 2 hours.*
- *Roll out and cut with cookie cutters.*
- *Bake at 425° for 5 to 10 minutes.*
- *Cool and decorate with icing.*

> **NOTE**
> The thicker you roll the dough, the softer the cookies will be.

57

CYCLOPS COOKIES

These have a large candy Kiss in the middle. Read the complete recipe as all of the ingredients are not listed together.

1/2 cup butter
1/2 cup creamy peanut butter
1/2 cup sugar
1/2 cup packed light brown sugar

- *Mix in large mixer bowl and beat until fluffy.*

Add:

1 egg
2 Tbsp milk
1 tsp vanilla

- *Beat well.*

In a medium mixing bowl, stir together:

1¾ cups flour
1 tsp baking powder
1/4 tsp salt
1/8 tsp baking soda

- *Slowly add this mixture to the peanut butter mixture.*
- *Cover and chill at least 1 hour.*
- *Drop by tablespoons onto cookie sheet.*
- *Bake at 375° for 10 to 12 minutes.*
- *Immediately press a chocolate kiss on top of each cookie.*
- *Place on a cooling rack.*
- *Makes approximately 5 dozen.*

PEANUT BUTTER COOKIES

This is a twist using whole wheat flour.

Cream together:

1/2 cup shortening
1/4 cup creamy peanut butter
1/4 cup light brown sugar
1/2 cup sugar
1 egg slightly beaten

Sift together:

1¼ cups wheat flour
1/2 tsp baking powder
3/4 tsp baking soda
1/4 tsp salt

- *Mix dry ingredients in with the creamed mixture.*
- *Chill for 1 to 2 hours.*
- *Roll into 1 inch balls and place 3 inches apart on a cookie sheet.*
- *Dip a fork in flour and make a crisscross mark on top of cookie.*
- *Bake at 375° for 10 to 12 minutes.*

MACAROON BARS

This is different as it uses refrigerated crescent rolls.

3 to 4 cups flaked coconut, divided
One 14 oz can sweetened condensed milk
1 tsp almond extract
One 8 oz tube of crescent rolls

- *Grease a 9 x 13 pan and sprinkle with 1½ cups coconut.*
- *Combine milk and almond extract, drizzle half of it over the coconut.*
- *Unroll crescent rolls and layer over coconut in a single layer.*
- *Drizzle with remaining milk mixture.*
- *Sprinkle with remaining coconut.*
- *Bake at 350° for 30 to 35 minutes or until brown.*
- *Refrigerate.*
- *Cool completely before cutting.*

PUMPKIN BARS

I cup sugar
I cup canned pumpkin (without any spices)
1/2 cup shortening (I stick)
I Tbsp grated orange peel
2 cups flour
I tsp baking powder
I tsp baking soda
I tsp cinnamon
1/4 tsp salt

- *Mix sugar, pumpkin, shortening and orange peel together. The mixture should be very soupy.*
- *Add the remaining ingredients. You can add raisins and nuts, if desired.*
- *Pour into a 9 x 13 baking dish or drop by spoonfuls onto a cookie sheet for cookies.*
- *Bake at 375° for 25 minutes for bars or 8 to 10 minutes for cookies.*
- *While the bars are cooling, make the following glaze.*

Glaze:

1/4 cup butter or margarine
2 cups powdered sugar
I tsp vanilla (substitute lemon or almond extract
   if desired)
I to 2 Tbsp milk

- *Melt margarine in a small saucepan and then remove from heat.*
- *Stir in powdered sugar and vanilla.*
- *Add milk for desired consistency.*

> **NOTE**
>
> For thicker bars or plenty of cookies, double the recipe.

SNICKERDOODLES

This is my favorite cookie but I like them crisp, not soft. The difference is in how long you bake them. You can cut this recipe in half if you don't want a bunch of cookies to eat, give away or freeze.

2 cups shortening (use the pre-measured sticks
   but do not use butter)
3 cups sugar
4 eggs
2 tsp vanilla
3½ cups flour
2 tsp soda
4 tsp cream of tartar
I tsp salt

- *Mix on low speed the shortening, sugar, eggs and vanilla.*
- *Mix dry ingredients together and add to shortening mixture.*
- *Separate into two balls and wrap in plastic wrap.*
- *Refrigerate for 1 hour.*

In the meantime, mix together:

1/2 cup sugar
2 Tbsp cinnamon

- *Preheat oven to 400°.*
- *Roll dough into balls about the size of a walnut.*
- *It is much faster and easier to use the smallest melon ball scoop for consistently sized cookies.*
- *Roll each ball in the cinnamon-sugar mix.*
- *Place on a cookie sheet.*
- *Bake at 400° for 8 to 10 minutes depending on if you want them soft (less time baking) or crisp (more time baking).*
- *Makes approximately 8 dozen.*

GIANT SUGAR COOKIES

These make large cookies which makes them great for decorating for holidays.

Cream together:

1 cup sugar
3/4 cup margarine
1/4 cup molasses
1 egg

Mix together:

2 cups flour
1/4 tsp salt
1 tsp clove
1 tsp ginger
1 tsp cinnamon
2 tsp baking soda

- *Combine both mixtures and mix well.*
- *Chill for 1 hour.*
- *Shape into balls about the size of a ping pong ball.*
- *Roll in sugar.*
- *Put four to a cookie sheet and flatten with the bottom of a drinking glass.*
- *Bake at 350° for 10 to 12 minutes*
- *Let cool.*
- *Frost with colored icing and decorate.*
- *Use candy corn, raisins, Life-Savers, or any other small candies to decorate.*
- *Makes 2 to 3 dozen.*

MY CHOCOLATE CHIP COOKIES

I cannot remember a good chocolate chip cookie since the ones from my childhood. I was determined to create one and this one comes pretty close to my childhood favorite.

1½ cups light brown sugar, packed
1 cup granulated sugar
1 cup buttered-flavored Crisco (one stick)
1 cup real butter
2½ tsp vanilla
3 eggs
5 cups flour
1 tsp salt
2 Tbsp baking soda
12 oz chocolate chips
Chopped nuts, optional

- *Using a large mixer bowl, beat on high speed the brown sugar, granulated sugar, Crisco, butter, vanilla and eggs until light and fluffy.*
- *Add flour, salt and baking soda and mix together.*
- *Put flour mixture in with the sugar mixture.*
- *Fold in as many chocolate chips as you like.*
- *Add nuts, if desired.*
- *Using a small melon ball scooper, place on a cookie sheet that has been sprayed with vegetable spray.*
- *Bake at 350° for 10 to 14 minutes depending on how soft you want them.*

NOTE

Do not over bake these. They are a soft and chewy cookie. If you want a smaller cookie, reduce the time accordingly.

OATMEAL COOKIES

These are lovely chewy cookies and come from Virginia Anderson back when we lived in Anaheim, California.

1 cup flour
3/4 tsp baking soda
1/2 tsp salt
1 tsp cinnamon
1/4 tsp nutmeg
3/4 cup shortening (use stick shortening)
1 1/3 cups packed brown sugar
2 eggs
1 tsp vanilla
2 cups regular oatmeal
1 cup raisins

- *Mix flour, soda, salt, cinnamon and nutmeg together.*
- *Add shortening, sugar, eggs and vanilla.*
- *Beat on medium speed for 2 minutes.*
- *Stir in oatmeal and raisins.*
- *Drop by heaping teaspoons onto a greased cookie sheet.*
- *Bake at 350° for 12 to 15 minutes.*

CHEWY GINGERSNAPS

From Jolyn Weathers in Gilbert, Arizona.

Cream together:

3/4 cup shortening
3/4 cup butter
2 cups sugar
2 large eggs
1/2 cup molasses

Sift together the following:

1/2 tsp ginger
1/2 tsp cloves
1 tsp cinnamon
1 tsp salt
4 tsps baking soda
4 cups flour

- *Chill for 1 hour.*
- *Shape into balls and dip in granulated sugar.*
- *Bake at 375° for 9 to 10 minutes on an ungreased cookie sheet.*

PUMPKIN CHOCOLATE CHIP COOKIES

Use yogurt for this recipe which was shared with me by Lana Richardson of South Jordan, Utah.

3/4 cup pumpkin (with no spices in it)
3/4 cup brown sugar
1/2 cup vanilla yogurt
2 Tbsp vegetable oil
1 tsp vanilla
2 cups white flour or 1½ cups wheat flour
1/2 tsp baking powder
1/2 tsp baking soda
1/2 tsp salt
1/4 tsp allspice
1/4 tsp nutmeg
1/2 tsp ginger
1½ tsp cinnamon
1 cup chocolate chips or white chocolate chips

61

- *Mix all ingredients together and drop by tablespoons onto a prepared cookie sheet.*
- *Bake at 350° for 15 minutes.*
- *Makes 3 to 4 dozen.*

NOTES

Desserts

Banana Cream Pie

This recipe is low in calories and fat.

Reduced calorie chocolate wafer cookies
1 Tbsp brown sugar
1 tsp canola oil

- *Pulse enough cookies in a food processor to make 1 cup of cookie crumbs.*
- *Add 1 Tbsp brown sugar and 1 tsp canola oil.*
- *Pulse to mix together, pat into a pie plate.*

For filling, mix together:

One 7 oz jar Marshmallow Cream
One 8 oz container reduced-fat Cool Whip

- *Fold in sliced bananas.*
- *Pour filling into pie crust.*
- *Top with shaved chocolate from a candy bar.*

64

Holiday Dessert

This comes from Margo Yerman of Paradise, California. She said at the end of the recipe to just eat what did not fit into the freezer container.

1/2 gallon of pineapple sherbet
4 ripe bananas, chopped
3/4 cup nuts, chopped (optional)
Maraschino cherries, chopped

- *In a bowl, combine the sherbet, bananas, nuts and cherries, stir and mix well.*
- *Return mixture to the original container or use a good plastic container with a tight fitting lid.*
- *Refreeze.*

Apple Burritos

This is one of the most unusual desserts. It is especially quick and easy. Watch the tortillas turn into a pastry treat before your eyes.

Small tortillas (as many as you want)
Canned pie filling (apple, cherry, blueberry or any other fruit you like)
Add cinnamon and sugar to the apples, if desired

- *Fry tortillas in a small amount of vegetable oil in a small skillet.*
- *Turn over in about 5 to 10 seconds but do not overcook as they become too crisp to handle.*
- *Remove and stack on paper towels to absorb excess oil.*
- *Put about 2 Tbsp of filling along the middle of the tortilla.*
- *Roll up as you would a burrito and place on a cookie sheet.*
- *Brush with soft butter and sprinkle with raw sugar (it is not fine sugar).*
- *Bake at 350° for 5 to 7 minutes, just enough to warm them.*
- *Serve immediately with vanilla ice cream.*

> ### Note
> These do not re-warm well. Only make what you think you will eat.

Bread Pudding with Fruit

2 dozen glazed day-old donuts, cut into bite sizes
2 eggs, beaten
1 can sweetened condensed milk
Pinch of salt
1 to 2 tsp cinnamon
Raisins
1 large can fruit cocktail, including juice

- *Mix all ingredients together and put in a large baking pan.*
- *Bake at 350° for 45 to 50 minutes. The center should be set.*
- *Hot Vanilla Sauce (page 33) is good over this.*

FOOD STORAGE APPLE CRISP

Use the dehydrated apples from your food storage.

6 cups of dried apples
3 cups boiling water

- *Add boiling water to the 6 cups of apples.*
- *Let sit while preparing the topping.*

Topping:

3/4 cup of oatmeal
3/4 cup brown sugar
1/2 cup flour
3/4 cup butter

- *Mix together and cut in butter.*

Add:

1 cup sugar
2 Tbsp cinnamon

- *Pour the topping over the apples and bake at 325°for 1 hour.*

APPLE CRISP

This is also known as Apple Betty.

10 large apples, peeled, cored and sliced (Granny Smith or Golden Delicious)
1/2 cup orange juice
1 cup sugar
1 tsp cinnamon
2 cups flour
2 cups rolled oats
1 cup brown sugar
1/2 tsp salt
3/4 cup butter or margarine (1½ sticks)

- *Arrange apples in the bottom of a 9 x 13 baking pan.*
- *Pour orange juice over the apples.*
- *Mix sugar and cinnamon together and sprinkle over apples.*
- *Make topping by mixing flour, oats, brown sugar, salt and butter together until moist and crumbly.*
- *Spread over apples.*
- *Bake 350° for 35 to 40 minutes or until topping is lightly browned.*
- *Serve with ice cream or whipped cream.*

BROWNIE TRIFLE

This trifle comes from Erica Williams of South Jordan, Utah.

1 package brownie mix or one dozen prepared brownies
One 3.9 oz package of instant chocolate pudding
1/2 cup water
One 14 oz can sweetened condensed milk
One 8 oz container of Cool Whip, thawed
One 12 oz container of Cool Whip, thawed
1 small chocolate bar to shave over the top

- *Make brownies as directions on box and let cool.*
- *Cut into 1 inch squares.*
- *Combine pudding mix, sweetened condensed milk and ½ cup water in a bowl and mix until well blended and smooth.*
- *Fold in the 8 oz container of Cool Whip and mix until well blended (no streaks).*
- *In a trifle bowl, or any clear decorative bowl, put half of the cut brownies in the bottom, half of the pudding mix and half of the 12 oz Cool Whip.*
- *Repeat one more time ending with the Cool Whip.*
- *Shave the candy bar over the top and refrigerate for 6 hours or overnight.*

65

FRESH PEACH PIE

From Jolyn Weathers in Gilbert, Arizona. She's had marriage proposals over this pie!

1 baked pie crust
One 3 ounce package of vanilla pudding (cooked)
1 cup canned peach nectar
1/4 cup sugar
1 Tbsp lemon juice
5 cups fresh peaches, sliced

- *Place pudding, nectar, sugar and lemon juice in a saucepan.*
- *Boil until thickened and clear.*
- *Let cool.*
- *Pour over peaches, glazing each slice.*
- *Refrigerate several hours.*

BROWNIES

5 Tbsp butter or margarine
1 oz unsweetened chocolate
2/3 cup unsweetened cocoa
1½ cup sugar
3 large egg whites, slightly beaten
1 large egg, lightly beaten
1 cup flour
1/2 tsp baking powder

- *In a large saucepan, melt butter and chocolate, stir in cocoa and cook for 1 minute.*
- *Stir in sugar. Cook an additional minute and cool slightly.*
- *Combine egg whites and egg.*
- *Add warm chocolate mixture to egg mixture.*
- *Whisk until well blended.*
- *Combine flour and baking powder, add to chocolate mixture, and stir well.*
- *Pour into a 9 inch square baking pan sprayed with vegetable spray.*
- *Bake at 325° for 25 to 30 minutes.*

CREAM PUFFS

1 cup water
1/2 cup butter
1/2 cup flour
1 tsp salt
4 eggs

- *In a large saucepan, bring the water, salt and butter to a boil.*
- *Reduce the heat and add the flour all at once, beating constantly with a wooden spoon until the mixture forms a ball.*
- *Remove from the heat and add the eggs one at a time, beating until smooth.*
- *Drop onto baking sheet with a large spoon, rounding the top, or make into long bars.*
- *Bake for 50 minutes unil light brown.*
- *Fill with chocolate pudding, vanilla pudding or custard.*
- *Spread with Chocolate Glaze (page 155).*

CHOCOLATE MOUSSE

This comes from Elaine Jack of Salt Lake City, Utah.

3 cups miniature marshmallows
1/2 cup whole milk
4 oz milk chocolate bar (with or without almonds) or you can use semi-sweet chocolate chips

- *Melt ingredients in microwave, stirring often.*
- *Remove and stir until smooth, let cool.*

1 cup whipped cream
9 inch prepared graham cracker crust (optional)

- *Gently fold 1 cup of the whipped cream into the marshmallow/chocolate mix.*
- *Pour into 6 serving bowls or a 9 inch prepared graham cracker crust.*

IMPOSSIBLE COCONUT PIE

This pie is also known as Impossible Pie because you can't believe it actually makes a crust by itself.

2 cups milk
1/2 cup Bisquick
1/4 cup butter
1½ tsp vanilla
3/4 cup sugar
4 eggs
1 cup flaked coconut

- *Preheat oven to 350°.*
- *Combine milk, sugar, Bisquick, eggs, butter and vanilla in a blender.*
- *Blend on low speed for 3 minutes.*
- *Pour into a greased 9 inch pie plate.*
- *Let stand for 5 minutes.*
- *Sprinkle with the coconut.*
- *Bake for 40 minutes.*
- *Serve warm or cold.*

CREPES

You can freeze the crepes you do not use.

3 eggs, slightly beaten
1/2 cup milk
1/2 cup water
3 Tbsp butter, melted
3/4 cup flour
1/2 tsp salt
2 Tbsp sugar (optional)
1 tsp vanilla (optional)

- *Add milk to beaten eggs.*
- *Gradually pour in flour, stirring constantly with a wire whisk until smooth.*
- *Add butter and salt and mix until smooth.*
- *Pour a thin amount of batter in an 8 inch non-stick skillet sprayed with vegetable oil.*
- *Tilt the skillet until the batter fills the bottom.*
- *Cook only until you can insert a pancake turner and turn the crepe—about 30 seconds.*
- *Remove and stack with waxed paper between each crepe.*
- *Makes about 12 crepes (use 3¾ tsps per crepe).*

Filling:

One 8 oz package of cream cheese, softened
1¼ cups powdered sugar, sifted
1 Tbsp lemon juice
1 tsp lemon rind, grated
1/2 tsp vanilla
1 cup heavy cream, whipped
3½ cups fresh or frozen strawberries, sliced
Three 8 inch crepes

- *Combine softened cream cheese, sugar, lemon juice, lemon rind and vanilla.*
- *Mix until well blended, then fold in whipped cream.*
- *Fill crepe with about 1/3 cup fruit and 1/3 cup cream cheese mixture.*
- *Roll up and top with remaining cream cheese mixture and remaining fruit.*

> **NOTE**
> The filling will make 3 large 8 inch crepes. Adjust to fill the number of crepes you want.

COCONUT CREAM PIE

It's almost embarrassing to be praised for this pie because it's so simple to make.

One 5.8 oz instant vanilla pudding mix
2½ cups whole milk
1 cup coconut

- *Make pudding recipe using the instructions on the box.*
- *Add coconut, stir and put in a prepared and baked pie shell.*
- *Cover with plastic wrap and refrigerate.*
- *When ready to serve, slice and top with whipped cream.*

> **NOTE**
> Use meringue topping instead of the whipped cream for a change. You may also use this recipe for banana cream pie, chocolate cream or chocolate coconut cream pie.

FRUIT ICE CREAM

This is the basic recipe for homemade ice cream.

4 eggs
2½ cups sugar
6 cups milk
4 cups heavy whipping cream (this will vary according to the amount of fruit used)
2 Tbsp vanilla
1/2 tsp salt
Two 10 oz packages of frozen fruit of your choice

- *Using an electric mixer, beat eggs until light.*
- *Add sugar gradually, beating until the mixture thickens.*
- *Add the remaining ingredients.*
- *Pour into an electric or hand ice cream freezer and process.*

GRILLED FRESH PEACHES

You can also grill pears, pineapple, apples or peaches dipped the same way. This makes a great dessert with a scoop of ice cream in the center.

Peaches
Butter, melted
Sugar

- Wash and let fruit dry on a paper towel.
- Cut in halves and dip in melted butter.
- Dip in white sugar.
- Place cut-side down on the grill and cook a few minutes, just until heated and the grill lines show.

LEMON BERRY MILKSHAKE

68

2 cups fresh or 10 oz partially frozen strawberries, raspberries or blueberries
1/4 cup sugar
2 cups milk
1 pint lemon custard ice cream (you may have to buy this from an ice cream parlor)

- Place berries, sugar and milk in a blender and blend for 5 seconds.
- Add ice cream and blend only until smooth.

LEMON ICE

This is an easy citrus ice that's very good with oranges, too.

2 lemons juiced
1 tsp of grated lemon rind
2 cups white sugar
4 cups milk

- In a medium bowl, stir together lemon juice and rind with sugar until smooth.
- Stir in milk and pour into a 9 x 9 dish.
- Place in freezer, stirring once when it begins to harden, until firm—about 2 hours.
- Or pour into the freezer canister of an ice cream maker and freeze according to manufacturer's directions.

LEMON MERINGUE PIE

The quick version.

One 4.3 oz package lemon Jell-O Cook and Serve

- Follow the pie filling recipe on box.
- Put in a bowl covered with plastic wrap and chill several hours.
- Prepare pie crust and let cool or use an already prepared shell.
- Pour the prepared filling into the pie shell.
- Cover with Meringue Topping (recipe below).

Meringue Topping:

3 egg whites
1/4 tsp cream of tartar
6 tsp sugar
1/2 tsp vanilla

- Beat egg whites, vanilla and cream of tartar until foamy.
- Beat in sugar, one tablespoon at a time, until stiff and shiny.
- Pour on top of prepared pie, piling into high peaks.
- Bake at 375° for 10 to 15 minutes until peaks are brown. Watch it closely as it browns quickly.

SAN FRANCISCO TREAT

This recipe is from Joan Thomsen who lived in Anaheim, California at the time.

1 package Oreo Cookies, crushed
1 pint Cool Whip
1/2 gallon chocolate chip mint ice cream

- Crush cookies.
- Put ¾ of the crushed cookies in the bottom of a 9 x 13 pan.
- Soften ice cream and spread on crushed cookies.
- Spread Cool Whip on ice cream.
- Top with remaining crushed cookies and freeze.
- Serves 15.

PAVLOVA

This is a wonderful Australian dessert given to me by Tiffany Nish of South Jordan, Utah.

Spray the bottom of a large cookie sheet with vegetable spray, sprinkle with corn starch, then follow the recipe.

8 egg whites (at room temperature)
1/4 tsp salt
1/2 tsp cream of tartar
2 cups Baker's Sugar (super fine white sugar)
1/4 tsp white vinegar

- *Mix egg whites, salt and cream of tartar in a mixer until thickened.*
- *Slowly add sugar and continue to beat until stiff peaks form.*
- *Fold in vinegar carefully.*
- *Place on the prepared cookie sheet. Use parchment paper if you have it. Build mixture into a large, high mound. The sides should almost touch the sides of the cookie sheet. <u>Do not spread thin; mixture should be high.</u>*
- *Bake at 250° for 1 hour and 15 minutes., turn off the oven and leave it there all day until ready to serve.*
- *Spread the top with real whipped whipping cream, not the spray or from a container and then place sliced fresh fruit over the top.*
- *Some suggested fruits are raspberries, blackberries, bananas, kiwi, strawberries or blueberries.*
- *Serve immediately.*
- *Serves 8 to 10.*

NOTE

When making the Peach Cobbler, if you're using a 12 inch Dutch oven, place 9 briquettes on the bottom along the edge and 15 on the top around the edge.

Check after 30 minutes until done. Do not place any briquettes in the middle under the bottom or on top of the Dutch oven as it will cause the cake to burn in spots.

FRESH PEACH ICE CREAM

This recipe was shared by Joan Thomsen of Provo, Utah. She found in one of the old Relief Society magazines from over forty years ago.

Prepare the first part of this recipe at least three hours before making the ice cream.

3 to 4 cups of diced fresh peaches or other fresh fruits
3 cups sugar
Juice of 2 lemons
Juice of 2 oranges

- *Combine all ingredients.*
- *Cover in a large bowl and let stand at room temperature for at least 3 hours.*
- *Pour mixture into a 4 or 5 quart ice cream freezer.*

2 quarts of half and half

- *Add the half and half.*
- *Process in an ice cream freezer.*

PEACH COBBLER

This works well for Dutch oven cooking.

Two 29 oz cans sliced peaches, including the juice
4 Tbsp tapioca
Ground cinnamon
Sugar
Yellow or white cake mix
1/2 cup of butter cut into 7 pieces

- *Put the peaches in a large pot with a tight lid. A Dutch oven is best.*
- *Sprinkle with tapioca, cinnamon and sugar.*
- *Put dry cake mix over peaches.*
- *Place cut up pieces of butter around top of the cake mix.*
- *Put the lid on and bake at 350° for 40 to 50 minutes or until the top is golden brown.*
- *See Note to the left.*

69

PEACH-PEAR COBBLER

This is my original recipe.

One 29 oz can sliced peaches, including the juice
One 29 oz can sliced pears, including the juice
1/2 cup butter, melted
1¼ cups sugar (you may substitute with Splenda)
1/2 tsp salt
1½ tsp baking powder
4 Tbsp dry tapioca
1 cup flour
1 cup whole milk

- *Melt the butter and put in a 9 x 13 baking dish.*
- *Combine the flour, sugar, salt, baking powder and tapioca and blend with a fork to mix.*
- *Stir in milk and mix until smooth.*
- *Pour mixture over melted butter.*
- *Drain juice from both peaches and pears, reserving the juice.*
- *Arrange the peaches and pears over the batter.*
- *Pour reserved juices over the fruit. Do not stir or mix together. Sprinkle topping over the fruit.*

Topping:

4 Tbsp sugar
3/4 tsp cinnamon

- *Bake at 350° for 40 to 50 minutes until top is brown*
- *Serve warm or at room temperature with or without ice cream.*

CHERRY CHEESE PIE

9 inch graham cracker crust
One 8 oz package of cream cheese at room temperature
1/2 cup lemon juice
1 tsp vanilla
1 (21 oz) can of cherry pie filling
One 14 oz can of sweetened condensed milk

- *Beat cream cheese until soft and fluffy.*
- *Add lemon juice and vanilla and put into pie shell.*
- *Chill at least three hours.*
- *When ready to serve top with pie filling.*
- *Serves 6 to 8.*
- *You may substitute other fruits for the topping.*

PEANUT BUTTER BROWNIES

This starts with a box of brownie mix and is fast as lightening to make.

1 box of brownie mix, any brand
(do not follow box instructions)

Add to brownie mix:

1/4 cup water
1/2 cup vegetable oil
2 eggs
1 cup peanut butter chips
1 cup miniature marshmallows

- *Pour into a 9 x 13 baking dish.*
- *Top with chopped nuts.*
- *Bake at 425° for 25 to 30 minutes.*
- *During the last minute cover the top with mini marshmallows and cook another minute to melt.*

PUMPKIN PIE

One 16 oz can pumpkin pie filling
3/4 cup sugar
1 tsp ground cinnamon (add more if you like)
1 tsp ground ginger
1 tsp ground nutmeg
1/2 tsp salt
3 eggs, beaten with a fork
2/3 cup evaporated milk
1/2 cup whole milk
1 prepared pie crust

Combine:

- *Pumpkin, sugar, cinnamon, ginger, nutmeg and salt in a large bowl.*
- *Add eggs to pumpkin mixture and stir with a whisk.*
- *Add evaporated milk and mix well.*
- *Pour into pie crust.*
- *Cover the edge of the crust with aluminum foil to prevent burning.*
- *Bake for 25 minutes at 375°.*
- *Remove foil from crust and bake for another 30 minutes or until a knife comes out clean when inserted into the center of the pie.*

PIE DOUGH SUPREME

This is the very best and easiest dough to work with. It is a combination of several recipes that I modified and makes two very large crusts or three small crusts. The dough freezes well and comes in handy later.

1¼ cups Crisco (butter-flavored or regular works, depending on the color of the crust you want)
1 Tbsp sugar
1/2 tsp baking powder
1 tsp salt
1 Tbsp nonfat dry milk
3 cups all purpose flour (do not sift)
1/2 cup cold water (it may require one additional tablespoon of water)

- *Using an electric mixer, cream Crisco, sugar, baking powder, salt and dry milk together.*
- *Mix on low speed until just mixed. Do not over mix as it will make the crust tough.*

Add:

- *Half of the flour and mix.*
- *Add water and remaining flour.*
- *Roll into 3 balls and refrigerate until cold.*
- *Using a floured pastry cloth, roll out half the pastry large enough to overlap the pie plate by 1 inch.*
- *Press lightly into the bottom and sides of the pie plate.*
- *Trim dough to ¼ inch of rim.*
- *Flute edges with fingers or a fork.*
- *For single crust, baked pie shells, prick the bottom and sides with a fork.*
- *Bake at 475° for 5 to 8 minutes.*

> ### NOTE
> Check every minute after five minutes as the crust will brown quickly.

RICE RAISIN PUDDING

Fast, rich and yummy.

One large package of instant vanilla pudding
2 cups whole milk
3/4 cup half and half

- *Mix together in a mixer bowl and beat on low speed for 2 minutes.*

Add:

1 cup rice, cooked and cold
Lemon zest (optional)
1 tsp vanilla
1/8 tsp nutmeg
1/2 cup raisins soaked in hot water, drained and towel-dried

- *Blend well and put in serving dishes.*
- *Top with whipped cream.*
- *Sprinkle with cinnamon or slivered almonds.*
- *Refrigerate for a few hours.*
- *Makes 5 custard cups.*

71

SHERBET DELIGHT

Joan Thomsen always had great, rich desserts so don't blame me.

One 8 oz container of Cool Whip (save enough for the top)
2 cups chopped nuts
2 dozen coconut macaroons, chopped (Mother's brand is good)
4 pints of different flavored sherbet

- *Fold together the Cool Whip, nuts and cookie pieces.*
- *Put in the bottom of a 10 x 13 pan.*
- *Cut each pint of sherbet into slices and arrange on top of Cool Whip and cookie mixture.*
- *Cover sherbet with remaining Cool Whip and freeze.*
- *Serves 15.*

STRAWBERRY PIE

This is delightful and different for a nice summer dessert.

32 large marshmallows
1/4 cup whole milk
1 pint whipping cream
1½ to 2 baskets of fresh strawberries

- *Either make or buy a prepared graham cracker crust.*
- *Melt marshmallows in milk in a heavy saucepan and set aside to cool.*
- *Prepare strawberries and drain well.*
- *Whip cream very stiff.*
- *Fold in cooled marshmallow mix with whipped cream.*
- *Fold in strawberries and pour into prepared crust.*
- *Chill for at least 4 hours.*

FRUIT COBBLER

Use fresh fruit in season for this cobbler.

Crust:

1/2 cup soft margarine or butter
1 cup flour
1/2 Bisquick
2 Tbsp baking powder
1/4 tsp salt
3/4 cup milk
Fresh fruit, your choice
1/2 cup sugar
1 cup hot water
1/4 cup dry small tapioca

- *Mix butter, flour, Bisquick, baking powder and salt.*
- *Add ¾ cup milk and blend well.*
- *Put fresh cut fruit in the bottom of a 9 x 11 pan, filling it 2/3 of the way.*
- *Sprinkle ½ cup sugar over the fruit. Adjust the amount of sugar to the sweetness of the fruit.*
- *Add 1 cup of water.*
- *Sprinkle ¼ cup of dry, small tapioca.*
- *Spread crust mixture over the top of the fruit.*
- *Pour an additional 1 cup of hot water on top.*
- *Bake at 350° for 35 to 40 minutes or until golden brown.*

STRAWBERRY PRETZEL DESSERT

This is from the best dessert friend I have—Joan Thomsen. If you haven't tried this before, share it with someone else who hasn't ever had it. It is a conversation dish.

- *Make crust ahead of time and let it cool.*

Crust:

4 cups pretzels
6 Tbsp unsalted butter at room temperature
3 Tbsp sugar

- *Crush the pretzels and mix with butter and sugar with a pastry blender. Press into a 9 x 13 baking dish sprayed with vegetable spray.*
- *Bake for 10 minutes at 350° and let cool completely.*

Filling:

One 8 oz package of cream cheese at room temperature
1 cup sugar
One 10 oz container of Cool Whip

- *Beat together the cream cheese and sugar until smooth.*
- *Fold in the whipped topping.*
- *Spread mixture over cooled crust.*

Two 3 oz packages strawberry Jell-O
2 cups boiling water
One 16 oz package frozen strawberries, or 1 pint of fresh berries, sliced lengthwise and sweetened with sugar

Topping:

- *Dissolve Jell-O in water, stir in thawed or fresh berries.*
- *Place bowl inside a larger bowl filled with ice water and refrigerate, stirring often, until just starting to thicken—about 10 to 15 minutes.*
- *Spoon strawberry mixture over cream cheese and refrigerate for 4 hours.*
- *Cut into squares and serve.*
- *Serves 12 to 15.*

73

CRUSTED FRUIT COBBLER

This cobbler makes its own crust as it bakes.

1 cup shortening (or sticks of pre-packaged shortening)
2 cup flour
2 tsp baking powder
1 tsp salt
1½ cups milk
One 25 oz can of fruit of your choice, drained or an equal amount of fresh or frozen fruit, thawed
1 cup sugar

- Mix all ingredients except the fruit and sugar and pour into a 9 x 13 baking dish.
- Cover with selected fruit.
- Pour 1 cup of sugar over the top.
- Bake at 375° for 1 hour or until the crust is golden brown.

74

LEMON ICE CREAM PIE

You can't find a faster ice cream dessert.

1 half gallon of your favorite vanilla ice cream
1 small can of frozen lemonade
1 prepared graham cracker crust

- Mix ice cream and lemonade with an electric mixer. Avoid it melting too much.
- Pour into pie crust and refreeze for 2 hours or longer.

MAI TAI PIE

You'll have people begging for this recipe.

Make the Macaroon Crust first and keep in refrigerator until the filling is ready to put in it.

Crust:

2 cups macaroon cookie crumbs
1/4 cup melted butter

- Press mixture into a 10 inch pie plate
- Refrigerate until ready to use

For the filling:

1 pint pineapple or lemon sherbet, softened
1 pint of vanilla ice cream, softened
1/4 cup lime juice
2 Tbsp orange juice
1 Tbsp grated lime peel
1 Tbsp grated orange peel
One 20 oz can of crushed pineapple, well drained

- Combine softened sherbet and ice cream with all juices and grated peel.
- Fold in pineapple.
- Pour into Macaroon Crust.
- Freeze until firm or overnight.
- Garnish with pineapple slices, if desired.

CHERRY COCONUT CRUMB PIE

1 prepared and baked pie shell
1 can of cherry pie filling

- Put cherry pie filling in a saucepan and bring to a boil.
- Pour into the baked pie shell.

Combine:

1/2 cup flour
1/4 cup sugar
1/4 cup butter (½ stick) melted
1 cup sweetened shredded coconut

- Mix well and sprinkle over pie.
- Bake at 375° for 20 minutes or until coconut has browned.
- Serve at room temperature.

RICE PUDDING

There are two rice pudding recipes in this book but both are very different. This one has a custard base and must be baked in the oven while the other has a pudding base which calls for instant pudding. Both are good but it depends on the taste you prefer or want at the time.

5 eggs
3¼ cups whole milk
1/2 cup sugar
Dash of salt
1 tsp cinnamon
1/2 tsp nutmeg
1/2 cup raisins, soaked in boiling water 10 minutes
1 cup cooked, cold rice

- *Whisk together all ingredients except the rice and raisins.*
- *Stir in rice and raisins.*
- *Carefully pour mixture into a buttered 8 x 8 square baking pan.*
- *Set that pan inside a larger pan that is half-filled with water.*
- *Bake for 1 hour at 350°.*
- *Refrigerate until cold. It will be wobbly but will set as it cools.*

GLAZED FRESH STRAWBERRIES

Use these berries for pies, tarts or strawberry shortcake.

5 to 6 cups of fresh strawberries cut into large pieces, saving 5 large berries cut in halves
1 cup sugar
4 heaping Tbsp cornstarch
1/2 cup water
One 9 inch baked pie shell, tart shell or shortcake
Whipped cream

Glaze:

- *Bring water, sugar and cornstarch to a boil in a 3 quart saucepan, stirring constantly for 2 minutes.*
- *Remove from the heat and let cool. Save 1/4 cup of the glaze for the decorative strawberry halves.*
- *Fold remaining cut berries into the cooled mixture.*
- *Pour into a prepared pie shell, tart shells, dessert dishes or over shortcake.*
- *Decorate with the strawberry halves dipped in the glaze and top with whipped cream when serving.*

BERRY CREAM PIE

This is a yummy summer dessert. Use only fresh berries for the best results.

1 prepared graham cracker pie crust
One 3 oz package of instant vanilla pudding
2½ cups fresh berries of your choice
1 cup sugar (more or less, depending on the sweetness of the berries)
1 Tbsp corn starch mixed with a little water

- *Make pudding as directed for pie filling, cover with plastic wrap and put in refrigerator.*
- *When cool, put pudding in pie shell, cover with plastic wrap and refrigerate.*
- *Put the berries and sugar in a saucepan and simmer for 5 minutes.*
- *Thicken with cornstarch. Put in a bowl, cover with plastic wrap and chill until ready to serve.*
- *When ready to serve, put chilled berries on top of pie.*

75

NOTE
You might prefer the consistency of the pudding you cook rather than the instant.

NUTTY PIE CRUST

If you are in a hurry, use the prepared crusts you find in the grocery store.

1 cup flour
1/2 cup butter or margarine
1/2 cup nuts, finely chopped
1/4 cup powdered sugar

- *Mix all ingredients in a bowl and pat into the bottom of a 9 x 13 pan.*
- *Bake at 350° for 15 minutes.*
- *Let cool before filling.*

NOTE
This is a terrific crust to use for any fruit or cream pies. The nutty flavor and texture make it truly delicious.

DANISH DESSERT

This is an old favorite used in my church's women's organization. It is from the 1960's but has become popular again.

1 yellow cake mix with no pudding in the mix
One 8 oz package of cream cheese at room
    temperature
1 pint whipping cream, not whipped
3 Tbsp sugar
1 tsp vanilla
1 box strawberry glaze (Junket Danish Dessert)

- *In a very large deep pan (10 x 15 x 2) bake the cake as directed on the box and let cool.*
- *Mix the cream cheese and whipping cream together and beat with an electric mixer until it forms peaks.*
- *Slowly add sugar and vanilla as you continue to beat.*
- *Spread over cooled cake.*
- *Follow the Strawberry Glaze recipe on the Junket Danish Dessert box.*
- *Pour strawberry glaze over the top of the cake and refrigerate at least 2 hours.*

> ### NOTE
> Use an extra large pan or the topping will overflow.

ENGLISH TRIFLE

There are a variety of trifles. This is only one of a few in this book. See page 79 for another recipe.

One 3 oz package Jell-O (any flavor)
One 3.4 oz instant vanilla pudding mix
Day-old angel food or white cake, broken into
    large bite-sized pieces
Fresh strawberries, cut into pieces
Bananas, sliced
1 large container of Cool Whip

- *Make Jell-O as directed on the package and chill. Then cut into cubes.*
- *Make instant pudding as directed.*
- *In a large glass bowl, layer broken-up cake, Jell-O cubes, pudding, bananas and Cool Whip.*
- *Repeat, ending with Cool Whip.*

LEMON PARFAIT

This recipe comes from an old friend, Leafy Gardner, whom I met in 1975 in Anaheim, California.

1/2 cup margarine
1/2 cup chopped nuts
1 cup flour

- *Blend ingredients together with a pastry blender or gently with a spoon.*
- *Press into a 9 x 13 pan.*
- *Bake at 350° for 15 minutes and let cool.*

In the meantime, mix together:

One 8 oz package of cream cheese at room
    temperature
1 cup powdered sugar, sifted
1 cup Cool Whip

- *Beat cream cheese and powdered sugar with a hand mixer.*
- *Blend in the Cool Whip.*
- *Spread over crust.*

In another bowl, mix the following:

Two 3 oz packages instant lemon pudding
3 cups whole milk

- *Beat the instant pudding with the milk on medium speed for 2 minutes.*
- *Spread over the cream mixture.*
- *Put additional Cool Whip on top.*
- *Sprinkle nuts on last.*
- *Refrigerate until ready to serve.*

STRAWBERRY-BANANA ICE CREAM

3 cups whole milk
3 cups half and half
3 cups sugar
3 cups orange juice
3 cups fresh, ripe or frozen strawberries
3 large ripe bananas, mashed

- *Mix all ingredients together, put in ice cream mixer and process.*

CHERRY CHEESECAKES

These petite little cakes are perfect for luncheons or desserts. They freeze well without the cherry topping which you put on when you're ready to serve.

Two 8 oz packages of cream cheese at room temperature
3/4 cup sugar
2 eggs
I Tbsp lemon juice
I tsp vanilla
24 vanilla wafers
One 21 oz can cherry pie filling

- *Beat cream cheese, sugar, eggs, lemon juice and vanilla together until light and fluffy.*
- *Line the bottom of muffin tins with paper baking cups.*
- *Place a vanilla wafer in the bottom of each cup.*
- *Fill each cup 2/3 full with the cream cheese mixture.*
- *Bake 375° for 15 to 20 minutes and chill.*
- *When ready to serve, remove from paper wrap and put a tablespoon of cherry pie filling on top.*
- *As an option, crush the cookies instead of keeping them whole.*
- *Makes 2 dozen individual cheesecakes.*

STRAWBERRY-BANANA CREAM PIE

I prepared pie shell (graham cracker, pastry prepared or homemade)
Sliced, fresh ripe bananas
I pint fresh or frozen, sweetened strawberries, sliced
I cup cold whole milk (for the pudding)
One 3.4 oz package instant banana cream or vanilla pudding
I ½ cups Cool Whip
Apple jelly, melted

- *Arrange 2/3 of the sliced bananas and strawberries on the bottom of the pie shell.*
- *Mix the pudding according to the directions.*
- *Fold in Cool Whip.*
- *Pour over the fruit and refrigerate.*
- *When ready to serve, take the remaining fruit and mix with melted apple jelly.*
- *Arrange 6 to 7 pieces of fruit per slice.*

77

ORANGE-BANANA SHERBET

This is a quick homemade ice cream and is also called "Six 3's" for obvious reasons.

3 cups of whole milk
3 cups of half and half
3 cups sugar
3 cups orange juice
3 lemons, the juice only
3 large ripe bananas, mashed

- *Put all ingredients in an ice cream maker and process.*

Nancy Miles

APPLE PIE

If you want the real deal, this is it—the best I have ever had anywhere. It was originally given to me by Tova Wilson of Red Bluff, California.

6 cups peeled, cored and sliced apples (Gravestein or Granny Smith)
2/3 cup sugar
1/4 tsp nutmeg
1 tsp cinnamon
1 tsp lemon juice
1/8 tsp salt
Touch of coriander
2½ Tbsp dry tapioca
1/4 cup butter (use ½ stick butter), cut into 6 pieces
Prepared pie crust

78

- *Prepare pie dough and press into the bottom of a large pie pan.*
- *Brush bottom of dough with a beaten egg white.*
- *Fill pie shell high with sliced apples.*
- *Pour spices and sugar over the top of the apples*
- *Sprinkle with the tapioca.*
- *Place the six pieces of butter on top.*
- *Adjust the top crust and cut a hole or design in it to allow for venting.*
- *Wrap foil around outside edge of crust to prevent it from burning.*
- *Put on a cookie sheet and bake at 425° for 40 to 45 minutes.*
- *Remove the foil and cook until the crust is golden brown.*

NOTE
Brush the remaining beaten egg white over the top crust and sprinkle it with sugar.

CHOCOLATE ICE CREAM

If you can recall the old fashioned Fudgecicles, this is it.

1 quart half and half
1/3 cup sugar
1½ pints of whipping cream
4 eggs
3¼ cups chocolate syrup
1/2 tsp salt
4½ Tbsp vanilla

- *Beat eggs and sugar by hand.*
- *Add remaining ingredients.*
- *Process in an ice cream maker.*

PEACH CUPS

- *Put the following in each hollow of the half peaches:*

1 Tbsp brown sugar
1/2 tsp butter
1/8 tsp cinnamon

- *Place peaches on a baking sheet.*
- *Bake at 350° for 20 minutes.*
- *Serve warm.*

PIE CRUST

Make this in your food processor. It's quick and easy.

2¼ cups flour
1 Tbsp sugar
1/2 tsp salt
1 egg
3 Tbsp sour cream
3/4 cup cold butter

- *Use the metal blade on your food processor.*
- *Put all ingredients in the food processor and pulse until the dough forms a ball.*
- *Remove immediately and roll into two 8 inch pie crusts.*

NOTE
Do not process over five seconds or it will make the crust tough.

In Good Taste

PINEAPPLE-RASPBERRY-BANANA SHERBET

This turns out to be an unusual dessert.

1½ gallons pineapple sherbet
One 10 oz package frozen raspberries
    (including the juice), thawed and mashed
3 ripe bananas, mashed

- *Let sherbet sit at room temperature until soft.*
- *Add raspberries and bananas.*
- *Put in tight freezer containers and re-freeze.*

PIE SHELLS

I have two pie dough recipes. One is made in the food processor and then this one by hand. It's easy to handle and the crust is nice and flakey. It also freezes well. Remember, the secret to light, flakey crust is to not handle or mix the dough too much.

2½ cups flour
2 Tbsp salt
1 cup shortening

Blend together and add:

2 Tbsp cold water
1 egg
1 Tbsp white vinegar and water to equal ½ cup
    liquid

- *Using a fork, mix all ingredients gently.*
- *Form into 2 balls.*
- *Roll out and put in pie pans.*
- *Prick with a fork to prevent the dough from bubbling.*
- *Bake at 400° for 10 to 12 minutes or until golden brown.*

NOTE
If you are not making pre-baked shells, do not prick or bake the bottom crust. Put the filling in and use the other crust for the top.

TRIFLE

I have two recipes for Trifle but they are different enough to have both recipes in the book.

1/2 of a pre-made cake in a flavor that
    compliments the rest of the ingredients or use
    leftover sweet rolls
One 3.4 oz instant vanilla pudding mix made
    according to the directions on box
5 ripe bananas, sliced
2 baskets of fresh strawberries, sliced
One 12 oz container of Cool Whip
Sliced almonds for flavor, optional
Jam, watered down a bit or use chocolate syrup
Chocolate bar, grated

- *Layer in a very large glass or decorative bowl starting with the cake and ending with the Cool Whip.*
- *Grate a chocolate bar on top.*

79

BASIC VANILLA ICE CREAM

This recipe comes from Jean Hartman many years ago. Our families used to get together at the beach on Monday nights. When Jean brought this creamy, delicious ice cream, she was the hit of the beach.

3 eggs
1 cup sugar
Dash of salt
One 5.9 oz package of instant Jell-O vanilla
    pudding mix
1 quart of half and half
1 can eagle brand milk
1 to 2 tsp clear vanilla

- *Mix all ingredients well and put in an electric ice cream freezer and process.*

CHERRY CHOCOLATE ICE CREAM

Add this to the Basic Vanilla Ice Cream for a nice change.

1 small jar of maraschino cherries, drained
1 large chocolate candy bar, chopped

- *Add to the Basic Vanilla Ice Cream recipe and process.*

BREAD PUDDING

Syrup:

3/4 cup light brown sugar
3/4 cup water
1/2 tsp cinnamon
1/4 cup raisins

- *Bring all ingredients to a boil; this is the syrup.*

2½ cups toasted bread, broken up and set aside
1/4 cup nuts, chopped (your choice)
One 15 oz can sliced peaches, drained
One 20 oz can pineapple chunks, drained
1/2 cup Jack cheese, grated

- *Using a 9 x 13 pan, starting with the bread and alternate fruits and nuts.*
- *Top with the cheese.*
- *Pour syrup over the top.*
- *Bake at 375° for 15 to 20 minutes.*
- *Serve warm or at room temperature.*
- *Top with whipped cream, optional.*

NOTE

My brother-in-law, Glenn Dyson, cannot turn bread pudding down even if he is stuffed. This recipe is particularly tasty because of the fruit and cheese.

CHEESECAKE

This is also known as Heavenly Cheesecake.

3/4 cup sugar
1/2 cup Bisquick
2 eggs
Two 8 oz packages of cream cheese, at room temperature
2 tsp vanilla
1/2 tsp grated lemon or orange peel

- *Put all ingredients in a food processor and process for three minutes.*
- *Pour into a 9 inch pie plate.*
- *Bake at 350° for 25 to 30 minutes.*

Cheesecake Topping:

1 cup sour cream
2 Tbsp sugar
2 tsp vanilla

- *Mix all ingredients and spread on top of cheesecake.*
- *Refrigerate until ready to serve.*

MERINGUE TOPPING

Add this topping to any cream pie in a pre-baked pie crust with instant pudding and pie filling.

2 egg whites
1/4 tsp cream of tartar
6 Tbsp sugar
1/2 tsp vanilla

- *Using an electric mixer on medium speed, beat the egg whites, cream of tartar and vanilla until it forms soft peaks.*
- *Switching to high speed, gradually add sugar and continue beating until stiff peaks appear and they are glossy.*
- *Spoon onto the top of the prepared pie, making certain the edges reach the sides. This will prevent the meringue from pulling from the sides.*
- *Using a knife, form peaks on top of meringue.*
- *Bake at 375° for 10 to 15 minutes or until golden brown. Keep an eye on it.*

CREAM CHEESE CHERRY PIE

Plan on this recipe making two pies.

2 pre-baked fresh or frozen pie shells, cooled
1 pint of whipping cream
One 8 oz package of cream cheese, softened

- *Whip the whipping cream and cream cheese until thick.*

Add:

2 tsp vanilla
1 cup powdered sugar

- *Beat until well blended.*
- *Divide mixture between the two pie shells.*
- *Cover pies with plastic wrap and refrigerate for at least 8 hours.*
- *When ready to serve, remove the wrap and top with canned cherry or blueberry pie filling.*

PECAN PIE

This is a mock version of pecan pie. No one could believe Kelley Wulff when she announced it wasn't the real thing.

3 eggs
3 cups sugar
1 cup margarine, melted
1 cup evaporated canned milk
2/3 cup cornmeal
1 cup pecans, chopped
1 Tbsp vanilla

- *Beat the eggs and add all remaining ingredients.*
- *Pour into two unbaked pie shells.*
- *Bake at 350° for one hour.*

MOUSSE

Got five minutes to spare? That'll do it.

One 4 oz package sugar free Jell-O chocolate Instant Pudding & Pie Filling
1½ cups 2% low-fat milk
1 cup Cool Whip, thawed

- *Prepare the pudding mix using 1½ cups low-fat milk.*
- *Fold in the Cool Whip, mix well.*
- *Put in dessert cups and chill.*

SHERBET

Juice of 3 oranges
Juice of 3 lemons
3 ripe bananas, mashed
1 can sweetened condensed milk
3 cups sugar
1 quart whole milk
1 pint whipping cream

- *Mix all ingredients together.*
- *Put in a freezer container and freeze.*
- *Stir once during freezing process.*
- *Freeze until solid.*

PEACH BETTY

2 lb (about 8 medium) fresh peaches
1 cup soft bread crumbs
1/2 cup sugar
1 Tbsp flour
1/4 tsp salt
2 Tbsp butter

- *Slice peaches and place in 1 quart casserole dish.*
- *Combine bread crumbs, sugar, flour and salt.*
- *Top peaches with half the bread crumbs.*
- *Dot with 1 Tbsp butter.*
- *Repeat.*
- *Bake at 375° for 40 minutes or until bread is golden brown.*

Nancy Miles

STRAWBERRY YOGURT PIE

People who don't even like yogurt will love this dish. From Leslie Tall.

16 oz strawberry yogurt (you can use other
    flavors; do not use an inexpensive brand)
1 cup regular oats
1/2 cup brown sugar
1/2 cup butter
1/2 cup walnuts, finely chopped
One 9 oz container of Cool Whip, thawed
Fresh strawberries

- Spray a glass pie plate with vegetable spray.
- Place oats and nuts in the pie plate.
- Microwave for 2 minutes, stirring after 1 minute.
- Melt butter, add sugar.
- Pour over the oats and nuts.
- Press into pie plate, let cool.
- Mix the Cool Whip with the strawberry yogurt.
- Fill pie plate and refrigerate.
- Just before serving add slices of strawberries around the edges and center of the pies.

DATE SPICE BARS

From Jolyn Weathers in Gilbert, Arizona.

Boil for five minutes in a large saucepan and cool slightly:

3 cups water
2 tsp Postum
2 cups white sugar
1/2 cup (rounded) Crisco shortening
2 cups chopped, pitted dates

Add:

1 heaping tsp of baking soda

Sift together and add:

3 cups flour
1 tsp cinnamon
1/2 tsp nutmeg
1 tsp cloves
1 tsp ginger
1 tsp salt

- Pour into a jelly roll pan.
- Bake at 350 for 23 to 25 minutes.
- When cool, spread with cream cheese frosting (p. 43).

82

LIME CREAM PIE

This is a nice, cool summer dessert and can be made in just a few minutes.

1 prepared graham cracker pie crust, or
    regular crust, baked and cooled
One 8 oz container of Cool Whip
1 can sweetened condensed milk
1 small can of frozen limeade

- Mix all ingredients and pour into pie shell.
- Refrigerate for several hours.

CHEESECAKE-TOPPED BROWNIES

These brownies come from Lana Richardson of South Jordan, Utah. Lana is my Emergency Food Partner. We're always experimenting with how to use our emergency food storage.

1 box fudge brownie mix (use cake-type mix)
One 8 oz package of cream cheese, softened
2 Tbsp butter, softened
1 Tbsp cornstarch
One 14 oz can sweetened condensed milk
1 egg
2 tsp vanilla
Ready-to-spread chocolate frosting (optional)

- Preheat oven to 350º.
- Prepare brownie mix as directed on box.
- Spread into a well-greased 9 x 13 inch baking pan.
- Beat in a large mixing bowl cream cheese, butter and cornstarch until fluffy.
- Gradually beat in sweetened condensed milk.
- Add egg and vanilla and beat until smooth.
- Pour mixture on top of brownie batter.
- Bake 40 to 45 minutes or until top is lightly browned.
- When cool, spread frosting on top.
- Cut into bars and store covered in refrigerator.
- Makes 35 to 40 bars.

Main Dishes

APRICOT CHICKEN

1 whole chicken or pieces of your choice
1 small bottle of Russian Salad Dressing
1 package dry Onion soup mix
1 small bottle of apricot jam

- Put all ingredients in crock pot and cook for 4 to 6 hours.
- Serve over rice.

ASIAN CHICKEN

I learned this in a cooking class. It's great for buffets.

2 to 3 lbs boneless chicken thighs cut into
    bite-sized pieces
1 cup soy sauce
1/2 cup brown sugar
2 tsp grated ginger
1 Tbsp red pepper flakes
4 garlic cloves, crushed, or minced garlic in a jar
1/2 cup orange juice

- Mix together and let marinate for 5 minutes.
- Bake chicken at 400° for 15 to 20 minutes and remove from oven.
- Dissolve ¼ cup cornstarch in a little water, add to chicken, and stir well.
- Return to oven and bake for 5 more minutes until sauce has thickened.
- Sprinkle with chives and serve over cooked rice.

BASIC MEATLOAF

2 lbs ground beef
1½ cups fresh bread crumbs (already prepared crumbs make the meat loaf tough)
2 eggs, slightly beaten
3/4 cup water
1/3 cup ketchup
1 envelope onion soup mix

- Mix well and shape into a loaf.
- Bake at 350° for 1 hour.
- Take the meatloaf out of the pan so it will not absorb the grease.

ASIAN FLANK STEAK

1 to 2 lbs flank steak

Marinade:

1/2 cup beef broth
1/3 cup Hoisin sauce
1/4 cup light soy sauce
2 green onions, sliced
3 Tbsp dry sherry, apple or orange juice
1 Tbsp sugar
1 tsp ginger, grated
4 garlic cloves, minced

- Mix marinade ingredients, then put marinade and steak in a ziplock bag.
- Put in refrigerator and marinate overnight.
- Drain marinade and either broil steak 4 to 5 inches from the broiler and cook for 15 to 18 minutes or you may cook on the grill for 17 to 21 minutes, turning only once.

OPTION

Prior to cooking, rub the steak with McCormick Montreal Seasoning Pepper.

BAKED TORTELLINI

My vegetarian daughter, Lori, loves this recipe.

Fresh cheese tortellini from the deli

- Cook in boiling water only until they float at the top—about 3 to 4 minutes.
- Remove and set aside.

2 cups marinara sauce
1/3 cup Mascarpone cheese (this makes the sauce creamy)
Fresh thyme, pulled off the stems
Fresh parsley, chopped
Smoky mozzarella cheese, sliced
Fresh Parmesan cheese

- Combine the tortellini, Mascarpone cheese and sauce in a baking dish.
- Cover with smoky mozzarella, thinly sliced.
- Cover with fresh grated Parmesan cheese.
- Bake 30 minutes at 350° until browned and bubbly.

BBQ Ribs

I can't count the times people have asked me for this recipe. It is so reliably good. When asked for this recipe, I am embarrassed at how little preparation it takes.

2 to 3 lbs boneless country-style ribs
2 small 18 oz bottles Kraft Thick & Rich Original Recipe BBQ sauce
Garlic salt
McCormick Montreal Steak Seasoning Pepper

- *Put garlic salt and pepper on both sides of the ribs.*
- *Place a single layer of ribs in a large crock pot.*
- *Cover layer with BBQ sauce.*
- *Repeat until all ribs are in the pot.*
- *Top with sauce.*
- *Cook on high for 4 to 5 hours or 6 to 8 hours on low.*
- *Just before ready to serve, remove ribs to a baking dish and place under the oven broiler until ribs are nice and browned—about 5 to 6 minutes.*
- *Serve with rice, any type of potato dish or fettuccini.*

NOTE
Don't substitute the brands as they are what make this recipe great.

Baked Bean Combo

This is a most unusual bean dish and can be called chili.

I lb ground beef, cooked and drained
1/2 lb cooked bacon
I onion, chopped
One 15 oz can of kidney beans
One 15 oz can butter beans
One 30 oz can pork & beans
1/2 cup water
1/3 cup brown sugar
1/3 cup white sugar
3 Tbsp molasses
1/2 cup BBQ sauce
1/4 cup catsup
1/2 Tbsp chili powder
I Tbsp prepared mustard
I tsp liquid smoke

- *Mix all ingredients and put in a large baking dish.*
- *Bake at 350° for 2 hours, stirring a few times.*

BBQ Brisket

5 lb beef brisket roast
3 Tbsp oil

Sauce:

1/4 cup Worcestershire sauce
2 cups chopped onion
1/2 cup white vinegar
2 cups ketchup
2 cups water
I tsp salt
1/4 tsp black pepper
1/2 cup brown sugar
I tsp dry mustard
2 Tbsp molasses
2 tsp paprika
1/4 cup BBQ sauce
I tsp liquid smoke seasoning

Crock pot method:

- *Sear brisket on all sides in hot oil.*
- *Put in crock pot and cook on slow 6 to 8 hours.*
- *Add sauce mixture and onions to the meat and continue to cook for 2 hours.*

Oven method:

- *Sear brisket on all sides in hot oil.*
- *Put in a roaster with lid on and bake overnight—10 pm to 6 am—at 225°.*
- *Drain the grease and remove any bones and fat.*
- *Add sauce mixture and onions to the meat.*
- *Bake 2 more hours at 250°.*

85

BBQ Tri-Tip

I large tri-tip or a brisket
I bottle of your favorite **BBQ** sauce (Mine is
   from Famous Dave's BBQ in South Jordan, Utah.
   They bottle it and you can buy some from their
   restaurant or in local stores.)
I large onion cut in thick slices

- *Rub meat with garlic salt and Montreal Seasoned Pepper.*
- *Put in crock pot and pour the bottle of BBQ sauce over the top.*
- *Cook on high for 4 to 5 hours or until a fork stuck into it comes out easily.*

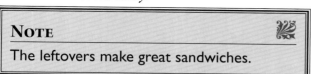

NOTE

The leftovers make great sandwiches.

86

Beef Pot Pies

You will be amazed at how easy and good these are.

One 12 oz can of fully cooked Premium Brisket
   Roast Beef in broth
I Tbsp olive oil
I Tbsp butter
2 Tbsp flour
I heaping Tbsp real beef base
I can cream of celery or mushroom soup
I½ cups of water
1/2 tsp Mrs. Dash Salt Free Seasoning
   Original Blend
Black pepper to taste
1/2 cup of frozen peas
1/2 cup of frozen corn
1/2 cup sliced carrots, boiled for 5 minutes
I small onion, chopped

- *In a large skillet, melt the olive oil and butter.*
- *Add meat and cook until meat is lightly browned.*
- *Add all remaining ingredients.*
- *Cook until comes to a boil.*
- *Pour into a large casserole dish and top with Bisquick recipe on the box.*
- *Bake as directed on the Bisquick instructions.*
- *Option: Make chicken pot pies by substituting canned chicken and chicken base instead of beef.*

Beef Stroganoff

With premium brisket roast beef available in cans now, this dish can be made in ten minutes flat. It is as good as if you took the time to cook a roast.

One 12 oz can of fully cooked Premium Brisket
   Roast Beef in broth
I Tbsp olive oil
I Tbsp butter
2 Tbsp flour
I heaping Tbsp real beef base
I can cream of celery or mushroom soup
I½ cups of water
1/2 tsp Mrs. Dash Salt Free Seasoning
   Original Blend
Black pepper to taste
I cup of frozen peas
I Tbsp dehydrated chopped onions
2 heaping Tbsp sour cream

- *In a large skillet melt the olive oil and butter.*
- *Add the canned beef and 2 Tbsp flour.*
- *Stir until the meat is lightly browned.*
- *Add all remaining ingredients except sour cream.*
- *Continue to cook until it comes to a boil.*
- *Reduce heat and simmer until ready to serve.*
- *Just before serving add the sour cream.*
- *Serve over cooked noodles or rice.*
- *Option: This is great over toast.*

Chalupa

This shredded Mexican meat is great for tacos, burritos, enchiladas, nachos, etc.

4 lbs of beef pot roast or pork loin roast
I lb small navy beans, canned or pre-cooked
2 cloves garlic, chopped
2 Tbsp chili powder
I Tbsp ground cumin
I tsp oregano
I small can chopped Ortega chilies
I Tbsp salt

- *Cook all ingredients in a crock pot until done. The meat should fall apart easily.*
- *Serve over chips with cheese, in tacos, burritos, etc.*

CARROT & RICE CASSEROLE

You may substitute sweet potatoes for the carrots.

3 cups shredded carrots, 6 to 8 medium
I cup water
1/4 cup long grain rice
2 green onions, sliced
1/4 tsp salt
1/8 tsp pepper
I¼ cups cheddar cheese, shredded and divided
3/4 cup milk
I egg, beaten

- *In a medium saucepan, combine carrots, water, uncooked rice, onions, salt and pepper.*
- *Bring to a boil and reduce heat.*
- *Cover and simmer 20 minutes. Do not drain .*
- *Stir in 1 cup of the cheese, milk, egg and put in a 9 x 9 baking dish.*
- *Bake at 350° for 20 minutes.*
- *Remove from oven and sprinkle with remaining cheese.*

BROCCOLI-LEEK QUICHE

I½ cups half and half or whole milk
3 eggs
One 9 inch pie shell, baked
1/4 tsp pepper
1/4 tsp salt
1/4 cup ham, diced
I½ cups cheddar cheese, shredded
One 10 oz package frozen chopped broccoli, thawed and very well drained
I package Knorr Leek Soup (dry)

- *Combine cheese, leek soup, ham, broccoli and pepper.*
- *Mix well and put into baked pie shell. Use the Pillsbury pie shells in the refrigerator section of the grocery.*
- *Combine cream and eggs and pour over mixture.*
- *Bake at 375° for 45 minutes or until a knife inserted in the center of the pie comes out clean.*

BLACK BEAN LASAGNA

This is delicious vegetarian lasagna using corn tortillas instead of lasagna noodles, layered with salsa, black beans, cheese, and guacamole. It seems like a long recipe.

I Tbsp vegetable oil
2 onions, chopped
4 cloves garlic, chopped
1/2 green bell pepper, diced
1/2 red bell pepper, diced
One 14.5 oz can chopped tomatoes
I cup salsa
Two 15 oz cans black beans, drained and rinsed
Salt and black pepper to taste
2 avocados, peeled, pitted, and mashed (optional)
I Tbsp fresh lemon juice
Twelve 6 inch corn tortillas, quartered
2 cups shredded cheddar cheese

- *Preheat oven to 400°.*
- *Lightly grease a 9 x 13 baking dish.*
- *Warm oil in a large skillet over medium heat.*
- *Stir in onions, 3 of the garlic cloves, and the green and red bell peppers.*
- *Sauté until the onions are soft and translucent.*
- *Stir in tomatoes with juice, salsa, and black beans.*
- *Season with salt and pepper, bring to a simmer and cook about 3 minutes.*
- *In a bowl, mash the avocados with the remaining clove of chopped garlic and lemon juice.*
- *Place a layer of tortillas on the bottom of the baking dish.*
- *Spread a third of the tomato/bean mixture on top.*
- *Spread half of guacamole on top, and then sprinkle with a third of cheese.*
- *Add another layer of tortillas.*
- *Top with half of the remaining tomato/bean mixture.*
- *Spread remaining guacamole on top.*
- *Sprinkle with half the cheese.*
- *Repeat with remaining ingredients.*
- *Bake at 350° for 35 minutes or until sauce is bubbly.*

87

CHEDDAR CHICKEN BAKE

This is good with rice.

2 whole chicken breasts split
2 Tbsp flour
1/2 cup butter
1 can condensed cheese soup
2/3 cup light cream
2 Tbsp lemon juice
1/2 tsp dried rosemary

- *Pre-heat oven to 350°.*
- *Coat chicken with flour.*
- *Melt butter in skillet and brown chicken lightly on all sides over moderate heat.*
- *Place chicken in baking dish.*
- *Blend cheese soup, cream, lemon juice and rosemary.*
- *Pour over chicken.*
- *Cover and bake 45 minutes or until chicken is tender.*

CHICKEN BAKE WITH SWISS CHEESE

6 chicken breasts, boneless and skinless
Melted butter
6 slices of Swiss cheese
1 small can cream of chicken soup
1 cup milk
1/8 tsp pepper
1 green onion, sliced
Pinch of garlic powder
2 cups seasoned bread crumbs
1 cup melted butter
Paprika

- *Wash chicken and pat dry. Cover in melted butter.*
- *Place in a 9 x 13 pan.*
- *Place a slice of Swiss cheese on top.*
- *Mix soup, milk, pepper, green onion and garlic powder.*
- *Pour over the top of the chicken.*
- *Mix together the bread crumbs and 1 cup melted butter and put on top.*
- *Sprinkle with paprika.*
- *Bake at 350° for 30 minutes, uncovered.*
- *Serve over rice.*

88

CHICKEN & FRUIT IN FOIL PACK

These are great to cook on the grill for family gatherings.

Boneless, skinless chicken breasts, sliced
Teriyaki sauce
Fresh peaches
Fresh pears
Fresh pineapple
Bananas, optional

- *Marinate chicken in teriyaki sauce for 20 minutes.*
- *Stir-fry chicken in a small amount of oil.*
- *Place all ingredients in a large piece of foil, roll the top and ends tightly.*
- *Grill until you hear ingredients cooking—about 5 minutes per side.*
- *Remove with BBQ tongs. Watch out for steam as you open package.*

CHICKEN & BROCCOLI DIJON

3/4 cup chicken broth
1 Tbsp soy sauce
4 cups broccoli flowerets
1 clove garlic, crushed
1 Tbsp vegetable oil
1 lb boneless, skinless chicken strips
3/4 cup Dijon mustard
4 cups pasta, cooked (penne is good)

- *Mix broth and soy sauce.*
- *Cook garlic and chicken strips in oil 3 to 5 minutes. Do not overcook.*
- *Add broccoli, stir in broth mixture and heat to a boil.*
- *Reduce heat and simmer 5 minutes.*
- *Stir in mustard, heat and serve over cooked pasta.*

CHEDDAR CHICKEN

4 boneless chicken breasts

- *Dredge chicken with ¼ cup flour, brown in butter.*

1 to 2 Tbsp rosemary
1 can cheddar Soup
1/4 cup lemon juice
1/4 cup white cooking wine
1½ cups half and half

- *Pour over chicken and bake, covered, at 350° for 30 to 40 minutes.*

CHICKEN ALFREDO QUICK STYLE

This is done quick style.

2 chicken breasts
1/2 cup margarine
One 8 oz package of cream cheese, softened
1 pint heavy whipping cream
1 Tbsp cooking sherry or rice vinegar
2 tsp garlic salt
4 Tbsp dried parsley
1/2 tsp salt
1/4 tsp black pepper
Dash of cayenne pepper
1/2 cup Parmesan cheese

- Season chicken breasts with garlic salt and McCormick's Montreal Steak Seasoning.
- Grill on a hot grill, turning once, about 3 minutes a side.
- Cut into strips, set aside and keep warm.
- In a medium skillet, mix together all the ingredients except the Parmesan cheese.
- Cook on low heat and simmer until thick.
- Add Parmesan cheese.
- Serve over hot, cooked fettuccini pasta.
- Top with grilled chicken.
- Optional: Add cooked broccoli or frozen peas.

CHICKEN SALAD SANDWICH

This is an open-faced sandwich.

One 8 oz can of white chicken chunks, drained
2½ cups celery
1¼ cups Miracle Whip (not mayonnaise)
1/2 cup slivered almonds
2 Tbsp lemon juice
2 Tbsp onions, chopped
1 cup longhorn cheese, shredded
Black seedless grapes cut into quarters, optional
Raisins, optional

- Mix all ingredients together and put on a sliced Kaiser roll.
- Broil until golden brown.
- Remove from oven and place fresh sliced tomatoes on top.

CHICKEN & WILD RICE CASSEROLE

1 box of Uncle Ben's rice and wild rice, cooked according to directions
1 roasted chicken from a grocery store, broken into small pieces, bone removed
1 large onion, diced
3/4 cup celery, diced
1 lb sliced mushrooms, optional
1 to 2 tsp curry powder
3 Tbsp butter
1 cup sour cream
1 can of cream of mushroom soup
Salt and pepper to taste

- Sauté onion, celery and mushrooms in butter until cooked and a little browned.
- Add curry powder, salt and pepper.
- In a medium bowl, mix together chicken bits, cooked rice and sauté.
- Mix well with 1 cup of sour cream and one can of soup.
- Put in 9 x 9 baking dish.
- Bake uncovered at 350° for 40 to 50 minutes or until brown and bubbly.

89

CHICKEN WITH PAPRIKA SAUCE

This is one of my very favorites. You may also use salmon in place of chicken and serve it over rice instead of pasta.

4 boneless, skinless chicken breasts
2 Tbsp olive oil
2 Tbsp butter

- Sauté chicken in olive oil and butter until lightly browned.
- Cover and simmer for 5 to 7 minutes. Do not overcook.
- Remove chicken, set aside and keep warm.

To the oil/butter mixture add:

Green onions, sliced
2 Tbsp paprika
2 cups whipping cream
Salt and pepper

- Simmer until thickened.
- Cook linguine, al dente, and put on serving platter.
- Pour sauce over pasta and top with chicken.

CHICKEN TORTILLA CASSEROLE

1 large onion, chopped
1 large green bell pepper, chopped
2 Tbsp vegetable oil
2 cups chopped, cooked chicken
1 small can cream of chicken soup, undiluted
1 small can cream of mushroom soup, undiluted
1 small can diced tomato and green chilies
1 tsp chili powder
14 tsp salt
1/4 tsp garlic powder
1/4 tsp pepper
12 six inch corn tortillas
2 cups shredded cheddar cheese, divided

- *Sauté onion and bell pepper in hot oil in a large skillet over medium to high heat for 5 minutes or until tender.*
- *Stir in chicken, soups, green chilies, chili powder, salt, garlic powder and pepper; remove from heat.*
- *Tear tortillas into one inch pieces. Layer a third of tortilla pieces in bottom of a lightly greased 9 x 13 baking dish.*
- *Top with a third of chicken mixture and 2/3 cup cheese.*
- *Repeat layers twice ending with cheese.*
- *Bake at 350° for 30 to 35 minutes until bubbly.*

CHICKEN RICE CASSEROLE

This is best if made the night before and refrigerated. Remove it from the refrigerator one hour before baking.

3 cups cooked, boneless chicken
1 cup celery, diced
2 cups cooked rice
3 Tbsp onion, minced (can be dehydrated onions)
1/2 cup cheddar cheese, cubed
2 Tbsp lemon juice
3/4 cup mayonnaise
2 cans cream of chicken soup
1 small can fried onion rings
1/2 cup slivered almonds

- *Mix together all ingredients except the fried onion rings and slivered almonds.*
- *Put in a buttered casserole dish and top with slivered almonds and fried onions.*
- *Bake at 325° for 1 hour.*

CHICKEN FLORENTINE

This looks like a lot of instructions but goes together quickly.

6 boneless, skinless chicken breasts, flattened to ½ inch
1/2 cup Parmesan cheese
1/2 tsp oregano
1/2 tsp basil
1 garlic clove, pressed
3 Tbsp butter
Salt and pepper to taste
1/2 cup milk
1 Tbsp chicken broth or cooking sherry
1 Tbsp flour
1 package frozen, chopped spinach, thawed and squeezed dry
1/2 cup sour cream
1 cup shredded mozzarella cheese

- *Combine Parmesan cheese, basil and oregano in a large ziplock bag.*
- *Add chicken one piece at a time to coat.*
- *Heat 2 Tbsp butter in a large skillet and cook chicken for 4 minutes per side.*
- *Remove and keep warm.*
- *After cooking all of the chicken, using the same skillet, add the other 3 Tbsp of butter and sauté the onions and garlic.*
- *Add flour, salt and pepper.*
- *Stir in the milk and broth or sherry, stirring until blended.*
- *Bring to a boil and reduce heat.*
- *Cook until thickened—about 2 minutes—stirring constantly.*
- *Stir in spinach and heat thoroughly.*
- *Remove from heat and stir in sour cream.*
- *Spoon over chicken.*
- *Top with mozzarella cheese*
- *Serve immediately.*

BREADED CHICKEN STRIPS

2 lbs chicken tenderloins
4 eggs
1/4 cup milk
2 cups Italian bread crumbs
1 cup grated Parmigiano Reggiano cheese
3 lemons, zest only
1 bunch fresh thyme, no stems and chopped
Salt and pepper
2 cups light olive oil

- *Heat 2 inches of oil in a deep skillet over medium heat.*
- *Whisk together the eggs and milk in a shallow dish.*
- *Combine the bread crumbs, cheese, lemon zest and thyme.*
- *Place the chicken strips in the bag with the egg mixture and shake.*
- *Transfer to the bread crumb bag and coat chicken.*
- *Fry in hot oil until brown.*
- *Remove and sprinkle with salt and pepper immediately.*

CHICKEN TURKEY ENCHILADAS

This is perfect with leftover turkey from Thanksgiving. Make this ahead of time and bake later.

Mix Together:

1/2 pint sour cream
2 cans cream of chicken soup
1 small can diced green chilies
1 lb grated cheddar cheese or mixed cheddar and Jack
Two 12.5 oz cans of chicken breast chunks
Garlic powder to taste

- *Save 1 to 2 cups of mixture to put on the top.*
- *Warm flour tortillas in microwave five at a time.*
- *Place ¼ cup of mixture on tortilla and roll up.*
- *Put in a 9 x 13 baking dish.*
- *Repeat until dish is full—10 to 12 tortillas.*
- *Spread remaining mixture over the top.*
- *Sprinkle with remaining cheddar cheese.*
- *Sprinkle with chives.*
- *Cover with foil and bake 40 minutes at 350°.*

GRILLED BACON-WRAPPED CHICKEN

This is my favorite BBQ chicken. I created this recipe after many attempts to reach just the right flavor.

Pre-cooked bacon, one strip per piece of chicken

Basic marinade:

1/2 cup balsamic vinegar
1/2 cup extra virgin olive oil
1 Tbsp minced garlic
1 Tbsp fresh oregano
1 Tbsp fresh basil
1 Tbsp fresh chives

- *Put chicken in a glass bowl with half of the marinade mixture. Let sit at room temperature for 20 minutes, turning once.*
- *Wrap the chicken with bacon, holding with a toothpick.*
- *Put chicken on a hot grill and charbroil for 4 minutes. Turn once. This gives it the grill marks.*
- *Remove chicken to the top cooking rack of the grill and turn the temperature to BBQ heat.*
- *Baste the chicken with the remainder of the marinade, turning and basting several times.*
- *Use a meat thermometer to make sure the chicken is done—165°.*

91

> **NOTE**
>
> The key to great chicken is don't overcook it. Inner temperature should be 165°. Boneless chicken cooks much faster and will be moist, unless you overcook it. Use skinless, boneless chicken breast halves or thighs and use precooked bacon for this recipe—one slice per piece of chicken.

MEXICAN TURKEY LASAGNA

This is much lower in fat.

1 lb ground turkey
1/2 red onion, chopped
4 cloves of garlic, chopped
1/4 tsp cumin
1/4 tsp chili powder
Flour tortillas

- *Brown turkey in 1 Tbsp vegetable oil, strain off liquid.*
- *In same skillet, add the following:*

1 small can diced green mild chilies
One 16 oz can stewed tomatoes with juice,
    chop the tomatoes finer than in the can
1 tsp salt
1 tsp pepper

Filling:

2 cups low fat cheddar cheese, not fat-free
1 pint light sour cream
Black olives

- *Line bottom of a 9 x 13 dish with small flour tortillas and layer as follows.*
- *Cheese mixture.*
- *Meat mixture.*
- *Green onions, chopped.*
- *Black olives, sliced (optional).*
- *Continue to layer ending with meat, fresh grated cheddar cheese and green tops of onions.*
- *Bake uncovered for 45 minutes at 350° or until bubbling.*

CHICKEN PEACHY

One 16 oz can peaches, drained, reserve liquid
2½ lbs skinned, boneless chicken parts
    in a large skillet
1/4 cup frozen orange juice concentrate
1/4 cup Heinz Malt vinegar
1 Tbsp brown sugar
1 tsp dried basil
1/2 tsp salt
1/4 tsp cloves
1/4 tsp cinnamon
1/8 tsp black pepper

- *Combine the liquid from the peaches with all of the ingredients except the chicken.*
- *Pour over chicken, cover and simmer for 30 minutes, or until chicken is cooked.*
- *Add peaches and heat.*
- *Thicken sauce with 2 Tbsp cornstarch mixed with 2 Tbsp water.*
- *Serve over cooked rice.*

CHILI VERSATILE

You can do so much with this chili if you use your imagination.

1 package chili seasoning, Lawry's or Schilling's
1 lb ground beef
Dried or fresh onions
One 15 oz can kidney beans, drained and rinsed
One 15 oz can navy beans, drained and rinsed
One 15 oz can black beans, drained and rinsed
1 can whole kernel corn, drained
One 15 oz can basil and garlic diced tomatoes
One 15 oz tomato soup
1 cup water
Salt and pepper to taste

- *Follow the directions on the chili seasoning package.*
- *Cook ground beef, drain and add seasoning.*
- *Mix all together and simmer 20 minutes.*
- *You can add small cooked pasta to this.*
- *Serve with crackers, French bread or over rice.*

CHILI CROCK-POT STYLE

Dana Hawes has won every chili bake-off she has entered with this recipe. I added the optional ingredients and served over rice which was a hit with our younger family members.

I to 2 lbs ground beef or sirloin
I tsp onion
I tsp each garlic salt and black pepper
I large onion, chopped
I green bell pepper, chopped
Four 8 oz cans tomato sauce
2 large cans stewed tomatoes
2 to 3 15 oz cans kidney beans, drained and rinsed
1/3 cup molasses
1/3 cup brown sugar
2 to 3 Tbsp chili powder
I Tbsp cumin
3 bay leaves

- *Brown the meat, adding onion and garlic salt.*
- *Place the remaining ingredients in a large crock pot and stir well.*
- *Cook 8 to 10 hours on low.*
- *Optional: Garnish with 1 cup corn, crushed taco chips, sour cream or cooked rice.*

> ### NOTE
> This is great with cornbread. See page 25 for the recipe.

CHILI CORNBREAD BAKE

Sandi Anderson of Paradise, California, and I have been working on recipes for years. This one is her's.

- *Use as many cans of chili based on the number of people you want to serve. I use Stagg Chili but any brand will do.*
- *Add green and red peppers, and onion, chopped.*
- *Top with Marie Callender's Corn Bread mixed as directed on the box and bake as the box directs.*
- *Serve in bowls, topping with sour cream, additional onions and shredded cheese.*

CHILI

Variety is the spice of cooking. Great in a crock pot, too.

2 lbs ground beef
One 29 oz can tomato sauce
One 29 oz can kidney beans (with liquid)
One 29 oz can pinto beans (with liquid)
I cup diced onion
1/2 cup diced green chili
I celery stick, diced
3 medium tomatoes, chopped
2 tsp cumin powder
3 Tbsp chili powder
1½ tsp black pepper
2 tsp salt
2 cups water

- *Brown and drain beef.*
- *Combine all ingredients in a large pot and simmer over low heat, stirring frequently for 2 to 3 hours.*

93

COD FILETS

4 cod filets
Salt and pepper
Flour
I egg, slightly beaten
1/2 tsp prepared mustard
Dried potato flakes
Herb of your choice, rosemary, tarragon, dill, etc.
Olive oil

- *Combine salt, pepper and flour in a bowl.*
- *Dip filets in a mixture of egg and prepared mustard.*
- *Dip each filet in the flour.*
- *Cover with a mixture of dried potato flakes.*
- *Fry in olive oil until browned, about 2 minutes a side.*
- *Remove and bake at 350º for 8 to 10 minutes.*

Sauce:

Sliced green onions
1/2 cup lemon juice
White rice vinegar
Salt and pepper
4 Tbsp butter

- *Heat until just coming to a boil, add butter and whisk well.*
- *Serve over cod.*

CORNED BEEF & CABBAGE

This version is done quick-style and so, of course, would never do for a St. Patrick's Day dinner.

1/2 lb bacon, fried crisp; remove but save drippings

Add to the bacon drippings:

1/2 stick butter
1 medium head of cabbage, cut into large pieces
Salt and pepper
1/3 cup water

Cover and simmer for 10 minutes, then add:

1 can Hormel Corned Beef, broken up, put on top of cabbage

- *Cover and heat through.*
- *Add crumble cooked bacon and serve.*

COWBOY TACOS

1 pound cubed or minced pork stew meat
One 1.25 oz package taco seasoning mix
1 Tbsp vegetable oil
1 cup chunky salsa
One 16 oz can chili beans
1/3 cup apricot preserves
12 taco shells
Shredded lettuce
Shredded cheese
Sour cream, optional
Canned corn, optional
One 10 oz can sliced ripe olives, optional

- *Toss pork with the taco seasoning mix until coated.*
- *Heat oil in a skillet cook meat until no longer pink.*
- *Stir the beans, salsa and apricot preserves.*
- *Reduce heat to low, and simmer until heated through, about 10 minutes.*
- *Spoon 1/3 cup of the pork mixture into each taco shell.*
- *Top with lettuce, cheese, sour cream, corn and sliced olives.*

CRANBERRY CHICKEN

4 boneless, skinless chicken breast halves
1 Tbsp vegetable oil
1/4 cup cranberry juice
1/4 cup orange juice
1 can cream of mushroom soup, undiluted
1 Tbsp dried cranberries
1 Tbsp sage
1/8 tsp pepper
4 cups hot cooked rice
Sliced green onions

- *Brown chicken in oil.*
- *Add juices, soup, cranberries, sage and pepper.*
- *Bring to a boil, cover and cook over low heat for 5 minutes.*
- *Serve over hot rice.*
- *Top with green onions.*

95

CREAMY CHICKEN LASAGNA

3 chicken breasts, cooked and shredded
6 lasagna noodles, cooked al dente (drain and put in cold water)
1 cube chicken bouillon
1/3 cup hot water
One 8 oz package of cream cheese, softened
2 cups shredded mozzarella cheese
One 26 oz jar of spaghetti sauce

- *Dissolve the bouillon cube in hot water.*
- *In a large bowl, mix the chicken, cream cheese, bouillon and 1 cup of mozzarella.*
- *Spread one third of the spaghetti sauce in the bottom of a 9 x 9 baking dish.*
- *Lay down half of the noodles and cover with half of the remaining spaghetti sauce, then half of the chicken mixture.*
- *Repeat with remaining noodles, sauce, chicken mixture and sprinkle with last of the mozzarella.*
- *Bake at 350° for 45 to 50 minutes.*
- *Serves 6.*

CREAMED CHICKEN

This recipe is very low in fat and really takes only five minutes to put in a crock pot.

2 boneless, skinless chicken breasts
I can cream of chicken soup, undiluted
I Tbsp dry Ranch Dressing mix
Salt and pepper to taste
I Tbsp dehydrated onions

- *Combine all ingredients, mix well and put in a crock pot.*
- *Cook on low for 4 to 6 hours.*
- *Serve over rice or noodles.*

PORK TENDERLOIN

96

I have been told this is a Cuban dish.

2½ lbs pork tenderloin, trimmed
4 cloves garlic
4 bay leaves
2 tsp anise seed
2 tsp ground coriander
I Tbsp ground cumin
2 limes, zest only
2 Tbsp McCormick Montreal Steak Seasoning
**   or coarse salt and pepper**
Extra virgin olive oil, to coat

- *Cut 4 slits in roast and put the garlic cloves in each slit.*
- *Combine all spices.*
- *Coat meat with oil.*
- *Rub spices over the pork and put in roasting pan.*
- *Cook at 375° for 25 to 30 minutes until internal temperature is 155°.*
- *Remove from oven and let stand for 10 minutes before slicing.*

CROCK POT CHICKEN

5 boneless chicken breasts cut in halves
I can cream of chicken soup, undiluted
I can cream of mushroom soup, undiluted
I package of dry Italian dressing mix
One 8 oz package of cream cheese cut into
**   ½ inch squares**

- *Combine both soups and dressing mix in crock pot.*
- *Place chicken breasts in mixture.*
- *Place cubes of cream cheese on top of chicken.*
- *Cook 6 to 8 hours on low heat. Stir occasionally.*
- *Serve over rice.*
- *Serves 6 to 8.*

DOUBLE CHEESE CASSEROLE

One 12 oz package uncooked egg noodles
I lb lean ground beef
I large onion, diced
One 15 oz can tomato sauce
4 oz cream cheese
12 oz cottage cheese
One 8 oz container sour cream
Salt and pepper to taste

- *Preheat oven to 350°.*
- *Cook egg noodles according to package directions.*
- *While noodles are cooking, brown the ground beef and onion in a large skillet over medium high heat.*
- *Reduce heat to low, add the tomato sauce, stir well.*
- *Simmer for a few minutes.*
- *Add the cream cheese and cottage cheese, stirring together until well blended.*
- *Stir in the egg noodles and sour cream until all ingredients are well mixed.*
- *Pour into a 2 quart casserole dish.*
- *Bake at 350° for 30 minutes.*

GREEN CHILI SAUCE ENCHILADAS

You can prepare this with cornbread on top or use corn tortillas and make it enchiladas.

Corn tortillas or cornbread mix

Mix together and sauté:

1 can chicken chunks, drained
2 Tbsp cilantro
One 20 oz can green chili sauce
2 Tbsp onion, chopped

As a baked dish with cornbread mix:

- *Place above mixture on bottom of a pan.*
- *Top with cornbread dough as directed on cornbread box.*
- *Bake at 350° or until top is golden brown.*
- *Serve with salsa on top.*

As enchiladas with corn tortillas:

- *Put mixture in corn, not flour tortillas and roll up tightly.*
- *Place in pan and cover with additional green chili sauce.*
- *Top with shredded cheddar cheese.*
- *Bake at 350° until hot and cheese is bubbling.*

FAJITA PITAS

These are great to serve while a crowd is gathered to watch a ballgame.

- *Thaw a loaf of frozen bread dough and cut into 10 slices.*
- *Roll each slice into a circle and fry in a non-stick skillet until brown on each side.*
- *Stack on paper towels.*
- *Cook as much of the stir-fry ingredients as you want.*

Fajita meat
Green and red bell peppers
Sweet onions
Garlic
Salt and pepper
Bottled stir-fry sauce to taste

- *When ready to serve, fill with stir fried mixture.*
- *Fold in half and enjoy.*

ENCHILADA CASSEROLE

This is another great crock pot dish.

1 lb cooked ground beef, drained
1 large can enchilada sauce
8 ounces of salsa, fresh or canned
1 can cream of celery soup, undiluted
1 small can diced green chilies

- *Mix all ingredients together and put in crock pot.*
- *Cut 1 dozen corn tortillas into quarters.*
- *Place on top of mixture in crock pot.*
- *Cover with shredded cheddar cheese.*
- *Top with diced green onions.*
- *Cook 4 to 6 hours on low.*

ORTEGA RICE CASSEROLE

97

This recipe is at least 35 years old. When I worked for the Farmers Insurance Home office, I loved this dish. I talked the cafeteria cook into giving me this recipe.

4 cups cooked and cooled rice
2/3 lb cheddar cheese, shredded
2/3 lb mozzarella cheese, shredded
1 small can sliced black olives
1 small can diced green chilies, mild
1 Tbsp dehydrated chopped onions
Salt and pepper to taste

- *Mix all ingredients together and put in an 11 inch round or a 9 x 9 square baking dish.*
- *Bake until hot and bubbling, about 40 to 45 minutes at 350°.*
- *When ready to serve, top with additional cheddar cheese and paprika.*
- *If you are using this dish with Mexican food, you may want to drizzle salsa on top.*
- *Serves 6 to 8.*

GORGONZOLA SAUCE WITH BEEF TENDERLOIN

Gorgonzola is an Italian cheese similar to blue cheese.

3 lbs beef tenderloin
1/4 cup butter
1/4 cup olive oil
1/4 cup fresh thyme, minced
Salt and pepper to taste

- *Heat butter and oil over medium high heat in an oven-proof skillet.*
- *Rub meat with salt, pepper and thyme.*
- *Sear for one minute on both sides in an oven-proof skillet.*
- *Put skillet in oven and bake for 30 to 45 minutes at 425°.*
- *While it is cooking, prepare the sauce.*

98

> ### NOTE
> Cooking the beef for fifteen to twenty minutes will result in a medium-done meat.

Sauce:

1 Tbsp butter
1 Tbsp flour
1 cup whipping cream
1/2 cup white cooking wine, divided
1/4 cup chicken broth
1 cup gorgonzola crumbles

- *Remove meat from oven and skillet.*
- *Add ¼ cup of the white wine to the skillet.*
- *Add butter and flour to the skillet which makes a roux. Mix well with a wire whisk.*
- *Slowly add the chicken broth, whisking until smooth.*
- *Add remaining wine and cream.*
- *Simmer up to 20 minutes, stirring occasionally.*
- *Add the cheese just before serving.*

FISH & CHIPS

Cod filets
Flour
Water
Baking soda
Panko bread crumbs
Vegetable oil

- *Make a thin batter using flour, water and a pinch of baking soda.*
- *Roll rinsed and dried cod fish in batter.*
- *Roll in Panko fine fresh bread crumbs, found in the Asian food section. of the grocery.*
- *Fry in vegetable oil.*
- *Serve with French-fried potatoes.*

GARLIC CHEDDAR CHICKEN

Erica Williams has shared some great recipes with me, including this one. She lives in South Jordan, Utah with our adopted grandchildren, Jack and Nixen.

1/2 cup butter, melted
4 cloves garlic, minced
3/4 cup dry bread crumbs
1/2 cup freshly grated Parmesan cheese
1½ cups shredded Cheddar cheese
1/4 tsp dried parsley
1/4 tsp dried oregano
1/4 tsp ground black pepper
1/8 tsp salt
8 skinless, boneless chicken breast halves, pounded thin

- *Add garlic to melted butter and put in a shallow pan.*
- *In another shallow bowl, mix the bread crumbs, Parmesan cheese, cheddar cheese, parsley, oregano, pepper, and salt.*
- *Dip each chicken breast in the garlic butter to coat then press into the bread crumb mixture.*
- *Arrange the coated chicken breasts in a 9 x 13 baking dish.*
- *Drizzle with any remaining butter and top with any remaining bread crumb mixture.*
- *Bake 30 minutes at 350° or until chicken is no longer pink and juices run clear.*

GREGG'S SPAGHETTI

This recipe comes from my nephew, Gregg Stuessi, of Leesburg, Virginia. Maybe the love for cooking is inherited as he is an Executive Chef and has prepared food fit for royalty for me and my husband. In his words, "Here's a very simple spaghetti sauce recipe that you can add other items to if you desire, such as mushrooms, eggplant, etc."

3/4 cup chopped onion
1 clove garlic, minced
3 Tbsp salad oil
Two 1 lb cans diced tomatoes, about 4 cups
Two 6 oz cans tomato paste
2 cups water
1 tsp sugar
1½ tsp salt
1/2 tsp fresh ground pepper
1½ tsp dried oregano
1 bay leaf

- *Cook onion and garlic in oil until tender but not brown.*
- *Stir in the other ingredients one at a time while the skillet is on medium to low heat.*
- *Simmer uncovered for 45 minutes.*

MACARONI BAKE

One 14 oz package Deluxe Macaroni & Cheese Dinner
2 cups broccoli florets
4 eggs
1 cup ham, diced
1/2 cup cheddar and Jack cheese, shredded

- *Cook macaroni until al dente.*
- *Add broccoli the last 2 minutes and drain.*
- *Beat eggs, stir in cheese and ham, stir well.*
- *Combine pasta and egg mixture.*
- *Put in a large pie pan sprayed with vegetable spray.*
- *Bake at 350º for 30 minutes or until lightly browned.*

GROUND BEEF BAKE

1 lb ground beef
1/2 cup diced onion

- *In a large, deep skillet, cook until meat is no longer pink; drain excess fat.*

Add the following:

1 cup uncooked rice (jasmine is a good rice)
2½ cups water
1 tsp beef base or 1 cube beef bouillon
1/2 tsp pepper

- *Simmer 25 minutes or until water is absorbed and rice is done.*

Add the following:

One 14.5 oz can diced tomatoes
1 cup diced green bell pepper

- *Continue to cook for 10 minutes.*
- *Transfer to a baking dish.*
- *Sprinkle top with mozzarella cheese.*
- *Bake until cheese is melted.*

GRILLED ROSEMARY PORK CHOPS

Marinade:

Zest of one orange
2 sprigs rosemary, chopped
3 Tbsp olive oil
3 Tbsp balsamic vinegar
1/4 cup molasses
Salt and pepper to taste

- *Marinate boneless chops for at least 2 hours.*
- *Put on a hot grill.*
- *Add pepper and kosher salt.*
- *Grill for 7 minutes per side until the internal temperature 165º.*

99

ITALIAN QUICHE

Using already prepared pie dough makes this recipe quick and easy.

- *Cut the top edge from a 9 inch prepared pie shell to remove the fluted crust.*
- *Using the directions on the package, bake the shell for half the time required.*

Filling:

1/4 cup grated Parmesan cheese, divided

- *Sprinkle 1 Tbsp Parmesan cheese on the bottom of the pie shell*
- *Whisk together the following:*

16 oz sour cream
3 eggs
1/4 tsp salt
1/4 tsp pepper

- *Pour into pie shell.*
- *Combine the following and sprinkle over egg mixture.*

3 Tbsp seasoned bread crumbs
1 tsp dried basil, crushed
3 cloves garlic

Top with:

One 14.5 oz can diced tomatoes, drained and squeezed well
1/4 cup olives, chopped
Remaining Parmesan cheese

- *Bake for 50 minutes at 350°.*

LASAGNA ROLL UPS

This is a nice change from regular lasagna and looks nice on a serving plate.

Pasta Sauce:

2 lbs ground beef
1 onion, chopped
2 cloves of garlic, pressed
Two 15 oz cans diced tomatoes, seasoned with basil, garlic and oregano
One 15 oz can tomato sauce, plus 1/2 can of water

- *Brown beef, onion and garlic and cook only until the onion is tender.*
- *Partially cook lasagna noodles and set aside.*

Cheese Mixture:

1 cup ricotta cheese
1/4 lb grated mozzarella cheese
1/2 cup Parmesan cheese
1 egg, slightly beaten with a fork
2 Tbsp parsley
1/2 tsp garlic salt
Salt and pepper to taste

- *Spread cheese mixture onto a noodle, roll up and place in a baking dish, standing up—not laying down. Continue until all noodles are used.*
- *Pour pasta sauce on top of the roll ups.*
- *Bake at 350° for 30 to 40 minutes until bubbly.*

MEXICAN LASAGNA

Mix together:

Black beans, drained and rinsed
Canned corn
Fresh tomatoes, cilantro and onion, chopped
Sliced black olives
Roasted chicken, diced (use leftover chicken)
Romano and Jack cheese
Flour tortillas
Salsa, red or green

- *Line a round baking pan with red and green salsa.*
- *Add a layer of soft tortillas to fill the bottom of pan.*
- *Put in layers of ingredients as listed above, ending with tortillas and grated cheeses.*
- *Cover with foil and bake at 350° for 30 minutes.*
- *Slice as a pie and top with salsa.*

MEATBALLS

These are the best in Spaghetti Sauce, as an appetizer, or even as Swedish Meatballs.

2 lbs ground beef
1 package Saltine crackers, crushed
1/2 cup grated Parmesan cheese
1/2 cup parsley
1 tsp garlic salt
2 large or 3 small eggs
1/2 tsp salt
1/2 tsp pepper
2 cloves garlic, finely minced
1/2 onion, finely chopped

- *Mix well with two forks.*
- *Using a large scoop, place balls on a greased cookie sheet.*
- *Bake at 350° for 15 minutes.*

NOTE

Only mix these ingredients with two forks. Do not use your hands and do not knead the mixture as this makes the meatballs tough. These meatballs are very moist and light due to very little mixing.

Also, it takes too long and it's too messy to cook these in a frying pan—and it takes too many batches. Use a cookie sheet and cook them all at once. Do not cook them completely. Just brown them and put them in the sauce to keep them tender. They will continue to cook in the sauce.

MINI HAMBURGERS IN BBQ SAUCE

Sauce:

1/2 cup pineapple preserves
1/2 cup BBQ sauce
1 heaping Tbsp brown sugar

- *Heat ingredints in a small saucepan until sugar melts.*
- *Make mini burgers, grill and baste in above sauce.*
- *Serve on small Hawaiian Sweet rolls.*

MANICOTTI SHELLS

When you make your own shells, the texture and consistency is unique, making the dish a new experience for your guests. Save time by making these ahead.

For batter, gradually add:

3 eggs, well beaten
1 cup flour
1 cup water
Pinch of salt

- *Use a small 5 inch skillet sprayed with vegetable spray, eyeball 1/8 cup of batter, spreading it quickly by rotating the skillet as you would a crepe.*
- *Cook over medium heat only on one side. Do not brown. The top will get a little bubbly, becoming solid like soft cooked pasta, which it is.*
- *Place between sheets of waxed paper.*
- *Makes between 12 and 14 shells.*
- *Freeze the shells you don't need and use them later.*

101

For Manicotti Filling, mix together:

Spaghetti sauce
2 cups ricotta cheese (I do not recommend cottage cheese as it makes the filling runny)
2 cups mozzarella cheese, grated
2 eggs
1 cup Parmesan cheese
4 Tbsp parsley
1 Tbsp garlic salt
1/2 tsp salt
1/2 tsp pepper

- *Place 2 Tbsp filling in each shell and roll up.*
- *Put in a baking dish.*
- *Spread with prepared spaghetti sauce.*
- *Cover with mozzarella cheese.*
- *Sprinkle with Parmesan.*
- *The filling freezes well and can be used for lasagna.*

NOTE

Buy pre-packaged shells to save time and after you cook them to al dente stage (firm but not soft), cut along the tops lengthwise, making it easier to put the filling inside. Place them in a baking dish cut edge down.

NANCY'S BEST MEATLOAF

This is the meatloaf I like the best.

3 slices white bread, crusts removed

- *Process the bread in food processor for 10 seconds and put in a large bowl.*
- *Put the following ingredients into the food processor and process for 30 seconds.*

I large carrot cut in ¼ inch rounds
I stalk of celery cut in ½ inch pieces
1/2 medium onion, chopped
2 cloves garlic, minced
1/2 cup parsley

Remove from food processor and add the following ingredients:

1/2 cup ketchup
2 tsp dry mustard
I½ to 2 lbs lean ground beef
2 large eggs, beaten
2 tsp salt
I tsp pepper
I tsp Tabasco sauce
1/2 tsp rosemary, chopped (optional)

- *Mix well by hand but do not over-knead as it will make the meatloaf dense and tough. The mix should be wet but still able to form into a loaf.*

Cover top of loaf with a mixture of:

3 Tbsp ketchup
I Tbsp olive oil
2 Tbsp dark brown sugar

- *Bake 1 hour at 400° until it reaches an internal temperature of 160°.*

BROILED MANICOTTI

This is an original dish that I created which is not the usual baked manicotti. This baked with no sauce over the top as you put it on the bottom. Bake it without sauce until well-heated and the top is golden brown. Read all the instructions prior to making this recipe. It calls for manicotti filling.

Pasta sauce
Manicotti filling (see recipe page 101)
Parmesan cheese
Paprika

- *Cover the bottom of a 9 x 13 baking dish with your favorite pasta sauce.*
- *Spread 1 to 2 Tbsp of manicotti filling on each manicotti shell.*
- *Roll up and place in a baking dish sprayed with vegetable spray, placing them close together.*
- *Sprinkle with Parmesan cheese and paprika.*
- *Bake uncovered at 375° for 25 to 30 minutes until the tops are golden brown.*
- *They should be crispy on the top with no additional sauce put on after baking. This is what makes the dish very unusual.*

MEATLOAF

This is one of several recipes for meat loaf but they are all different and give you a variety.

I egg
2 Tbsp sour cream
2 Tbsp flour
I package of dry onion soup mix
I lb ground sirloin
Ketchup

- *Mix together the egg, sour cream and flour with a wire whisk until smooth.*
- *In medium bowl combine the beef and egg mixture, being careful not to overmix.*
- *Shape into one large or two small loaf pans.*
- *Cover with ketchup.*
- *Bake at 400° for 45 minutes.*

102

MEXICAN CASSEROLE

You won't believe how fast this casserole goes together.

1 lb ground beef, cooked and drained
2 Tbsp cumin
2 Tbsp chili powder
1 small onion, chopped or 1 tsp dehydrated chopped onions
Garlic salt to taste
One 16 oz can zesty Jalapeño chopped tomatoes
One 8 oz bottle taco sauce (Taco Bell brand is good)
1/2 can corn, drained
1 can black beans, drained and rinsed
1 lb cheddar cheese, grated, leaving some for the top
Black olives, sliced
Spinach tortillas cut in halves
Sour cream

- *Layer 9 x 13 baking dish with half of meat mixture, half of the cheese and some olives.*
- *Cover with the spinach tortillas and repeat layers.*
- *Finish with extra cheese.*
- *Bake covered at 375° for 20 minutes.*
- *Remove cover and cook an additional 10 minutes.*
- *Slice and serve with sour cream, salsa, chips and salad.*

PESTO CHICKEN PASTA

1 lb boneless, skinless chicken breasts, cubed
- *Cook chicken in butter until browned.*

2 Tbsp butter
One can cream of chicken soup
1/2 cup pesto sauce (see recipe page 148)
1/2 cup milk
3 cups bow tie pasta, cooked and drained

- *Bring butter, soup, pesto and milk to a boil.*
- *Cover and cook over low heat for 5 minutes.*
- *Mix together with cooked pasta.*
- *Heat thoroughly and pour into a large serving dish.*
- *Place chicken on top.*
- *Serves 6.*

MEXICAN MEAT MIX

When you make this, separate it into individual packages and freeze it for future Mexican dishes.

5 pounds boneless chuck roast
3 yellow onions, chopped
1/4 tsp garlic powder
4 Tbsp flour
4 tsp salt
1 tsp cumin
One 4 oz can green chilies, chopped
Two 7 oz cans green chili salsa

NOTE

Use a pressure cooker to lessen the cooking time. Slow cook it at 275°. Another option is to cook it in a large Dutch oven. Do not add salt or water. Cover and cook for 8 to 10 hours.

Pressure cooker method:

- *Use 1 cup water.*
- *Cook for 55 to 60 minutes.*
- *Drain meat and keep the juices.*
- *Shred meat with two forks and set aside.*
- *Sauté onions and green chilies in olive oil.*
- *Add remaining ingredients.*
- *Cook for a few minutes, add meat juices and cook until thickened.*
- *Cool, package in 2 cup ziplock bags and freeze for later use.*

NOTE

The reason you don't add water or salt is that the meat lets out its own juices and the water will weaken the flavor in the juices and the salt has a tendency to draw the juices out too quickly. making the meat tough. But if you salt the meat several hours beforehand and let it sit, it will act like a tenderizer.

103

NAVAJO TACOS

This is a very different version of a taco and it's great.

Frozen dinner rolls
Vegetable oil
Canned or homemade chili (or make your own)

- *Place as many frozen dinner rolls as you need for your meal separately on a greased cookie sheet and let thaw.*
- *Roll each roll into a circle about the size of a small tortilla.*
- *Fry the flattened rolls in a small amount of oil until brown on each side.*
- *Drain on a paper towels.*
- *Put your favorite chili on the fried bread and then your favorite taco toppings.*

104 *Toppings:*

Diced tomatoes
Chopped onions
Salsa
Shredded lettuce
Grated cheese
Sour cream
Guacamole

NOTE

Use fresh, homemade bread dough with this recipe if you have the time.

PAN-FRIED PORK CHOPS

5 to 6 boneless pork chops 1 inch thick

- *Salt and pepper chops.*
- *Cover bottom of skillet with olive oil, put chops in skillet on medium high heat.*
- *Cook for 5 minutes on each side. Do not overcook as it will make them dry and tough.*
- *Remove chops from skillet.*

Add:

1/2 cup apple juice
Salt and pepper

- *Pour over pork chops.*
- *Serve hot.*

PAD THAI

1/2 lb cooked linguine
1/2 lb skinless chicken strips cut lengthwise (optional)
3 Tbsp vegetable oil, divided
1/2 lb fresh bean sprouts, rinsed and drained
1/3 cup sliced green onions, including the tops
2 cloves garlic, minced
1 Tbsp fresh cilantro

Combine and set aside:

3/4 cup tomato juice
3 Tbsp Lite Soy Sauce
1 Tbsp vinegar
2 tsp sugar
1/4 tsp cornstarch

- *Add chicken, stir-fry for one minute, remove and set aside.*
- *Heat remaining 2 Tbsp oil in the same pan.*
- *Add bean sprouts, green onions and garlic.*
- *Stir-fry one minute.*
- *Stir in linguine and cook until heated through.*
- *Add all ingredients together and cook until sauce boils and thickens.*
- *Serve immediately.*
- *Serves 4.*

PAN PIZZA

1 lb ground beef
1/4 lb sliced pepperoni sausage
One 14 oz can pizza sauce
Two 12 oz packages refrigerated buttermilk
    biscuit dough
1/2 onion, sliced and separated into rings
One 10 oz can sliced black olives, sliced
One 4.5 oz can sliced mushrooms (optional)
1½ cups shredded mozzarella cheese
1 cup shredded cheddar cheese

- *Preheat oven to 400°.*
- *Grease a 9 x 13 inch baking dish.*
- *Cook ground beef over medium high heat until evenly brown.*
- *Stir in pepperoni and cook until browned, drain.*
- *Stir in pizza sauce, remove from heat, and set aside.*
- *Cut biscuits into quarters and place in the bottom of baking dish.*
- *Spread meat mixture evenly over the biscuits.*
- *Sprinkle the top with onion, olives, and mushrooms.*
- *Bake uncovered at 400° for 20 to 25 minutes.*
- *Sprinkle with mozzarella and cheddar cheeses.*
- *Bake an additional 5 to 10 minutes until cheese is melted.*
- *Let stand 10 minutes before serving.*

RUEBEN SANDWICH

Ham or other deli lunch meat
Rye or sour dough bread
Swiss or cheddar cheese, sliced
Dill pickles, sliced
Leftover or prepared coleslaw

- *Assemble in same order as listed.*
- *Butter both sides of bread.*
- *Grill until golden brown.*

NOTE
These sandwiches are great with a Panini grill. For Panini style, instead of buttering the bread, brush on a mixture of pressed garlic and olive oil.

PARMESAN CHICKEN

6 thin chicken cutlets

- *Rub oil on chicken and salt and pepper each side.*
- *Grill 3 minutes per side, remove from heat and tent with a piece of foil.*

Prepare sauce in a medium saucepan:

2 cloves of garlic, chopped
1 medium onion, chopped
    1 sprig of thyme, including stem; remove stem before using sauce
1 Tbsp red pepper flakes

- *Combine and let simmer for 10 minutes.*

Add:

1 large can of fire-roasted diced tomatoes
    (in the organic section of the grocery)
3 pieces of fresh basil, broken into large pieces
Salt and pepper

105

- *Assemble half of the sauce in the bottom of a baking dish, place chicken breasts and add remaining sauce.*
- *Sprinkle with grated Parmesan cheese and top with fresh smoked mozzarella cheese (comes in a ball), thinly sliced.*
- *Put under broiler until melted and bubbly.*
- *Serves 6.*

Nancy Miles

PARMESAN-CRUSTED CHICKEN

6 boneless chicken breasts
1½ cups bread crumb mixture (see below)
1 egg, beaten
2 cups fresh (not dry) bread crumbs
2 Tbsp parsley
1/4 cup Parmesan cheese
1/2 tsp garlic salt
1/2 tsp pepper

- Break several pieces of bread in food processor to make fresh bread crumbs.
- Add parsley, Parmesan, garlic salt and pepper.
- Dip chicken in egg and then in bread crumb mixture and set aside for 30 minutes.
- Sauté chicken in olive oil for 3 minutes until brown.
- Place in baking dish and cook at 350° uncovered for 20 minutes. Serve plain or with chicken sauce below.

Chicken Sauce:

1 can cheddar soup
1 tsp chicken bouillon
1 Tbsp butter
1 cup water
1 Tbsp dehydrated onions
Salt and pepper

- Whisk all ingredients together and cook over medium heat for 10 minutes.

PESTO SPINACH FETA PIZZA

Pesto sauce
Thin slices of sweet onion
Fresh spinach
Feta cheese
Mozzarella cheese

- Preheat oven to 450°.
- Prepare your favorite pizza crust or use a prepared crust.
- Layer the pesto, onion, spinach and cheeses on the crust.
- Bake at 450° for 10 to 15 minutes, remove and put the following toppings on:

Fresh sliced tomatoes
Red pepper flakes
Fresh grated Parmesan cheese

PIZZA SAUCE

One 6 oz can tomato paste
1 can warm water (use tomato paste can)
3 Tbsp grated Parmesan cheese
1 tsp minced garlic
2 Tbsp honey
3/4 tsp onion powder
1/4 tsp dried oregano
1/4 tsp dried marjoram
1/4 tsp dried basil
1/4 tsp ground black pepper
1/8 tsp cayenne pepper
1/8 tsp dried red pepper flakes, optional
Salt to taste

- Combine all of the ingredients in a small bowl. Do not heat.
- Let it sit in bowl for at least 30 minutes before using.

MEXICAN RICE CASSEROLE

My daughter, Diane Wilson of Cottonwood, California gave me this recipe.

1½ cups long grain rice, cooked and cooled
1 small can Cream of Chicken Soup
1/2 cup milk
1 cup sliced mushrooms, optional
1 small onion, diced
1/2 tsp salt
1/2 tsp pepper
3/4 tsp chili powder
Sliced black or green olives
3 cups cooked, diced chicken
One 16 oz bottle of Pace Picanté Sauce
Jack cheese

- Add chicken and Picanté sauce to the rice.
- Layer rice mixture with Jack cheese.
- Top with extra cheese.
- Bake 35 to 40 minutes at 375°.

106

PIZZA WITH HOMEMADE DOUGH

Pizzas make fun parties. We often have people over and let them all make their own individual pizzas.

4 cups bread flour
1½ cups lukewarm water
1 Tbsp olive oil
1½ tsp kosher salt
1 Tbsp instant yeast

- *Preheat oven to 500°. Use a pizza stone if you have one and preheat stone for 30 minutes.*
- *Put all of the ingredients in electric mixer with the dough hook.*
- *Process for 8 minutes.*
- *Sprinkle a pizza paddle with corn meal.*
- *Prepare pizza on the pizza paddle, keep it turning to prevent sticking and easy release from paddle to the pizza stone.*
- *Top with any of the following ingredients or your own favorites.*

Prepared pizza sauce or just olive oil with pressed garlic
Fresh pressed garlic
Sliced red, yellow or green bell pepper
Sliced olives
Small pieces of broccoli and cauliflower
Pepperoni
Onions, green or yellow
Ham
Pineapple

- *Bake at 500° for 6 to 7 minutes. Timing varies as to thickness of dough, check it often.*

SLOPPY JOES

1 pound ground beef or ground turkey
1 small onion, chopped (optional)
1 cup ketchup
2 Tbsp white sugar
2 Tbsp white vinegar
2 Tbsp yellow mustard

- *Brown and drain ground meat and onion.*
- *Add remaining ingredients.*
- *Toast buns and fill with Sloppy Joe mixture.*

PORK CHOP & POTATO CASSEROLE

1 Tbsp olive oil
6 boneless pork chops
One 10.75 oz can cream of mushroom soup
1 cup milk
4 potatoes, thinly sliced
1/2 cup chopped onion
1 cup shredded cheddar cheese

- *Preheat oven to 400°.*
- *Sear pork chops in the oil.*
- *In a medium bowl, combine the soup and the milk.*
- *Place potatoes and onions in a 9 x 13 baking dish.*
- *Place the browned chops over the potatoes and onions and then pour the soup mixture over the top.*
- *Bake 30 minutes, top with the cheese, and then bake for an additional 30 minutes.*

PORK CHOPS IN ORANGE GLAZE

2 boneless pork loin chops, ½ inch thick
1/2 tsp salt
1/8 tsp pepper
1 Tbsp vegetable oil
1/2 cup brown sugar
1/2 cup orange juice concentrate (not diluted)

- *Sprinkle pork chops with salt and pepper.*
- *Brown in oil on both sides.*
- *Combine brown sugar and orange concentrate and pour over chops.*
- *Bring to a boil, reduce heat, cover and simmer for 8 minutes.*
- *Serve over rice.*

ROASTED CHICKEN

1 whole chicken
Rub with olive oil
Sprinkle with coarse salt
Fresh ground pepper or lemon pepper

- *Bake uncovered at 450° for 45 minutes.*
- *Cover and continue baking for 15 minutes.*

PULLED PORK TOSTADAS

Refried beans
Mango Salsa
Pulled pork mixture
Shredded lettuce
Cheese
Chopped tomatoes
Garlic Salt, salt and pepper to taste

Using a pressure cooker:

- *Cut 4 lbs of pork tenderloin into 3 to 4 inch pieces, put in a pressure cooker with 1 cup water.*
- *Cook for 50 to 60 minutes and let cool naturally.*
- *Shred pork with two forks.*
- *Add garlic salt, salt and pepper to taste.*
- *Enough mango salsa to make the meat easy to use on a tostada shell, in a burrito or taco shell.*
- *Mix well, heat through.*
- *Spread flat tostada shell with refried beans, pork mixture, shredded lettuce, cheese and tomatoes.*
- *This will keep in a crock pot on low heat.*

> ### NOTE
> Use the pulled pork for burritos and tacos but the regular salsa does not go well with mango salsa. Don't mix them.

PORK CHOPS IN GRAVY

4 boneless pork chops
I can cream of celery soup and ½ cup water
1/2 package dry onion soup mix
Black pepper to taste

- *Brown pork chops in a small amount of olive oil, about 4 minutes per side.*
- *Remove from skillet.*
- *Whisk remaining ingredients until well blended.*
- *Return chops to skillet.*
- *Cover and simmer for 7 minutes.*

> ### NOTE
> Do not add salt. The soup mix has enough in it.

QUESADILLAS

Serve this as an appetizer or main dish.

Mozzarella cheese, shredded
Chicken, cooked and diced, optional
Black beans, drained and rinsed
Corn
Salt and pepper to taste

- *Using flour tortillas, place on a cookie sheet and fill with the cheese, chicken, beans, corn and seasonings.*
- *Place another tortilla on top and broil until the top is crisp.*

Serve with the following sour cream mixture:

Sour cream
Touch of lime juice
Fresh salsa

- *Briefly mix in a small food processor.*
- *Serve with quesadillas.*

109

SALMON WITH CREAMY DILL SAUCE

6 salmon steaks, skin side down, on a greased piece of foil
Sprinkle with lemon pepper and onion salt
Top with sliced onion and lemon
Dot with butter

- *Fold foil around salmon tightly.*
- *Bake at 350° for 20 minutes.*
- *Open foil and broil 4 to 6 inches from heating element for 8 to 12 minutes.*

Sauce:

1/3 cup sour cream
1/3 cup mayonnaise
I Tbsp finely chopped onion
I tsp lemon juice
I tsp horseradish
3/4 tsp dill weed
1/4 tsp garlic salt
Salt and pepper

- *Cook over medium heat until thickened.*
- *Serve over salmon.*

Rice Ham Pie

2 cups cooked rice
3 Tbsp Parmesan cheese
1/8 tsp salt
1/8 tsp white pepper
1 Tbsp dried parsley
1 egg, slightly beaten

- *Mix the above ingredients well and press into a greased 9 inch glass pie plate.*
- *Bake 15 minutes at 350° or until lightly browned.*

2½ cups cooked ham, cubed
1/2 medium white onion, cut up

- *In a food processor, pulse the ham and onion only until blended, but still very chunky.*
- *Remove and place in a mixing bowl.*

Then add the following to the mixing bowl:

2 Tbsp sweet pickle relish
1/4 cup mayonnaise (not salad dressing)
1 heaping Tbsp prepared mustard
Salt and pepper to taste

- *Put the mixture on top of the rice.*

Add to the top:

Jack cheese, grated

- *Bake for 20 minutes at 350° uncovered.*
- *Remove from oven and let sit for 10 minutes.*

Salsa

- *When ready to serve, sprinkle salsa on top of the cheese and serve.*
- *Makes 6 large slices.*

Note

There is a distinct difference in the flavor between salad dressing and mayonnaise. Salad dressing is more tart than mayonnaise.

Taco Chili

This is easy on the waistline and very good.

8 oz ground beef
1 small onion, chopped
One 28 oz can crushed or diced tomatoes
One 4 oz can diced green chilies
1 package taco seasoning mix
Two 15 oz cans red kidney beans, drained and rinsed
One 15 oz can corn, drained
1 cup water
1 package dry Ranch Dressing mix

- *Cook ground beef with onion and drain.*
- *Add remaining ingredients and simmer for 30 minutes.*
- *Makes about 12 one cup servings.*

Spaghetti Carbonara

This is rich with a lot of flavor.

1/2 lb Italian bacon (pancetta) cut in 1 inch pieces
Spaghetti, fettuccine or penne

- *Cook spaghetti, fettuccine or penne al dente, drain and keep warm.*
- *Cook bacon until crisp, remove and save drippings.*

1 tsp olive oil
2 garlic cloves, minced
1 small onion, diced
2 slightly beaten eggs
Salt and black pepper
1/2 to 1 cup Parmesan cheese
2 Tbsp parsley
1/4 tsp red pepper

- *Add olive oil, garlic and onion to drippings and sauté until soft.*
- *Add eggs to the warm pasta and mix well.*
- *Mix pasta with the sautéed onions and garlic.*
- *Add the bacon and enough drippings to make a good consistency to the pasta, about ¼ cup.*
- *Add seasonings, Parmesan, parsley and red pepper.*
- *Heat on low heat until well blended and hot.*
- *Serve immediately.*

STEAK WITH GARLIC BUTTER

The butter makes this steak melt in your mouth.

1/2 cup butter
1 tsp garlic powder
4 cloves garlic, minced
4 rib steaks, filet mignon or any good cut of meat
Salt and pepper to taste

- *Preheat an outdoor grill on high heat.*
- *In a small saucepan, melt butter over medium to low heat with garlic powder and minced garlic and set aside.*
- *Brush steaks with oil and sprinkle both sides with salt and pepper.*
- *Grill steaks 4 to 5 minutes per side or to desired doneness and transfer to warmed plates.*
- *Brush tops generously with the garlic butter and allow to rest for 2 to 3 minutes before serving.*

SWEET CHILI

Instead of a hot chili powder taste, this has a nice sweet taste and works well in a crock pot.

1 lb ground beef, cooked and drained
1 small onion, chopped
1/2 lb cooked bacon, crumbled
One 15 oz can of kidney beans
One 15 oz can pinto beans
One 30 oz can pork & beans
1/3 cup brown sugar
1/3 cup white sugar
2 Tbsp molasses
1/4 cup BBQ sauce
1/4 cup ketchup
1/2 Tbsp chili powder
1 Tbsp prepared mustard
1 tsp liquid smoke
1 can of corn, drained

- *Mix all ingredients and simmer 30 minutes.*

SHEPHERD PIE

Use all your leftovers from Thanksgiving for this dish.

Dressing (stuffing)
Cranberry Sauce (either whole berries or jelly)
Turkey
Gravy
Carrots
Mashed potatoes

- *Using a deep large pie plate, layer the dressing, cranberry sauce, turkey, gravy, carrots and mashed potatoes.*
- *Bake at 350° for 30 to 35 minutes.*

TAMALE PIE

The corn meal is mixed into the pie instead of a crust.

111

1 lb ground beef, partially cooked and drained
1 small onion, chopped
2 cloves of garlic, minced
1 Tbsp chili powder
1 package taco seasoning (prepared or use the recipe on page 149)
One 16 oz can crushed tomatoes, with juice
1 can corn, drained
1 can sliced olives, drained
Salt and pepper to taste
Grated cheese

- *Add the onion, garlic, chili powder, taco seasoning, tomatoes, corn, olives and seasonings to the ground beef.*
- *Prepare the cornmeal mixture below.*

2 eggs
1 cup milk
1/2 cup cornmeal

- *Mix the eggs, milk and cornmeal.*
- *Drop the cornmeal mixture over the meat mixture in a 9 x 13 pan.*
- *Bake at 350° for 45 minutes.*
- *Remove from oven and top with grated cheese.*

VEGGIE TOSTADA

This is quick, easy and healthy.

Tostada shells
I large can refried beans
I tsp dehydrated onions
1/4 cup salsa
Jack cheese, shredded
Assorted vegetables, chopped

- *Mix beans, onion and salsa together in a medium saucepan.*
- *Chop assorted vegetables such as broccoli, tomatoes, zucchini, squash, cauliflower, bell peppers, etc.*
- *Monterey Jack cheese, shredded.*
- *Spread beans on tostada shell, cover with vegetables and top with cheese.*
- *Put on cookie sheet and broil until cheese melts.*

TRACY'S LASAGNA

Erica Williams raved about this lasagna. She gave me the recipe and I traced it to Tracy Eberline, right in my own neighborhood.

I lb ground beef
I jar spaghetti sauce
I box lasagna noodles
Grated mozzarella cheese
One 8 oz package of cream cheese
One 16 oz container of small curd cottage cheese
One 8 oz sour cream
I small onion, chopped (optional)

- *Brown beef and onion, then drain off fat.*
- *Boil noodles and drain.*
- *Mix cream cheese, cottage cheese and sour cream.*
- *Combine meat and spaghetti sauce.*
- *Layer as follows: small amount of sauce in the bottom of the baking dish, noodles, cream mixture, meat sauce and cheese.*
- *Repeat once or twice, depending on the size of dish you use.*
- *Bake at 350° for 30 to 35 minutes or until bubbling.*

NANCY'S TRI-TIP

This will always be known as my signature recipe. Any one that knows me knows my Tri-Tip. This is for Mark Anderson and the Carter kids who grew up with it.

One large, lean Tri-Tip
Teriyaki sauce
Garlic salt
McCormick Grill Mates Montreal Steak Seasoning
Olive oil

- *Marinate at least overnight in teriyaki sauce.*
- *The next day, rub olive oil on the Tri-Tip.*
- *Sprinkle a heavy amount of garlic salt all over.*
- *Then rub in McCormick Grill Mates Montreal Steak Seasoning.*
- *Put on rotisserie and cook 15 minutes per pound.*
- *Let stand for 15 minutes before slicing.*

NOTE

Tri-Tip is not a tender cut so the marinade is a must.

CHICKEN RICE-A-RONI CASSEROLE

2 cups cooked chicken or turkey, diced
I package of Chicken Flavored Rice-A-Roni
I cup celery, chopped
1/2 cup onion, chopped
I can cream of chicken or mushroom soup
I cup mayonnaise
1/4 cup slivered almonds
I tsp lemon juice
Potato chips, crushed

- *Prepare the Rice-A-Roni as directed on the box.*
- *Mix all remaining ingredients except the chips and put in a large casserole dish.*
- *Bake at 350° for 40 minutes.*
- *Top with potato chips for the last 5 minutes.*

WHITE SAUCE LASAGNA

Lana Richardson of South Jordan, Utah shares this true Italian recipe. It's very different from the traditional lasagna. It appears long but is not too involved and well worth it. I have altered it to better fit my family's taste but the basic ingredients are the same.

I to 2 lbs ground beef
Salt and pepper
Garlic salt
I small onion, chopped

- *Brown beef and drain, add onion.*
- *Season to taste with salt, pepper, and garlic salt.*
- *Make the white sauce with the following:*

3/4 cube of butter
6 Tbsp olive oil
Two 8 oz packages of cream cheese, softened
4 Tbsp cooking sherry or rice vinegar
I quart whipping cream or half and half
2 tsp minced garlic
1/2 tsp garlic salt
1/4 tsp cayenne pepper
1/4 cup parsley
3/4 cup Parmesan cheese

- *Over low heat, melt all of the ingredients except the Parmesan cheese.*
- *Simmer until thickened.*
- *Add the Parmesan cheese.*
- *Mix sauce and meat mixture together.*
- *Prepare the following.*

One 8 oz package lasagna noodles, cooked and drained (do not overcook)
6 hard boiled eggs, peeled and sliced
4 cups grated mozzarella cheese
Broccoli or spinach, optional

- *Layer ingredients in four parts.*
- *Place a layer of noodles in a 9 x 13 or baking dish.*
- *Pour half of the meat mixture over the noodles.*
- *Slice 3 hard boiled eggs and place over the meat.*
- *Layer of mozzarella cheese.*
- *Repeat the layers, ending with noodles.*
- *Top with mozzarella cheese.*
- *Bake at 350° for 45 to 50 minutes or until bubbling in middle.*

CREAMED TUNA

Many people don't like creamed tuna but if there is someone out there you know who does, here is a recipe that is very good and very easy.

I small can of white Albacore tuna in water, drained
1/4 cup butter or margarine
2 Tbsp flour mixed with enough water to make a thick paste
1/2 tsp dehydrated chopped onions
Dash of white pepper
2 cups whole milk
Salt and pepper to taste
I cup frozen peas
Cooked rice, English muffins or cooked noodles

- *Sauté tuna and butter in medium skillet for 5 minutes.*
- *Add flour and water mixture and stir until thickened.*
- *Add onions, milk, salt, pepper and frozen peas.*
- *Continue to cook for 5 minutes, stirring often.*
- *Serve over steamed rice, cooked noodles or toasted English muffins.*

113

> ### NOTE
> If you add cooked noodles to the mixture, you can put it in a casserole, top with ½ cup shredded cheddar cheese and bake at 350° for 25 to 30 minutes.

CHICKEN HAM-BAKE

This comes from Donna Knowlton. We lived in Paradise, California at the same time. She now resides in St. George, Utah. It makes enough to serve a large crowd.

6 boneless chicken breasts
4 Tbsp butter
1 cup onions, chopped
2 envelopes of dry chicken noodle soup mix
1 1/3 cups long grain rice
1 cup wild rice
1 tsp rosemary
4 cups water
12 slices of ham, thinly sliced
2 envelopes of dry mushroom soup mix
One 6 oz can broiled mushrooms, drained (optional)

- *Brown chicken in the butter in a large skillet, remove and set aside.*
- *Add onion to the skillet and cook until tender.*
- *Add dry chicken noodle soup mix, long grain rice, wild rice, rosemary and the 4 cups of water.*
- *Bring to a boil.*
- *Pour into a 9 x 9 baking dish.*
- *Top with chicken.*
- *Bake covered for 50 minutes at 350°.*
- *Prepare the mushroom soup according the package directions, adding mushrooms if desired.*
- *Lift chicken and slide ham under each chicken breast.*
- *Pour soup mixture over the top of the chicken.*
- *Continue to bake uncovered for 15 more minutes.*

TOSTADA PIZZA

Looking for a fun family dinner? Let them make their own crust and put toppings on. Adults will like this too.

1 lb ground beef, optional
1/2 cup water
One 4 oz can green, chopped chili peppers, drained (use as much as you like)
1 tsp chili powder
2 Tbsp taco seasoning mix
One 15 oz can refried beans, heated with enough water to make it spread easily
Cheddar cheese, shredded
Cabbage or lettuce, shredded
Green onion, sliced
2 cups Bisquick
1/2 cup water
1 tomato, chopped

- *Preheat oven to 450°.*
- *Cook ground beef, drain.*
- *Add water, chili peppers, chili powder and taco seasoning and simmer.*
- *Spray a 12 inch round pizza pan and sprinkle with cornmeal.*
- *Mix Bisquick and enough water to make the dough form a ball.*
- *Using vegetable oil, form dough in bottom of the pizza pan.*
- *Spread with refried beans.*
- *Layer remaining ingredients, as desired, ending with cheese.*
- *Bake at 450° for 15 to 20 minutes or until golden brown.*
- *Remove and put cabbage or lettuce on top.*

> **NOTE**
>
> For those who like fresh tomatoes, they are great added to the top of this pizza after is has fully cooked. Vegetarians may substitute fresh chopped broccoli, cauliflower and bell pepper for the ground beef prior to baking.

114

KIELBASA SKILLET DINNER

This is a very healthy dish. Kielbasa is a Polish Sausage.

2 Tbsp olive oil
1 small yellow onion, thinly sliced
1/2 head cabbage, shredded
1 Kielbasa (smoked Polish sausage)
Salt and pepper to taste

- *Cover the bottom of a large skillet with the onions.*
- *Salt and pepper.*
- *Add shredded cabbage on top of the onions.*
- *Cover with sliced Kielbasa.*
- *Add 1/3 cup water.*
- *Cover and simmer for 15 minutes.*

CHICKEN ENCHILADAS

This is great with leftover turkey from Thanksgiving.

12 flour tortillas
1/2 pint sour cream
2 cans cream of chicken soup
Garlic powder to taste
3 to 4 cups chicken or turkey, diced
One 6 oz can diced green chilies
1 lb cheddar cheese, shredded

- *To make the sauce, mix soup, sour cream, garlic powder, chilies and ¾ of the cheese together.*
- *Put chicken on the tortilla and 2 Tbsp of prepared sauce.*
- *Continue to roll up each tortilla and place in a buttered baking dish.*
- *Spread remaining sauce over the top and sprinkle with cheese.*
- *Bake at 350º for 30 minutes or until bubbling hot.*

NOTE

Add frozen vegetables or used canned chicken chunks as a variation.

CHICKEN DIVAN

6 large chicken breasts cut in half
One 10 oz package frozen broccoli spears, steamed and drained
1 tsp lemon juice
1/2 tsp curry powder (optional)
1 cup salad dressing (not mayonnaise)
1/2 cup sour cream
1 can cream of chicken soup, undiluted
1 cup cheddar cheese, shredded
Salt and pepper to taste
Corn flakes or potato chips

- *Place broccoli in a greased 9 x 13 baking dish.*
- *Layer chicken over broccoli.*
- *Mix salad dressing, lemon juice, soup, salt, pepper and curry.*
- *Pour over chicken.*
- *Sprinkle with cheese and cover with crushed corn flakes or potato chips.*
- *Bake 30 minutes at 375º.*
- *Make 6 to 8 servings.*

115

SPICY SAUSAGE HASH

I got this from my neighbor in Paradise, California when Melissa and Kirsten Kelly were just little girls.

1 lb ground sausage or ground beef
1 large onion, chopped
2 cups uncooked elbow macaroni
One 15 oz can diced tomatoes
2 Tbsp sugar
2 tsp chili powder
1½ cups sour cream

- *Brown sausage or ground beef and onion together.*
- *Add macaroni to the meat mixture and cook 5 minutes. Drain.*
- *Stir in the remaining ingredients and continue cooking until it comes to a boil.*
- *Simmer 20 to 30 minutes until macaroni is tender.*

CHINESE HAYSTACKS

This recipe is fun for a large crowd. It will serve 8 to 10 people. Prepare as much as you think you'll need of each ingredient.

8 cups cooked rice, keep warm in a rice cooker or crock pot
2 large cans of chow mien noodles
4 cans cream of chicken soup, with one can of water added, heat in a medium saucepan
3 large tomatoes, diced
5 stalks celery, sliced diagonally
Cooked ham, diced
Cooked chicken or turkey, diced
1 lb mild cheddar cheese, shredded
2 bunches green onions, sliced, including the tops
Slivered almonds
2 large cans crushed pineapple, drained
2 cups shredded coconut
Maraschino cherries cut in halves

- *Put each ingredient in individual serving bowls and line up in buffet-style.*
- *Start with the rice, meat, hot soup mixture. This makes the gravy.*
- *Then top with the remaining ingredients, ending with the cheese and cherries.*

> ### NOTE
> This dish requires the rice and soup to be hot and the rest of the ingredients at room temperature.

CHINESE FRIED RICE

This recipe includes the instructions I use in food demonstrations. Once you know how to make it, you won't have to refer to all of the instructions.

Heat oil in wok
Add cold rice
Salt
Sugar
Scrambled eggs
Vegetables
Soy sauce
Oyster sauce
Green onions

- *In advance, cook 1 cup of rice, according to package directions. Cover with plastic wrap and refrigerate for several hours or the night before. This is a very important step.*
- *Use long grain white rice or brown rice. I like Calrose rice as it has a nice texture.*
- *Prepare the vegetables you want to use such as frozen peas, blanched carrots and celery, Napa cabbage, also known as Chinese cabbage, and green onions.*
- *Prepare the meat such as steak, shrimp, chicken, or pork. Dice the meat the same size as the frozen carrots.*
- *Blanching is a procedure where you partially cook the vegetables. Without blanching the carrots and celery, they would not cook to the same consistency as the rest of the ingredients. To blanch, bring a pot of water to a boil and add the sliced carrots. Boil for about 3 minutes, remove and immediately put into ice cold water, to stop them from cooking any further.*
- *Pour olive oil in a ring once around the wok and heat on high heat.*
- *Add cold rice, breaking it up with your hands.*
- *Sprinkle with salt and a touch of sugar.*
- *Add soy sauce, or Liquid Aminos, to lightly color the rice. If you put too much soy sauce in, it will overpower the flavor of the other ingredients.*
- *Add scrambled eggs, one Tbsp oyster sauce, meat and vegetables, adding the green onions and their tops the very last.*
- *Serve immediately.*

LEMON CHICKEN

This has a fabulous lemon sauce.

4 boneless, skinless chicken breasts
2 Tbsp butter
2 Tbsp olive oil

- *With a meat cleaver or the bottom of a heavy pan pound the chicken until ¼ inch thick.*
- *Put butter and oil in large skillet and cook chicken on high heat for 3 to 4 minutes per side. Do not overcook as the chicken will get dry and tough.*
- *Remove and set aside.*

To make the sauce, combine the following:

1 cup heavy cream
1 green onion, finely chopped
2 tsp dried lemon peel or fresh zest of a lemon
3/4 tsp thyme
1/2 tsp dry tarragon
3 Tbsp tarragon vinegar or white wine vinegar
2 Tbsp lemon juice
Salt and pepper to taste

- *Pour cream into the same skillet you cooked the chicken in and bring to a boil over high heat.*
- *Boil until browned chicken bits come loose. This is called deglazing.*
- *Add the remaining ingredients except for the lemon juice, stir until cream is thickened, about 3 minutes.*
- *Stir in lemon juice, salt and pepper.*
- *Spoon over chicken and serve immediately.*

CHICKEN & DRESSING BAKE

4 large boneless, skinless chicken breasts, cooked
1 can cream of chicken soup
1/2 pint of sour cream
1 box of Stove Top chicken flavored dressing
Salt, pepper and onion powder to taste
1 cup frozen, chopped broccoli
1 cup cheddar cheese, shredded

- *Put cooked chicken in a 9 x 13 baking dish.*
- *Mix soup, sour cream and seasoning and spread over chicken.*
- *Prepare dressing as directed on box put over chicken, then cover with cheese.*
- *Bake at 375º for 40 minutes or heated through.*

FIVE MINUTE QUICHE

Five minutes is all it takes to put this quiche together.

One 10 oz package frozen broccoli
1/2 cup onions, chopped
1/2 cup green bell pepper, chopped (optional)
1 cup cheddar cheese, shredded
3/4 cup Bisquick
3 eggs
1 tsp salt
1/4 tsp pepper

- *Preheat oven to 400º.*
- *Lightly grease a large pie pan or two small pans.*
- *Mix broccoli, onions, green pepper and cheese.*
- *Put in the bottom of pie pan.*
- *Beat the Bisquick, eggs, salt and pepper until smooth and pour into pan.*
- *Bake 35 to 40 minutes or until lightly brown and a knife comes out clean when inserted in the middle.*
- *Let stand 5 minutes before serving.*

117

BURRITO BAKE

1 lb ground beef
1 cup Bisquick Mix
1/4 cup water
One 16 oz can refried beans
1 Tbsp chili powder
1/4 tsp garlic salt
Salt and pepper to taste
Salsa, a thick salsa
1½ cups cheese, shredded
Sour cream, optional
Green onion, sliced (optional)

- *Cook ground beef and drain.*
- *Add garlic, salt and pepper.*
- *Mix Bisquick, water and beans.*
- *Spread on a large, greased pie plate.*
- *Layer ground beef, salsa and cheese.*
- *Bake at 375º for 30 minutes.*
- *Top with sour cream and green onions, optional.*

Nancy Miles

POT ROAST MEXICALI

What a hit this is with the younger generation and it serves a big crowd.

4 lb chuck roast
1 cup red cooking wine
1 package dry onion soup mix
One 15 oz can ranch style beans, drained
One 15 oz can garbanzo beans, drained
One 15 oz can pinto beans, drained
One 30 oz can chili with beans
One 30 oz can tamales cut into bite-sizes
One 30 oz can green chili sauce
One 10 oz can red chili sauce
1 lb grated cheddar cheese

- *Place roast in heavy pot like a Dutch oven with the wine and soup mix.*
- *Cover and bake at 350° for 3 to 4 hours until very tender.*
- *Shred meat and add all remaining ingredients but the cheese.*
- *Put in a very large casserole baking dish and refrigerate overnight.*
- *Remove from refrigerator and skim off fat. Let the dish become room temperature.*
- *Bake at 350° for 45 minutes.*
- *Sprinkle with cheese and bake an additional 15 to 20 minutes.*

118

CROCK POT BBQ BRISKET

Five minutes to crock pot is all this takes.

3 lb beef brisket, Tri-Tip works well
One 18 oz bottle Kraft Original Barbecue Sauce
1 large onion, cut in half and then into slices

- *Rub brisket with salt, pepper and garlic salt.*
- *Brown in a little oil in a large skillet.*
- *Place fat-side up in crock pot and cook on low 4 to 6 hours.*

MEXICAN CHEESE TORTE

Arrange this torte in three layers.

Layer One

Flour tortillas, fried and drained on paper towels
Spicy canned refried beans
Chopped onions
Green peppers
Tomatoes
Monterey Jack cheese

Layer Two

Layer of fried tortillas
Sharp cheddar cheese

- *Bake at 350° only until the cheese is melted.*

Layer Three
Fresh lettuce, sliced thin
Salsa
Sour cream

- *Cut as you would a pizza.*
- *Serves 8 to 10.*

BEEF BURGUNDY

This is quick and delicious but you do have to allow three hours of baking time. It makes its own gravy.

2 lbs stew meat
1 can golden mushroom soup
1/2 cup water
1/2 cup burgundy wine
1 package dry onion soup mix
1 can water chestnuts, sliced

- *Mix all ingredients together in a Dutch oven or roasting pan with a tight lid.*
- *Bake for 3 hours at 300°.*
- *Serve over cooked noodles or rice.*

Salads

Nancy Miles

APPLE LETTUCE SALAD

This recipe comes from Taralee Enger of South Jordan, Utah.

Variety of salad greens
Sliced red onions
Craisins
Green Golden Delicious apples, peeled and shredded
Glazed walnuts or cashews cut in large pieces
Salt and pepper to taste

- *Use any amount of the above ingredients and mix well with Poppy Seed Dressing.*

ASIAN CHICKEN SALAD

3 to 4 cups cooked and shredded chicken
1/4 cup chopped roasted peanuts
1 Tbsp toasted sesame seeds, optional
1 cup red bell pepper, diced
1/2 cup green onions, sliced
1 can mandarin oranges, drained

Dressing:

2 Tbsp canola oil
1 Tbsp sesame oil
1 Tbsp rice wine vinegar
1 Tbsp light soy sauce (or liquid Aminos)
2 tsp fresh ginger, grated

- *Just before serving, mix all above ingredients together.*

BROCCOLI SALAD

Use fresh broccoli or spinach, bite-sized pieces
1/2 pound bacon, cut in small pieces and cooked crisp
Thinly sliced red onion
Glazed almonds (see recipe page 11 or 124)

Dressing:

1/2 cup Best Foods mayonnaise (the brand makes a difference in this recipe)
1/4 cup balsamic vinegar
1/4 cup sugar

BBQ CHICKEN SALAD

This is one of my originals and I have had some good feedback. I have no measurements for this salad so just wing it. You can't go wrong.

Variety of lettuces, chopped
Black beans, drained and rinsed
Sweet corn
Jicama, diced
Cilantro
Basil
Feta cheese, crumbled
Won Ton skins, sliced and quick-fried in a small amount of oil
Tomatoes, diced
Scallions, sliced
BBQ chicken, cut in strips

- *Mix all in Herb Ranch Dressing.*
- *Top with BBQ chicken breasts, diced tomatoes and scallions.*
- *Drizzle with a little more BBQ sauce.*

CHICKEN & LETTUCE SALAD

1 cup of leftover cooked chicken, cubed
Celery, sliced
Red onion, sliced
Tomatoes, cubed
Cheddar cheese, cubed
Mandarin oranges

Mix the following ingredients:

3 to 4 Tbsp mayonnaise
1 to 2 tsp prepared mustard
2 Tbsp ketchup
Salt and pepper
1 Tbsp pickle relish

- *Spoon over a bed of lettuce.*

NOTE

Salads are always are great entrée, especially if you add a little protein in the form of nuts or meat.

120

CHICKEN LETTUCE SALAD

1/2 head lettuce sliced in 1 inch slices and
   then into cubes
1 cup of cooked chicken ortuna
1/4 head of cabbage sliced in half inch slices
2 stalks celery sliced
1 Fuji apple cut in small pieces
2 green onions sliced
Seedless red grapes cut in halves
Cheddar cheese cubed
Fresh green peas
2 hard boiled eggs sliced
Corn off the cob, already cooked
Pickled beets (add only when ready to serve as
   they will turn the lettuce red)

- *Use as much of any of the above ingredients that do not have a measurement noted.*

Dressing:

1/2 cup real mayonnaise
1/8 cup prepared mustard
2 Tbsp sweet pickle relish
2 Tbsp rice vinegar
1 tsp sugar
Salt and pepper

- *Make this dressing and use as much as you want for the salad. There is usually enough for another serving.*

CHICKEN RICE SALAD

1 package Rice-A-Roni Chicken Flavored Rice
2 Tbsp oil
1 package deli sliced chicken breasts, roasted
   (leftover chicken works)
One 16 oz can black beans, rinsed and drained
1 cup canned peas, drained
1/2 cup prepared Italian dressing

- *Prepare Rice-A-Roni as package directs but substitute oil for the margarine.*
- *Add chicken the last 10 minutes of cooking time.*
- *Cool 10 minutes an add the rest of the ingredients.*
- *Just before serving, add ½ head of lettuce, toss lightly and serve.*

HOT CHICKEN SALAD

This is wonderful for a luncheon with homemade muffins.

Two 8 oz cans of white chicken chunks, drained
2½ cup celery
1¼ cup Miracle Whip (not mayonnaise)
1/2 cup slivered almonds
2 Tbsp lemon juice
2 Tbsp onions, chopped
1 cup longhorn cheese, shredded
1 small can of French Fried Onion Rings

- *Mix all ingredients together except for the onion rings and put in a baking dish.*
- *Bake at 400° for 10 minutes.*
- *During the last minute add dried onions.*

121

> **NOTE**
> Don't overheat this dish. When you bite into it, you should notice that it is warm and cool in spots.

CHICKEN SALAD

Here's your big event salad.

1 lb vermicelli pasta
4 cups chopped chicken
1 cup diced celery
1/2 cup chopped green onion
4 sweet pickles (I usually double this)
6 hard boiled eggs
2 cups mayonnaise
3 Tbsp vegetable oil
4 Tbsp apple cider vinegar
Salt, pepper, seasoning salt and paprika

- *Cook vermicelli as package directs. Drain, blanch (put in cold water) and chill.*
- *Marinate in oil and vinegar plus seasoning to taste with salt, pepper, season salt and paprika.*
- *Add other ingredients and toss together.*
- *Serves 15.*

COLESLAW

This recipe is from Joan Thomsen of Provo, Utah.

I bag of prepared coleslaw
I apple chopped
I small can pineapple tidbits, drained
Miniature marshmallows, as many as you want

Dressing:

Mayonnaise
Cool Whip

- *Mix equal amounts of the mayonnaise and Cool Whip together.*
- *Add to the coleslaw, apple, pineapple and marshmallows and chill.*

122

CURRY CHICKEN SALAD

Cube prepared BBQ chicken, using breasts only
2 green onions, sliced
2 celery stalks, sliced
Red seedless grapes cut in half
Shredded carrots
I Tbsp curry powder
Black pepper
I pint plain yogurt

- *Mix well and serve.*

FRUIT JELL-O SALAD

I put this in the book, not because I live in Utah, but because a lot of people like a good Jell-O salad.

One 3.5 oz package peach flavored Jell-O
Fresh peaches, peeled and cubes
Large seedless grapes cut lengthwise
Cantaloupe balls
Mini marshmallows

- *Prepare Jell-O minus ¼ cup water.*
- *Put all fruit in Jell-O and partially let it set.*
- *Stir in marshmallows and mix well with fruit.*
- *Refrigerate and let set firm.*

FRESH FRUIT SALAD

You'll figure out that I like good, quick and easy.

- *Use the fruit of your choice.*
- *Add equal amounts of cream cheese and Jet Puff Marshmallow Cream.*
- *Add a touch of nutmeg.*
- *Mix well and refrigerate.*

FRUIT SALAD

This is what is called Texas Style—meaning a lot of it.

I can sweetened condensed milk
I small can frozen lemonade, or juice of 2 lemons
One 16 oz container of Cool Whip
I can cherry pie filling

Fold in Cool Whip and add the following:

I can pineapple, drained
I can mandarin oranges, drained
3 bananas, sliced thick
1/4 cup nuts, optional

> **NOTE**
> Use any kind of fruit. Be creative. The can size depends on how much salad you want to prepare.

FRUIT & VEGGIE CHOPPED SALAD

Select and chop fruits and vegetables of your choice.

Tomatoes
Celery
Green onions
Persimmons (Fuji only)
Carrots
Pears
Fuji or Gala apples
Oranges
Cranapples or Craisins
Cantaloupe

- *Chop everything evenly into small pieces. Do not use any salad dressings. The combination of the fruits and vegetables makes the flavor unique.*

MANDARIN ORANGE SALAD

8 cups of assorted lettuce greens such as romaine, red leaf, butter, iceberg, etc.

3 green onions or sliced red
One 15 oz can mandarin oranges, drained
1 cup slivered, sugared almonds (recipe page 124)
1 can French-fried onions

Dressing:

1/2 cup fresh-squeezed orange juice
1/2 cup vegetable oil
2 Tbsp cider vinegar
3 Tbsp sugar
2 tsp poppy seeds

- *Mix dressing ingredients thoroughly and let chill for several hours.*
- *When ready to serve, place chilled greens and onions in a salad bowl, along with the mandarin oranges.*
- *In a small skillet, sprinkle almonds with sugar and cook over medium heat until almonds are coated and sugar is dissolved.*
- *Just before serving, sprinkle with the sugared almonds and French-fried onions.*
- *Try an optional dressing with the ingredients below.*

1 cup oil
1/2 cup vinegar
1/2 cup sugar
1 tsp each celery seed, dry mustard and salt

ORANGE OREGANO SALAD

3 oranges, peeled and sliced
2 sprigs of fresh oregano, chopped
1/4 red onion, thinly sliced
Extra virgin olive oil
Red wine vinegar

- *Place orange slices on a serving plate.*
- *Sprinkle with fresh oregano.*
- *Add red onion.*
- *Drizzle extra virgin olive oil over the top.*
- *Drizzle with red wine vinegar.*
- *Salt and pepper.*
- *Serve chilled.*
- *Substitute tomatoes for the oranges for a wonderful tomato salad.*

MACARONI FRUIT SALAD

This comes from Marge Matthews from years past.

1/2 cup small shell macaroni, cooked, rinsed and cooled
Red grapes, halved
Celery, diced
Pineapple tidbits, drained, reserve juice for apples
Diced apples, soaked in above pineapple juice

- *Add to the macaroni as many grapes, as much celery, pineapple and apples as you like.*

Dressing:

1/2 cup mayonnaise
1/2 cup Kraft Coleslaw Dressing

- *Add the dressing to the macaroni and fruit.*
- *Add any of the following optional ingredients, mix well and chill.*

Cashew nuts, unsalted
Chunks of cooked chicken
Raisins
Water chestnuts

CHRISTMAS JELL-O SALAD

Two 3 oz packages of cherry or strawberry Jell-O
2 cups boiling water
One 10 oz package frozen strawberries, with juice
1 small can crushed pineapple, with juice
2 bananas, mashed with 1 tsp lemon juice
1 cup sour cream

- *Combine all ingredients except the sour cream and mix well.*
- *Pour half of the mixture into an 8 x 8 glass dish.*
- *Refrigerate until firm.*
- *Spread with sour cream.*
- *Pour remaining mixture on top.*
- *Refrigerate until firm.*

123

Oriental Chicken Salad

Skinless, boneless chicken breasts
Teriyaki sauce
Green cabbage
Red cabbage

- Grill teriyaki chicken breasts or use pre-packaged cooked ones until done or 160º.
- Slice into strips, put in a serving bowl and set aside.
- Slice enough green cabbage to serve the amount of guests you are serving.
- Add a small amount of red cabbage for contrast.
- Combine the following ingredients in a bowl.

1 can mandarin oranges, drained
1/2 carrot, julienned or shredded
1 green onion, sliced
1 to 2 Tbsp sliced almonds, roasted or glazed
1/3 cup narrow chow mien noodles

- In a large serving bowl, mix oranges, carrot, onion, almonds, chow mein noodles and cabbages together.
- Mix the salad dressing (recipe below) and add to the above fruits and vegetables.
- Pass chicken around in a separate serving bowl.

Salad dressing:

3 Tbsp honey
1½ Tbsp white vinegar
4 tsp mayonnaise
1 Tbsp Dijon mustard
1/8 tsp sesame oil

124

Tomato Oregano Salad

3 large fresh tomatoes, sliced
2 sprigs of fresh oregano, chopped
1/4 red onion, thinly sliced
Extra virgin olive oil
Red wine vinegar

- Place tomato slices on a serving plate and sprinkle with fresh oregano, add the red onion, drizzle with the extra virgin oil and red wine vinegar, and salt and pepper.
- Substitute oranges with the tomatoes for variety.
- Serve chilled.

Pasta Pesto Salad

1 box of bow tie pasta, cooked and cooled
1/2 pint container of pesto (see page 148)
1/4 cup pine nuts, sautéed in olive oil
1 small jar sun-dried tomatoes, drained, chopped
1 can black beans, drained
1 small red onion, chopped
1 tomato, cut up
1/3 cup fresh Parmesan cheese
Salt and pepper

- Mix all ingredients together and serve at room temperature.
- Serves 8 to 10

Pear Salad

Dressing: mix together and refrigerate.

1/4 cup apple juice
2 Tbsp balsamic vinegar
2 Tbsp olive oil
1 tsp Dijon mustard
1/2 tsp salt
1/4 tsp pepper

Salad:

Mixed greens
2 Bosco pears, thinly sliced
1/3 cup pecans, roasted
2 small red onions, thinly sliced
2 oz blue cheese

- Roast 1/3 cup pecans at 200º for 15 minutes.
- Add to mixed greens.
- Add pears, red onions and blue cheese.
- Pour chilled dressing over the salad and toss well.

Glazed Nuts

- In a skillet, cover pecans, walnuts or almonds with granulated sugar. Over medium heat, stir until sugar has absorbed and the nuts have turned a light brown. Let cool before using in salad.

POTATO SALAD

I took the best parts of many recipes and created my own potato salad recipe.

6 medium russet potatoes, boiled
1/4 cup Bernstein's Italian Dressing
1 small onion, chopped
8 hardboiled eggs, chopped finely
3 sweet pickles, cut in large pieces
1/3 cup sweet pickle juice
1/2 cup mayonnaise
2 Tbsp prepared mustard
Salt and pepper to taste
1 tsp celery seed

- *After potatoes are cooked, peel and cut into small pieces.*
- *While still warm, put Italian dressing on cut potatoes and cover with a plate.*
- *Let stand at room temperature until potatoes have cooled down.*
- *Add the remaining ingredients and mix well.*
- *Chill for several hours or overnight.*
- *Serves 8 to 10.*

RED POTATO SALAD

This is made with no mayonnaise. Serve warm or cold.

1 to 2 lbs red potatoes cut in quarters
Handful of sun-dried tomatoes
1 cup broccoli flowerets
2 Tbsp dried parsley
Kosher salt
Montreal Seasoned Pepper

- *Put potatoes and sun-dried tomatoes in a medium saucepan.*
- *Cover with cold water and cook until potatoes are tender.*
- *Add broccoli and cook only until the broccoli is tender. Do not overcook.*
- *Drain all water and return ingredients to the pot.*
- *When ready to serve, add parsley, salt and pepper.*
- *Serve hot or cold.*

RICE SALAD WITH RAISINS & SCALLIONS

1 cup long-grain white rice, cooked
1/3 cup golden raisins
1 Tbsp olive oil
3 Tbsp fresh lemon juice
1 small head radicchio or red Belgian endive, thinly sliced crosswise
2 scallions, thinly sliced on the diagonal

- *Add raisins and oil to rice while still hot and fluff with a fork.*
- *Put in a shallow bowl, cover loosely with plastic wrap, and refrigerate until cool.*
- *With a fork, mix in lemon juice, radicchio, and scallions. Season with salt and pepper.*

NOTE

Adding the golden raisins to the hot rice helps soften them. They plump up as they absorb moisture from the rice.

125

SALAD GREENS WITH PEARS

Selected mixed greens
2 Fuji pears, peeled, cored and thinly sliced
1 small red onion, thinly sliced
2 oz blue cheese
1/3 cup glazed pecans or almonds (recipe page 11 or 124)

Dressing:

1/4 cup apple juice
2 Tbsp balsamic vinegar
2 Tbsp olive oil
1 tsp Dijon mustard
1/2 tsp salt
1/4 tsp pepper

- *Mix together and chill.*
- *Just before serving, mix dressing with greens and serve.*

RUSSIAN SALAD

Don't let this long list of ingredients stop you from trying this great salad. This is my own version but taken from a young woman who served a mission in Russia for 18 months—Kirsten Anderson. Use any fruit or vegetable together. That is what makes it so unusual. Dice all the ingredients the same small size as this is what gives its pretty presentation.

Use any of the following ingredients:

Fresh tomatoes, seeded and chopped
Sweet red, yellow and green peppers, diced
Carrot, diced
Green onion, sliced (including the green tops)
Jalapeno pepper, seeded and diced
Fresh cilantro, parsley and dill (optional)
Garlic cloves, minced
Fresh or frozen corn
Black beans, drained and rinsed
Celery, diced
Cucumber, seeded and diced
Fuji apple, cored and diced
Fresh Asian pears, cored and diced (Asian pears are firm like an apple. Don't use regular pears.)
Drizzle lemon juice
Kosher salt
Black pepper
Drizzle olive oil

- *Mix all ingredients together in a large bowl.*
- *When ready to serve, drizzle a small amount of Russian Salad Dressing in salad. Do not use too much dressing. You want to be able to taste the fruits and vegetables.*

126

SALSA SALAD

This is very good over baked potatoes.

Tomatoes (not canned)
Onions

Chop as many tomatoes and onions as you would like into very small pieces and add:

Canned black beans, drained
Fresh cilantro
Canned corn
Small amount of V-8 to moisten
Garlic salt to taste

SALAD TOSS-UP

When we had dinner at Erica and Chad William's home, I wasn't the only one who asked for this recipe so thanks, Linda Pino, for sharing it with Erica and me.

1 bag or 1 head of romaine lettuce, cut up
1 bag spinach
1 bag coleslaw
1 bag Craisins
1 small can honey roasted peanuts
1 Jar of Brianne's Poppy Seed Dressing (in the cooler section of the produce department)

- *Mix all the greens together and refrigerate until ready to serve.*
- *Add all salad ingredients together and toss with salad dressing.*

NOTE

When we moved to Utah from Paradise, California, Brianne's Salad Dressings were just becoming known in this area. I use Brianne's Blush Wine Vinaigrette in a lot of salad recipes. If you haven't used these before, you're going to love them.

SALAMI PASTA SALAD

- *Cook and rinse spiral pasta or any other pasta*

2 oz hard salami cut in julienne strips
8 oz garbanzo beans, drained and rinsed
1/4 lb smoked mozzarella, cubed
5 to 7 peperoncini peppers, sliced
1/4 tsp red pepper flakes
1/2 cup chopped parsley
3/4 cup sun-dried tomatoes in oil or soaked in hot water to soften
1 bottle of Bernstein's Italian Dressing

- *Assemble ingredients in large bowl and pour dressing over them. Toss well.*
- *Refrigerate for several hours or prepare the night before.*
- *Serve cold.*

Nancy Miles

SOUTHWESTERN CHICKEN SALAD

This makes a salad large enough for several people. You can consider this a dieter's wonderful low-fat salad.

4 to 6 cups salad greens
1/4 cup corn
1/4 cup black beans, rinsed and drained
1/4 cup salsa or Pico De Gallo
3 oz cooked chicken, chopped
1 Tbsp Parmesan cheese
3 green onions, sliced, including the greens
2 to 3 Tbsp of your favorite fat-free dressing
Handful of light or baked corn chips, crushed

- *Mix all ingredients together and serve immediately.*

SPINACH SALAD

128

1 bunch of fresh spinach
1/2 lb bacon, fried crisp and crumbled
4 hard boiled eggs (optional)
1/2 cup raisins
Sunflower seeds (optional)
Red onions, very thinly sliced
Glazed almonds (see recipe page 11 or 124)
Poppy seed dressing, to your liking (prepared or
    see recipe below)

Balsamic Vinegar Dressing:

Balsamic vinegar
Real mayonnaise
Sugar

- *Mix all ingredients together when ready to serve.*

Homemade Poppy Seed Dressing:

3/4 Tbsp poppy seeds
1/3 cup white vinegar
3/4 cup vegetable oil
1/3 cup sugar
3 Tbsp salt
1 Tbsp Dijon mustard

- *Combine all ingredients in a jar, shake well and refrigerate.*

SPINACH & WHITE BEAN SALAD

This is unusual as it uses maple syrup as a sweetener.

1/2 cup green onions, sliced
1/2 cup finely chopped red bell pepper
5 bacon slices, cooked and crumbled
1 small can of mandarin oranges, drained
1/2 cup sugared walnuts (see recipe)
One 15.5 oz can of Great Northern beans
Two 7 oz packages fresh baby spinach

- *Combine all ingredients in a large bowl.*
- *Prepare the dressing below.*

Dressing:

1/4 cup real maple syrup
3 Tbsp cider vinegar
1 Tbsp extra virgin olive oil
1 Tbsp Dijon mustard
1/4 tsp salt
1/4 tsp ground black pepper

- *Combine in a microwave-safe bowl and cook on high for 1 minute.*
- *Stir with a whisk.*
- *Heat the beans in the microwave.*
- *Add the dressing and beans to the salad and toss well.*
- *Serve immediately.*

SUGARED WALNUTS

- *Put powdered sugar in the bottom of a skillet.*
- *Add walnuts and cook on medium to high until sugar melts into walnuts.*
- *Let cool.*

TOMATOES WITH BASIL SAUCE

This makes a refreshing salad.

Tomatoes, any kind, sliced into thick slices

Drizzle tomatoes with the following mixture:

1 Tbsp fresh, chopped basil leaves
2 Tbsp olive oil
2 Tbsp grated Parmesan cheese

FRUIT & SPINACH SALAD

1/2 cup balsamic vinegar and oil dressing
1/4 cup orange marmalade
3 kiwi, peeled and sliced
1 orange, peeled and diced
2 cups fresh strawberries, sliced
1/4 cup green onions, sliced
Roasted glazed walnuts (recipe page 124)

- *Whisk together the dressing and marmalade.*
- *Add the kiwi, orange, strawberries, green onions and walnuts and toss together lightly.*
- *Serve immediately.*

TOMATO, BASIL & MOZZARELLA SALAD

Pesto salad dressing:

2 cups fresh basil leaves
6 cloves garlic
1/2 tsp crushed red pepper flakes
1/2 cup pine nuts, toasted
1 cup fresh Parmesan cheese, not grated
1/2 cup red wine vinegar
Salt and pepper

- *Put above ingredients in a food processor.*
- *Pulse until blended.*

1 cup virgin olive oil

- *While processor is running, pour 1 cup virgin olive oil in shoot to keep it from separating.*

Slices of fresh mozzarella
Thick slices of fresh tomatoes
Lettuce leaves

- *Spread slices of mozzarella with the pesto dressing.*
- *Alternate a slice of tomato with a slice of mozzarella.*
- *Place on a bed of lettuce leaves on a large oval platter.*
- *Drizzle additional dressing on top.*
- *Add Italian meats, if desired.*

TROPICAL CHICKEN SALAD

2½ cups small pasta shells, cooked
2 green onions cut in pieces
3 to 4 chicken breasts, cooked and cut into bite-sized pieces
2 cups apples, chopped
2 cans pineapple tidbits, drained
1 can sliced water chestnuts, drained
1 can mandarin oranges, drained
1½ cups coarsely chopped almonds, toasted or glazed (add last)
2 cups dressing made with a combination of
    Mayonnaise
    Lighthouse Coleslaw dressing
    Lighthouse Poppy Seed dressing

- *Mix pasta, chicken, green onions, apples, pineapple, water chestnuts, and mandarin oranges in a large bowl.*
- *Add the dressing and toss.*
- *Add the almonds last.*
- *Serve immediately.*

129

TUNA LETTUCE SALAD

You may substitute tuna with chicken.

1/2 head lettuce, sliced in 1 inch slices
   and then into cubes
1/4 head of cabbage, sliced in ½ inch slices
2 stalks celery, sliced
1 Fuji apple cut in small pieces
2 green onions, sliced
Seedless red grapes cut in halves
Cheddar cheese, cubed
Fresh green peas
2 hard-boiled eggs, sliced
Corn off the cob, already cooked (or canned corn)
Pickled beets (add when ready to serve as they
   will turn the lettuce red)

Dressing:

1/2 cup real mayonnaise
1/8 cup prepared mustard
2 Tbsp sweet pickle relish
2 Tbsp rice vinegar
1 tsp sugar
Salt and pepper

CHICKEN ALMOND SALAD

Make the dressing for this salad the night before. It's great with fresh muffins, too.

6 cups boneless, skinless chicken, cooked, cubed
2 cups pineapple chunks, drained
1 cup water chestnuts, sliced
2 cups celery, diced
2 cups seedless Flaming Red grapes cut in halves
1 cup toasted almonds, slivered

Dressing:

1 cup mayonnaise (do not use salad dressing)
1 cup sour cream
1½ tsp curry powder
1 tsp soy sauce
1 Tbsp lemon juice

- *Mix all ingredients together and let sit overnight.*
- *Toss with salad just before serving.*

CRANBERRY-APPLE JELL-O SALAD

This has become a traditional Christmas salad for our family and for many others.

One 6 oz package strawberry Jell-O
1/4 tsp salt
2½ cups boiling water (different from the box
   directions)
Two 1 lb cans jellied cranberry sauce
4 cups finely chopped apples, about 5 small apples

- *Put the chopped apples in lemon water until ready to use.*
- *Dissolve Jell-O in boiling water and salt.*
- *Break cranberry sauce into large pieces with a fork. Don't mash as you want actual chunks in the salad.*
- *Chill until mixture is thick but not set, about 1 hour.*
- *Drain the apples and fold into the Jell-O.*
- *Pour in a large 9 x 13 glass dish.*
- *Chill until firm.*

GERMAN COLESLAW

Known as the twenty-four hour German Slaw, this recipe has been in my family on my father's side since he was a little boy, which would make it over 110 years old. My Aunt Evelyn gave it to me. All of my German recipes are either from her or my father, Warren Stuessi.

1 large or 2 small heads of cabbage, thinly sliced
2 small onions, sliced thin
1 cup sugar

- *In a large plastic bowl, alternate the cabbage, onions and sugar and then add the following ingredients:*

1 tsp each dry mustard and celery seed
2 Tbsp sugar
1 Tbsp salt
3/4 cup each white vinegar and salad oil

- *Bring all ingredients to a boil and pour over the layered cabbage.*
- *Let stand at room temperature for 4 hours with no cover on the bowl.*
- *After the 4 hours, cover with a tight fitting lid. Do not stir or mix, but refrigerate overnight.*
- *Do not disturb the layers at any time until it's ready to serve. This keeps well for up to one week.*

PASTA SALAD

I had my hands on this recipe way back when the thought of eating cold pasta made people cringe. Now there are a bunch of varieties of this great side dish. I haven't seen it with Salad Supreme seasoning in it before which makes it a bit different from all the rest.

1 large box of pasta bows, colored twists
   or thin spaghetti
1 large bottle of Bernstein's Italian Restaurant
   Style Dressing
1 small bottle of Salad Supreme Seasoning

- *Cook and drain pasta but do not overcook it.*
- *Add the complete bottle of Salad Supreme Seasoning to the pasta and mix well.*
- *Cover and let sit at room temperature overnight. Do not refrigerate.*
- *The next day, add all ingredients and refrigerate until chilled.*
- *Use any of the ingredients below for your salad.*

1 cucumber, diced
1 red or green bell pepper, sliced
1 can black or green olives, drained
Pepperoni, sliced
Cheddar cheese, diced
Tomato wedges
Snow peas
Broccoli flowerets
Cauliflower, same sizes as the broccoli
Shredded carrots
Artichoke hearts
Pepperocinis, chopped with some of the juice

NOTE
If the salad is too dry, add some olive oil and water just to loosen it up. Taste it to see if you need to add salt and pepper.

THREE BEAN SALAD

This recipe has been around for eons but all new cooks will want it.

One 16 oz can kidney beans, drained
One 16 oz can green beans, drained
One 16 oz can yellow waxed beans, drained
1 small onion, cut in half and sliced
1 small green bell pepper, diced
1 Tbsp sugar
One 12 oz bottle of Italian salad dressing
Salt and pepper to taste

- *Mix sugar, salad dressing, salt and pepper with the Italian salad dressing.*
- *Mix beans with dressing mixture and let marinate for several hours, even overnight.*
- *Just before ready to serve, drain liquid and add onions and peppers.*
- *Serve cold.*

131

SEVEN-LAYERED SALAD

Many people have had this salad and like it, especially men. It is good enough to repeat for those young, new cooks who may never have tasted it.

One head of lettuce, torn (do not cut)
1 bell pepper, diced
1 cup celery, diced
10 oz frozen peas
1 red onion, diced
1 Tbsp sugar, sprinkled over the top
2 cups mayonnaise (not salad dressing)
1 lb cheddar cheese, shredded
1 lb bacon, cooked and crumbled
Cauliflower, optional

- *Layer the ingredients in a large glass bowl, in the order above but do not mix together.*
- *Cover with plastic wrap.*
- *Refrigerate for several hours, overnight if possible.*
- *When ready to serve toss lightly or not at all.*

NOTE
Let your guests mix this beautiful salad as they serve it.

FRUIT & CABBAGE SALAD

2 oranges, peeled and cut up
2 apples, peeled, cored and cut up
2 cups shredded cabbage (about ¼ head)
1 cup seedless green grapes
1/2 cup whipping cream
1 Tbsp sugar
1 tsp lemon juice
1/4 tsp salt
1/4 cup mayonnaise or salad dressing

- *Beat whipping cream.*
- *Fold in sugar, lemon juice and salt.*
- *Mix with other ingredients and serve.*

HOT GERMAN POTATO SALAD

132

This German recipe has been in my family for generations.

6 to 8 red or white potatoes (do not use
  Russet potatoes as they get too mushy)
1 large onion, chopped fine or sliced thin
1 tsp celery seed
1/2 lb of bacon, fried until crisp, broken into pieces

- *Remove bacon from pan and save drippings.*
- *Boil potatoes just until semi-tender as they will cook more in the sauce.*
- *Peel potatoes and cut in slices.*
- *To the bacon drippings add 2 heaping Tbsp flour and stir until well mixed.*

Add the following to the drippings and flour:

2 cups of water
1/2 cup vinegar
2/3 cup sugar
Salt and pepper

- *Stir until the mixture thickens and looks like gravy.*
- *Transfer gravy to a large pot and add potatoes, onion, celery seed and bacon.*
- *Heat well until the potatoes are tender.*

NOTE
Check the gravy and adjust to your taste. If too sweet, add more vinegar. If too sour, add sugar. Add more water as the potatoes continue to cook, if necessary. And you may need more salt and pepper.

STRAWBERRY JELL-O SALAD

Two 3 oz packages strawberry Jell-O
2 cups boiling water (do not add any cold water)
1 pint frozen strawberries
1 cup mashed bananas
1 small can crushed pineapple, including juice
1 cup sour cream

- *Mix Jell-O and water and stir until dissolved.*
- *Combine all except the sour cream.*
- *Pour half of the mixture into a flat glass dish and let it set.*
- *Spread with sour cream.*
- *Put remaining Jell-O over the sour cream.*
- *Refrigerate until set.*

BROCCOLI MEDLEY SALAD

This salad is attractive and goes well with a hot summer night's BBQ. It comes from my good friend, April Carter, of Paradise, California.

2 bunches of broccoli, cut in flowerets
One 16 oz can diced, pickled beets, drained
One 27 oz can of kidney beans, drained and rinsed
1 cup cheddar cheese, shredded
1 large tomato, diced and seeds removed
1/2 onion or several green onions, diced
Salt and pepper to taste
One 12 oz bottle of Catalina Dressing

- *Combine all ingredients and marinate for several hours, stirring often.*
- *Keep refrigerated until ready to serve.*

PUDDING FRUIT SALAD

1 small can fruit cocktail, drained
1 can pineapple chunks drain and save juice
Sliced bananas
One 3.4 oz box of instant lemon pudding

- *Mix saved pineapple juice with pudding, stir until thickened.*
- *Add remaining ingredients and chill.*
- *Use fruits like oranges, pears, apples, and coconut.*

FROG'S EYE SALAD

Since I use this recipe every summer, I have to put it in the book. It got its name from the type of pasta used which looks kind of "bug-eyed." Plan on starting this one the night before and you need to keep it cold.

The night before, combine:

1 cup sugar
2 Tbsp flour
1 ¼ tsp salt
1 ¾ cups pineapple juice (from the pineapple used tomorrow)
2 eggs, beaten

- In a large saucepan, mix all the ingredients and cook over medium heat, until thickened.
- Cool to room temperature.

The next day, combine:

One 8 oz package of Acini De Pepe pasta
1 Tbsp vegetable oil
1 ¼ tsp salt

- Cook pasta as directed on package and cool to room temperature.
- Add pasta to the egg mixture from last night.

Then combine:

3 cans mandarin oranges, drained
2 cans chuck pineapple, drained
1 can crushed pineapple, well drained
1 large carton of Cool Whip, thawed
1 cup miniature marshmallows
1 cup shredded, sweetened coconut

- Mix all ingredients together in a very large serving bowl.
- Substitute rice for the pasta as a variation.

JELL-O CHIFFON SALAD

This can be doubled or even tripled. For a variety use different flavors of Jell-O or use fruit cocktail instead of oranges.

One 3 oz package or orange Jell-O, dry
One 8 oz container of cottage cheese
One 8 oz container of Cool Whip, thawed
One 11 oz can mandarin oranges, drained
½ cup nuts, chopped (optional)

- Mix oranges, cottage cheese and nuts.
- Fold in Cool Whip.
- Fold in dry Jell-O.
- Put in serving bowl and refrigerate for at least 30 minutes.

RED CABBAGE SALAD

133

1/2 head red cabbage, shredded
1/2 cup olive oil
1/2 cup plus 2 Tbsp red wine vinegar
3 Tbsp sugar
4 tsp salt
1 tsp seasoned salt
1/4 tsp black pepper
1/4 tsp onion powder

- Mix all ingredients together and serve.

PINEAPPLE-CARROT TOSS

2 cups carrots, shredded
One 8.75 oz can pineapple tidbits, drained
1/2 cup raisins, pre-boiled in water and drained
Mayonnaise

- Mix all ingredients together and chill.
- Just before serving, add enough mayonnaise to moisten.

ORIENTAL COLESLAW

I medium head of cabbage, shredded
3 to 4 green onions, chopped
1/2 cup toasted sliced almonds
3 Tbsp toasted sesame seeds or sunflower seeds
I package of chicken-flavored Top Ramen noodles, broken into small pieces

Dressing:

1/2 cup olive oil
1/4 cup rice vinegar
Chicken flavoring packet from the noodles

- *Mix all ingredients together only when ready to use.*
- *Do not mix before ready to serve as you want the noodles to be crunchy.*

> ### NOTE
> Mix the cabbage and onions together and keep refrigerated until ready to toss with the dressing and serve.

134

TABOULI SALAD

This is a healthy hearty salad made from wheat berries.

2 cups of cooked whole wheat kernels (berries)*
1/2 cup chopped green onions, including the tops
2 to 3 Roma tomatoes, diced with seeds removed
1/4 cup fresh parsley, chopped
I to 2 cans garbanzo beans drained, optional
1/2 cup bell pepper, chopped, optional
Corn, optional
Broccoli, optional
1/4 cup olive oil
1/4 cup Italian Salad Dressing
2 Tbsp lemon juice
2 tsp salt
Black pepper to taste
1/2 tsp cumin
1/8 tsp garlic powder
Diced mild cheddar cheese

- *Mix all ingredients together and let marinate for at least one hour.*
- *Serve cold.*

WHEAT SALAD (BULGUR)

This recipe comes from April Carter of Paradise, California. She was always experimenting on new recipes so I grabbed some good ones. This one is like the Tabouli Salad and uses cooked wheat.

2 cups of cooked whole wheat kernels (berries)*
3 Tbsp sweet pickles, chopped
1/8 tsp pepper
1/2 cup green bell pepper, chopped
2 Tbsp onion, chopped
3 Tbsp French dressing
1/2 tsp salt
1 1/2 cups celery, sliced
2 eggs, hard boiled and chopped
2/3 mayonnaise

- *Mix all ingredients together.*
- *Serve on a bed of lettuce with tomato wedges.*
- *If you want to make this a main dish, add diced chicken or tuna.*

> ### NOTE
> * For cooking instructions, see the recipe for Cooked Wheat Berries on page 22.

SHRIMP-MACARONI SALAD

4 cups uncooked macaroni, like salad pasta
1/4 cup French dressing
1 1/2 cups celery, diced
1/2 cup green onion, chopped
Pimento, chopped (optional)
1/3 cup sweet pickles chopped or use pickle relish
1 cup cheddar cheese, cubed
2 cans shrimp
2/3 cup mayonnaise

- *Cook macaroni and drain.*
- *Toss macaroni with French dressing and let cool.*
- *Add remaining ingredients.*
- *Refrigerate until well chilled.*

TACO SALAD

1 head lettuce, torn
1/2 lb cheese, grated
1/2 to 1 lb ground beef
1 tsp chili powder
1/4 tsp cumin
1 tsp oregano
One 8 oz can tomato sauce
Salt and pepper to taste
Bottled taco sauce to taste (recipe page 149)
1 cup crushed corn chips

- *Brown meat, drain.*
- *Add oregano, chili powder, cumin, tomato sauce, salt and pepper.*
- *Simmer for 5 minutes.*
- *Mix all remaining ingredients, toss lightly.*
- *Serve immediately.*
- *Serve with Ranch or Catalina Dressing if desired.*

WATERGATE SALAD

This salad is from the 70's when the Watergate Scandal took place. I still see the name on other dishes from this same period so I decided to leave the name the way it is.

One 3.4 oz package of Instant Pistachio Pudding
One 9 oz container of Cool Whip, thawed
One 20 oz can of crushed pineapple, with juice
1 cup miniature marshmallows
1/2 cup chopped nuts

- *Mix dry pudding mix and Cool Whip until blended.*
- *Stir in pineapple and juice.*
- *Fold in the marshmallows and nuts.*
- *Put in serving bowl and refrigerate until it sets.*

HOT GERMAN RICE SALAD

1/2 cup onions, chopped
2 Tbsp butter
3 cups cooked rice
1 cup celery, diced
1½ Tbsp flour
2/3 cup salad dressing
2 tsp prepared mustard
Salt and pepper to taste
3/4 cup whole milk
3 hard boiled eggs

- *Sauté onions and butter until golden brown.*
- *Add cooked rice and celery.*
- *In a separate bowl, blend the flour, salad dressing, mustard, salt and pepper and the milk together.*
- *Combine all ingredients in a 1½ quart casserole.*
- *Cover and bake for 30 minutes at 350°.*
- *Garnish with 3 sliced hard-boiled eggs.*

135

PANTRY COLESLAW

The original Pantry Restaurant is a landmark in downtown Los Angeles. They made this recipe available to the public. It's still at 877 South Figueroa.

3/4 cup mayonnaise
3 Tbsp sugar
1¼ Tbsp white wine vinegar
1/3 cup canola oil
1/8 tsp each garlic powder, onion powder, dry mustard and celery salt
Dash of black pepper
1 Tbsp lemon juice
1/2 cup half and half
1/4 tsp salt
1 large head of cabbage, finely shredded

- *Blend mayonnaise, sugar, vinegar and oil.*
- *Add remaining ingredients except the cabbage and stir until smooth.*
- *Pour over shredded cabbage in a large bowl.*
- *Toss until well-coated.*
- *Store in refrigerator.*

FROZEN FRUIT COMPOTE

This delicious compote comes from good 'ole Leslie Tall.

3 lbs fresh peaches, about 12 medium
1½ cups sugar
1 lb seedless grapes
1 can pineapple tidbits (including juice)
1/2 cup fresh lemon juice, 2 lemons including pulp)
1½ cups fresh orange juice, 3 oranges, including pulp

- *Peel peaches, cut into bite-size pieces and sprinkle with sugar.*
- *Pour citrus juices over peaches, including the pulp from the lemon and oranges.*
- *Add grapes and pineapple.*
- *Put into freezer containers and freeze.*
- *Do not thaw completely to serve.*
- *Thaw 2 to 2½ hours on the counter or 1 to 2 minutes in the microwave.*
- *Makes 3 quarts.*

GARLIC CROUTONS

Make a lot of these and keep them in an airtight container. They also make a great gift with some homemade salad dressing.

1/4 cup butter
1 Tbsp grated parmesan cheese
1 tsp garlic powder
4 cups cubed French bread with the crust removed

- *Preheat oven to 350°.*
- *Melt the butter and cheese and add the garlic powder.*
- *Put bread cubes in a large bowl.*
- *Add melted mixture to the bread and stir until all the cubes are coated.*
- *Spread the cubes on an ungreased baking sheet.*
- *Bake for 20 minutes, stirring frequently.*
- *Store in an airtight container.*

Dressings
Seasonings and Sauces

ASIAN SESAME SOY DRESSING

This is just a good combination for your Asian dishes.

2 Tbsp canola oil
1 Tbsp sesame oil
1 Tbsp rice wine vinegar
1 Tbsp light soy sauce, or liquid aminos
2 tsp fresh ginger, grated

- *Mix well and store in refrigerator.*

BALSAMIC VINAIGRETTE

1 cup canola oil
1/3 cup balsamic vinegar

- *Shake well and chill several hours before using.*

138 ## THOUSAND ISLAND DRESSING

This is as good as you can find. My husband's nephew, Rick Weaver, got it from a hotel chef from the old Hotel Utah. Find people who love Thousand Island dressing and then make it for them as a gift.

5 cups mayonnaise (not salad dressing)
One 12 oz bottle of Homemade Chili Sauce (that is the brand name and it comes in a round jar)
1 cup sweet pickle relish
Onion salt, to taste

- *Mix all ingredients together and store in refrigerator.*
- *Makes 2 quarts.*

NOTE

For a more tart flavor, use one cup of Miracle Whip rather than the mayonnaise.

COLESLAW DRESSING

1 cup salad dressing (not mayonnaise)
2 Tbsp milk
2 Tbsp brown sugar
1/2 tsp dry mustard
2 Tbsp cider vinegar
Salt and pepper to taste
Celery seed, optional

- *Mix well and store in refrigerator.*

BLUE CHEESE DRESSING

1 pint sour cream
1 pint mayonnaise (not salad dressing)
1/4 lb blue cheese, crumbed
1 to 2 cloves of garlic, use juice only
2 Tbsp green onions, finely chopped
1 Tbsp lemon juice
Salt and pepper to taste
1/4 cup dried parsley

- *Mix all ingredients together and store in an airtight container.*
- *Keep refrigerated.*

FRUIT SALAD DRESSING

This will keep well for several weeks in the refrigerator. If you use too much dressing, you will not taste the fruit and it won't be a very good salad. Less is better.

2 cups sugar
1 cup Miracle Whip (not mayonnaise or salad dressing)
2 Tbsp paprika
1/4 cup sugar
1/8 cup pineapple juice or lemon juice

- *Mix all ingredients together and beat with a fork.*
- *Prepare fruit of your choice for a salad.*
- *When ready to serve, use just enough dressing to coat the fruit, about 2 tablespoons of dressing to 8 cups of fruit.*

HOT BACON DRESSING

8 strips of bacon

- *Cut bacon into small pieces and fry until crisp in a large skillet.*

Combine the following ingredients:

1½ cups sugar
3 Tbsp cornstarch
1/2 tsp salt
1 tsp dry ground mustard

Add the following:

1¼ cups water
1/2 cup cider vinegar

- *Pour combined mixtures into the skillet with the bacon and drippings. Watch for splattering.*
- *Cook, stirring constantly, until thickened.*

Serve over:

A prepared lettuce salad
Cabbage
Fresh spinach
Cucumbers
Green beans

FRENCH DRESSING

1 cup olive oil
1/4 cup vinegar
1 tsp salt
1/3 cup sugar
1 tsp paprika
1 tsp dry mustard
1/4 cup chili sauce
1/4 tsp parsley flakes (optional)
1/2 cup ketchup
1 clove minced garlic or ½ tsp minced garlic
1/4 tsp celery salt
1 Tbsp onion, minced
1 Tbsp Worcestershire Sauce

- *Blend all ingredients together in a food processor or blender.*
- *Store in a jar with a tight lid.*

LIME CILANTRO SALAD DRESSING

This is wonderful on a taco salad.

5 tomatillos, or green tomatoes
1 package Hidden Valley Buttermilk Ranch dressing (dry mix only)
1/2 cup sour cream
1/2 cup mayonnaise
1/2 cup buttermilk
1 cup cilantro, chopped
2 cloves garlic, crushed
1/2 tsp cayenne pepper
1/2 tsp salt
2 Tbsp lime juice
1/2 tsp cumin
2 to 4 drops Tabasco sauce

- *Put all ingredients in a blender and puree. Chill.*

139

CREAMY ITALIAN DRESSING

1/2 cup mayonnaise
1/3 cup white vinegar
1 tsp oil
2 Tbsp corn syrup
2 Tbsp Parmesan cheese
2 Tbsp Romano cheese
1/4 tsp garlic Salt
1/2 tsp Italian seasoning
1/2 tsp parsley flakes
1 Tbsp lemon juice

- *Mix all ingredients in a blender until well mixed.*
- *Add a bit of sugar if this is too tart for you.*

ITALIAN SALAD DRESSING

This is an original Italian recipe from a real Italian—Joe Ingoglia of Paradise, California.

1 clove of garlic
1/4 cup fresh parsley
1 Tbsp oregano, fresh
1 Tbsp thyme, fresh
1/2 cup extra virgin olive oil
4 Tbsp white balsamic vinegar
Juice of one lemon

- *Put all ingredients in a blender and mix well.*
- *Refrigerate well before serving..*

HACIENDA SALAD DRESSING

This is really good on a taco salad.

1 egg
1 cup mayonnaise (not salad dressing)
1/2 cup sweetened condensed milk
4 Tbsp lemon juice
2 cloves garlic

- Cook together.
- Add cooked mixture to blender and blend until smooth and refrigerate.

HONEY DRESSING

1/4 cup vinegar
1 cup mayonnaise
1 tsp prepared mustard
1 tsp sugar
1 tsp onion, chopped
1/2 cup honey
Pinch of parsley
Salt and pepper
1/2 cup vegetable oil

- Using a food processor mix vinegar, mayonnaise and mustard until smooth.
- Add all but the oil and mix.
- Slowly add oil while blender in running until well blended.
- Store in refrigerator.

RANCH DRESSING

When our son, John, was a kid he used to eat this by the spoonful.

2 cups mayonnaise
2 cups buttermilk
1/4 tsp onion salt
1 tsp salt
1 tsp garlic powder
1/2 cup parsley flakes

- Whisk together and refrigerate several hours before using.

RASPBERRY VINAIGRETTE

This is great with fresh spinach, red leaf or butter lettuce.

1 cup grapeseed oil
1/4 cup fresh or frozen raspberry juice
1/4 cup raspberry vinegar
2½ Tbsp fresh lemon juice
1 Tbsp honey

- Whip until well blended.
- Chill before using.

ONION POPPY SEED DRESSING

Good on spinach strawberry salad.

1/2 cup light corn syrup
1 tsp dry mustard
1 tsp salt
1/3 cup vinegar
1 tsp onion juice
1/2 Tbsp poppy seeds
1 cup olive oil

- Place all, but poppy seeds and oil in a blender.
- Cover and blend.
- Remove lid and gradually add the oil.
- When thick, add the poppy seeds and mix well.
- Chill before serving.

FRENCH BLENDER DRESSING

Put this in a blender and blend until smooth.

1 cup sugar
1 cup oil
1 cup vinegar
1 Tbsp salt
1½ inch slice of onion

Add the following:

1 large carrot, cut into 1 inch pieces
1 green pepper, cut into 1 inch pieces

- Blend until vegetables are coarsely chopped.

GARLIC MUSTARD DRESSING

I clove of garlic
I Tbsp Dijon mustard
3 Tbsp red wine vinegar
I Tbsp balsamic vinegar
1/2 Tbsp water

- *Put all ingredients in a blender and mix well.*

While blender is running add:

1/2 cup olive oil
Salt and pepper

THAI SALAD DRESSING

This is great with thinly shredded cabbage, carrots, peppers, red onions or just use in stir-fry.

3 Tbsp red wine vinegar
I Tbsp sugar
I Tbsp soy sauce
1/2 Tbsp crushed pepper or to taste
1/2 tsp sesame oil
1/2 tsp sesame seeds
Salt and freshly ground black pepper

- *Whisk ingredients together well.*
- *Keep refrigerated.*

SOUR CREAM DRESSING

This is an authentic Amish recipe.

3 Tbsp salad dressing
I tsp salt
2 Tbsp sugar
4 to 5 Tbsp vinegar
I cup buttermilk
1/3 tsp celery salt
1/4 tsp black pepper
I cup sour cream

- *Combine all ingredients and beat well.*
- *This will keep for several days in the refrigerator.*

POPPY SEED DRESSING

This is superb on pasta salad, spinach salad or lettuce salads.

3/4 Tbsp poppy seeds
1/3 cup white vinegar
3/4 cup olive oil
1/3 cup sugar
3/4 Tbsp salt
I Tbsp Dijon mustard

- *Combine all ingredients in a pint canning jar.*
- *Shake until well blended.*
- *Store in the refrigerator.*

MAYONNAISE

Many people have never tried homemade mayonnaise. 141
They'll be in for a pleasant surprise. A food processor is needed to make this.

I egg
I Tbsp Dijon mustard
I Tbsp lemon juice
Pinch of salt
I cup safflower or virgin olive oil

- *Using a metal blade in your food processor, process the egg, mustard, lemon juice and salt.*
- *While processor is still on, slowly pour the oil through the feeding port and do not stop processing until the oil is all absorbed.*
- *Store in a canning jar in the refrigerator for only a few days. It is best if you can make it around a recipe you know it will be used in such as a potato or macaroni salad.*

NOTE

Add the oil slowly.

CHICKEN & PORK RUB

The brown sugar will give the meat a sweet glaze.

1½ Tbsp chili powder
2 tsp ground cumin
2 tsp brown sugar
1 tsp dried oregano
1 tsp coarse salt

- *Mix all ingredients together and store in an airtight container.*

MARINADE

Good for BBQ or shish ka bobs.

1/2 cup olive oil
1/3 cup soy sauce
4 green onions, including the stems
2 cloves of garlic
4 Tbsp lemon juice
1/2 tsp red pepper flakes
1/2 tsp cumin
3 Tbsp dark brown sugar

- *Put in blender and process.*
- *Use with beef or chicken.*

142

FLANK STEAK MARINADE

1 cup Grey Poupon Mustard
1 cup soy sauce
2 cloves of garlic, minced

- *Mix all ingredients together.*
- *Marinate steak overnight.*
- *Spray the grill with vegetable spray before you turn it on. Turn it to 600°.*
- *Put steaks on the grill, close the lid and reduce heat to 350 to 400°.*
- *Cook for 5 to 7 minutes per side.*
- *Remove and loosely cover with foil.*
- *Let stand for 10 minutes.*
- *Slice thinly across the grain.*

SPICY PEPPER RUB

Great on steaks.

2 tsp sea salt
2 tsp sweet paprika
2 tsp dried oregano leaves
2 tsp dried thyme leaves
1 tsp garlic powder
1 tsp onion powder
1 tsp ground black pepper
1 tsp ground white pepper
1/2 tsp ground red pepper

- *Combine all ingredients.*
- *Store in an airtight container.*
- *Shake before using.*

ADOBE MARINADE

Great for shish ka bobs.

1 cup soy sauce
1 cup white sugar
Fresh ginger, sliced
Fresh garlic, sliced
1/2 cup brown sugar

- *Put all ingredients in a small saucepan and simmer until thickened.*
- *Marinate cut-up chicken 20 to 30 minutes.*
- *Grill about 3 minutes per side.*

FLANK STEAK RUB

2 tsp ground cumin
2 tsp chili powder
1 tsp kosher salt
3/4 tsp black pepper
1/2 tsp dried crushed red pepper
1/4 tsp cinnamon

- *Mix the above ingredients together.*
- *Rub 1½ to 2 lbs of flank steak with vegetable oil on both sides.*
- *Rub dry mixture over both sides of steak and let sit for 10 minutes.*
- *Using a hot grill (600°), place the steaks on the grill, close the lid and reduce heat to 350 to 400°.*
- *Cook for 5 to 7 minutes per side.*
- *Remove and loosely cover with foil.*
- *Let stand 10 minutes before slicing thinly across the grain.*

ROAST RUB

2 tsp garlic pepper seasoning
2 tsp dried basil
2 tsp thyme
1 tsp dried parsley

- *Combine all ingredients and store in an airtight container.*

To use on a roast:

- *Rub onto a 3 to 4 lb boneless round rump roast.*
- *Put roast in a roaster pan. Do not cover or add water.*
- *Roast 1½ to 2 hours at 325°.*
- *Remove when internal temperature is 140°.*
- *Remove from pan, tent with foil and let meat rest for 15 to 20 minutes before slicing.*

RIB SEASONING

This is a dry rub that can be used on any type of beef.

1 cup white sugar
1/2 cup salt
2 Tbsp paprika
2 Tbsp red pepper
1 Tbsp celery seed
1 Tbsp cumin

- *Mix all ingredients together, rub on meat and let sit 15 minutes. If you let the meat sit any longer, it will cause the rub to become runny.*

RUB SEASONING

1 cup white sugar
1/2 cup salt
2 Tbsp paprika
2 Tbsp red pepper
1 Tbsp celery seed
1 Tbsp cumin

143

- *Mix all ingredients together, rub on meat and let sit 15 minutes.*
- *Cook according to the recipe you are using.*
- *Cook immediately as delaying will cause the rub to get runny.*

GRILLING BLACKENED SEASONING

2 Tbsp sweet paprika (use Penzey's Hungarian, if you can find it)
2 Tbsp garlic powder
2 tsp onion powder
3/4 tsp ground coriander
3/4 tsp salt
1/4 tsp cayenne pepper
1/4 tsp ground black pepper
1/4 tsp ground white pepper

- *Mix all ingredients and store in an air tight jar.*
- *Rub on fish, chicken or pork 10 to 20 minutes prior to cooking.*

KANSAS CITY BBQ SAUCE

The only thing I know about this recipe is that it came from a great restaurant in the capital of the best BBQ in the U.S.—Kansas City. It has been in my family for so long I can't give credit to anyone. Make it and give it as gifts. It makes a large batch of about three quarts.

1 cup white sugar
1/4 cup coarse salt
2 Tbsp celery seed
2 Tbsp ground cumin
2 Tbsp garlic powder
2 Tbsp red pepper
1 Tbsp chili powder
2 quarts ketchup
2 cups apple cider vinegar
1½ tsp liquid smoke
1 tsp lemon juice

- *Mix dry ingredients separately in a small bowl.*
- *In a large bowl, combine the remaining ingredients and add to the dry mixture.*
- *Store in the refrigerator for two months or freeze it.*

BEEF GRAVY

People are always telling me they can't make gravy. I came up with this quick, fool-proof recipe. You do not need any meat drippings to make it.

1 Tbsp beef bouillon paste
1 small can cream of celery soup
1/2 tsp dried, chopped onions
1 cup water
Salt and pepper to taste

- *Heat in a small saucepan.*
- *Put in food processor and process until smooth.*
- *Return to pan and simmer 10 minutes.*

CHICKEN GRAVY

Use this recipe when you don't have chicken drippings.

1 Tbsp chicken bouillon paste
1 small can Cream of Chicken Soup
1/2 tsp dried, chopped onions
1 cup water
Salt and pepper to taste

- *Mix well with a wire whisk and simmer 10 minutes.*
- *If you do not like the chunky look, after it is heated, put it in a food processor to remove lumps.*

CHICKEN SAUCE

1 small can cheddar soup
1 tsp chicken base
1 cup water
1 Tbsp dehydrated onions
Salt and pepper

- *Whisk and cook over medium heat for 10 minutes.*
- *Serve over cooked Parmesan-Crusted Chicken or other cooked chicken.*

SWEET CHILI SAUCE

This is very good with egg rolls.

One 7 oz bottle hot chili sauce with garlic (Asian food section of your grocer)
1/2 cup water
1/2 cup rice wine vinegar
1/4 cup sugar
1/4 cup lemon juice
2 Tbsp chili paste (Asian food section)

- *Stir together all ingredients until blended and chill.*

CHEDDAR SAUCE

This is tasty over cooked vegetables.

1 Tbsp butter
1 Tbsp flour
2 tsp Dijon mustard
1 cup milk
1/3 cup shredded cheddar cheese
Kosher salt
1/4 tsp pepper

- *In a small saucepan melt butter until foamy.*
- *Whisk flour into the butter and cook. Whisk until mixture darkens.*
- *Add mustard and milk and simmer while whisking until thick.*
- *Remove from heat and stir in cheese.*
- *Season with salt and pepper.*

MISO SALMON SAUCE

2 tsp light Miso sauce (in the Japanese food section of your grocer)
1 Tbsp prepared Dijon mustard
2 Tbsp Chinese rice cooking wine
1 medium sized onion, cut in half and sliced
3 cloves of garlic, minced
1/2 Tbsp minced fresh ginger or 1/4 tsp dried
2 tsp soy sauce
Salt and white pepper to taste
Green onion, chopped, to taste

- *Put all ingredients in a small saucepan and simmer for 5 minutes.*
- *Prepare salmon according to your recipe.*
- *Drizzle Miso sauce over the top of the salmon and serve immediately.*

CHICKEN & CHEESE SAUCE

2 lbs chicken tenderloins
2 cans cream of chicken soup
1 cup water
1 cup of real mayonnaise (not salad dressing)
1 Tbsp lemon juice
1 tsp dehydrated onions
1 tsp paprika (sprinkle on top)
Rice, cooked

- *Mix the soup, water, mayonnaise, lemon juice, and onion together.*
- *Layer a 9 x 13 pan with chicken tenderloins.*
- *Pour soup mixture over the chicken and sprinkle with paprika.*
- *Bake uncovered at 400° for 45 minutes.*
- *Serve over rice.*

145

LEMON SAUCE

Use on seafood, chicken or vegetables.

Zest of 3 lemons
2 Tbsp sugar
1 Tbsp salt
1/3 cup plus 1 tsp freshly squeezed lemon juice
3 Tbsp chopped fresh dill

- *Heat all ingredients in a saucepan and cook until slightly thickened.*

DUTCH OVEN SPAGHETTI SAUCE

Four 15 oz cans of tomato sauce
3 cans water
1 can Italian tomato paste
2 Tbsp Italian seasoning
1/2 tsp salt
1/2 tsp pepper (add red pepper flakes if you like it
    a bit spicier)
1/2 tsp garlic powder
1/2 tsp onion powder or dehydrated or fresh onions

- *Put the all of the ingredients in a Dutch oven and simmer for 3 to 4 hours.*

TERIYAKI PEANUT SAUCE

Use this with Asian dishes.

2 tsp peanut butter, creamy style
2 Tbsp honey
3 Tbsp Tamari, dark soy sauce
1 Tbsp sesame oil
1 tsp ground ginger, fresh if available
Oriental rice noodles
4 Tbsp Soy Vay Island Teriyaki (Oriental food
    section at grocer)
1 Tbsp lightly toasted sesame seeds (optional)
Red pepper flakes, to taste

- *Heat the peanut butter in the microwave on high until melted, about 15 to 20 seconds.*
- *Whisk the honey and Tamari into the peanut butter.*
- *Whisk in remaining ingredients.*
- *Toss the noodles with the sauce.*
- *Top with the sesame seeds.*

PEANUT SAUCE

This sauce is perfect with angel hair pasta, rice or noodles. My vegetarian daughter loves it with steamed vegetables and brown rice.

2 tsp creamy peanut butter
1 Tbsp honey
2 Tbsp tamari
1 to 2 cloves of garlic, minced
1 tsp red pepper flakes, optional
1 tsp sesame oil
1 Tbsp toasted sesame seeds
1 tsp ground ginger or fresh ginger, peeled
    and grated

- *In a medium saucepan, heat peanut butter.*
- *Whisk honey and tamari into peanut butter.*
- *Add sesame oil and ginger.*

PASTA SAUCE

2 lbs ground beef
1 onion, chopped
2 cloves of garlic, pressed
Two 15 oz cans diced tomatoes, seasoned with
    basil, garlic and oregano
One 15 oz can tomato sauce, plus one can water

- *Brown beef, onion and garlic. Cook only until the onion is tender.*
- *Add tomatoes, tomato sauce and water.*
- *Simmer 10 minutes.*

NOTE

If you prefer spicy sauce, add Italian seasoning and some red pepper flakes or substitute a spicy sausage for half of the ground beef.

PORK CHOP SAUCE

1 can cheddar soup
1 tsp bouillon
1 cup water
1 Tbsp dehydrated onions
Salt and pepper to taste

- *Cook over medium heat for 10 minutes.*
- *Serve over cooked, breaded pork chops.*

PESTO SAUCE

1 ½ cup fresh basil leaves
1 cup fresh Parmesan cheese, grated
1/4 cup pine nuts
6 cloves of fresh garlic
Olive oil

148

- *Combine all but oil in food processor and process until blended.*
- *While blender is still running, add olive oil until a good consistency.*
- *Add additional Parmesan cheese, salt and pepper to taste.*
- *Makes about ½ cup.*

PIZZA SAUCE

One 6 oz can tomato paste
1 can warm water (use tomato paste can)
3 Tbsp grated Parmesan cheese
1 tsp minced garlic
2 Tbsp honey
3/4 tsp onion powder
1/4 tsp dried oregano
1/4 tsp dried marjoram
1/4 tsp dried basil
1/4 tsp ground black pepper
1/8 tsp cayenne pepper
1/8 tsp dried red pepper flakes, optional
Salt to taste

- *Combine all ingredients in a small bowl.*
- *Do not heat. Let it sit in the bowl for at least 30 minutes before using.*

QUESADILLA SAUCE

Serve with quesadillas. How easy it this!

Sour cream
Touch of lime juice
Chipotle sauce

- *Use as much of the ingredients as you like according to your taste.*
- *Briefly mix in a small food processor and chill before serving.*

RAISIN SAUCE

This is good on ham or other meats.

1/2 cup brown sugar
2 Tbsp each cornstarch and lemon juice
1 ½ cups water
1 Tbsp cider vinegar
1 cup raisins

- *Mix brown sugar, cornstarch and dry mustard together in a medium saucepan and slowly add water, lemon juice, vinegar and raisins.*
- *Bring to a boil and serve over cooked ham.*

EASY SPAGHETTI SAUCE

This is the easiest yet.

1/2 to 1 lb ground beef
4 cloves of fresh garlic, pressed
1 medium onion, chopped
1 small green bell pepper, chopped

- *Sauté meat, garlic, onion and bell pepper in olive oil.*

Add the following and simmer several hours:

4 cans Italian-style stewed tomatoes, pureed
   in food processor
One 6 oz can tomato sauce
Salt and pepper to taste
1 Tbsp sugar (optional, it cuts down the acidity)
1/2 tsp cocoa powder (another secret ingredient)

NOTE

You may also cut the acidity by using baking soda.

TACO SAUCE

From my daughter-in-law, Maria Miles, who can really cook up a storm. Thanks, Maria.

4 to 5 dried small red peppers (packaged)
2 to 3 dried California Chili Pods (packaged)

- *Remove stems and some of the seeds as they make it hotter.*
- *Roast in a skillet, without any oil or liquid.*

2 cloves of garlic, minced
Salt to taste
1 small can of tomato paste

- *Add garlic, salt and tomatoe paste.*
- *Put all ingredients in a blender and puree.*
- *Add water to make the correct consistency.*

> **NOTE**
> This is much better than bottled or canned taco sauce from the grocery.

TACO SEASONING MIX

Make individual packages of this mix for future use. In the meantime, use it in tacos, burritos, enchiladas, tostadas, etc.

1 tsp chili powder
2 tsp dried minced onion
1 tsp salt
1/2 tsp crushed dried red pepper
1/2 tsp cornstarch
1/2 tsp cumin
1/2 tsp instant minced garlic
1/4 tsp dried oregano

- *This makes one package of seasoning mix. Pre-cut pieces of foil, lay them out and put the ingredients in each piece of foil. Fold tightly and store in a ziplock bag.*

To make taco meat:

- *To each package of seasoning, add 1 lb cooked ground beef and ½ cup water.*

SPICY BBQ SAUCE

1 cup apple cider vinegar
1 cup ketchup
1/4 cup packed light brown sugar
1 Tbsp molasses
1 Tbsp brown sugar
1 Tbsp yellow mustard
2 tsp Worcestershire Sauce
2 tsp minced garlic
1/2 tsp kosher salt
1/4 tsp cayenne pepper
1/4 tsp freshly ground black pepper

- *Mix all ingredients in a saucepan and simmer 10 minutes.*

SWEET & SOUR SAUCE

149

1/2 cup brown sugar
1 cup white vinegar
1/2 cup ketchup
1/2 cup stock or water
1/2 cup pineapple juice or water
2 Tbsp oil
1/2 tsp salt

- *Heat and bring to a boil.*

4 Tbsp cornstarch and 4 Tbsp water

- *Add corn starch mixture of 4 Tbsp cornstarch to 4 Tbsp cold water, stirring constantly, until thickened.*

TARTAR SAUCE

1½ cups mayonnaise
1 medium dill pickle, diced or 1 tsp pickle relish
One shake of Worcestershire sauce
Cayenne pepper to taste
2 tsp chives (fresh or dried)
1/4 tsp seasoning salt

- *Mix all ingredients together and keep refrigerated.*

SPAGHETTI SAUCE SURPRISE

There is a variety of spaghetti sauces, in this book but each one is different. I concocted this version by adding an ingredient you would never expect.

1 lb ground beef, cooked and drained
One 6 oz can tomato puree
One 15 oz can tomato sauce
1 small can of Manwich Sandwich Sauce (the secret ingredient)
1/4 tsp garlic salt
1 Tbsp dehydrated onions
1 cup water
Salt and pepper, to taste
1/2 tsp oregano

- *Combine all ingredients and simmer for 15 to 20 minutes.*
- *Serve over cooked spaghetti.*

MEATLOAF SAUCE

I can still taste from many moons ago the meatloaf that my brother, Neal, made for us. He used this sauce on top of his meatloaf and it made the dish very tasty. Thanks, Neal.

One 6 oz can Penny's White Sauce
1 pint sour cream
1 tsp horseradish
Ketchup to color (about the color of cream tomato soup)
1/2 tsp prepared mustard

- *Combine all ingredients in a medium saucepan.*
- *Cook until well-heated.*
- *Serve warm over meatloaf or in a serving bowl.*

AUTHENTIC ITALIAN SPAGHETTI SAUCE

This is the Italian sauce that I use with the meatball recipe on page 160. It comes from Jim Cozy who passed away years ago. I got all of his hints for this wonderful sauce and meatballs. This is probably the longest recipe I have but I wanted to be sure it was available in this book.

Three 28 oz cans of Italian tomatoes (Progresso brand, if you can find them)
2 lbs stew meat
6 hot and 6 mild Italian sausages
1/2 cup parsley
3 cloves of garlic, minced
1 onion, finely chopped
Three 6 oz cans tomato paste (again, Progresso)
1 tsp oregano
Dash of baking soda
1/4 cup of sugar
Salt and pepper to taste

- *Chop tomatoes in a food processor.*
- *In a large pot, bring tomatoes to a boil.*
- *Add 2 cups water and a dash of baking soda, then reduce to a simmer.*
- *Add parsley, oregano, salt, pepper and sugar.*
- *In a large skillet, brown the sausage, stew meat and meatballs (recipe on page 160) in a small amount of oil and add all meat to the sauce.*
- *In the same skillet you browned the meat in, sauté garlic and onions, stirring until browned.*
- *Add tomato paste and 1 cup of water and simmer for 15 minutes and add to other mixture.*
- *Continue to cook on low heat for 3 to 4 hours or longer, stirring occasionally.*

NOTE

Don't use a lid while this is cooking as you want it to thicken.

BBQ Spareribs Sauce

Originally I made this for spareribs but it is a good sauce for any meat you want to grill.

2 cups Hoisin sauce (Oriental food section)
1½ cups sugar
1/4 cup honey
1/4 cup soy sauce
2 Tbsp vinegar
1 tsp five spice powder (Oriental food section)
1/2 cup ketchup
2 Tbsp salt
1/4 tsp pepper (more, if you like it spicier)

- *Combine all ingredients well.*
- *Partially cook ribs, steaks, hamburgers, etc. on high heat on the grill, turning once.*
- *Baste with BBQ sauce and move meat to upper rack, lower heat.*
- *Turn and repeat until meat is the desired internal temperature.*

BBQ Sauce

2/3 cup ketchup
1/3 cup cider vinegar
1/4 cup dark corn syrup
1 tsp Worcestershire sauce
Pepper to taste

- *Heat all ingredients together in a medium saucepan on medium high heat.*
- *Stir until it comes to a boil.*
- *Lower heat and simmer 5 minutes until slightly thickened.*

Teriyaki Sauce

3/4 cup soy sauce
1/2 cup water
1/4 cup olive oil
1 tsp sugar
1/2 tsp ginger

- *Mix all ingredients together.*
- *Marinate meat for several hours before cooking.*

Alfredo Sauce

1/2 cup butter
One 8 oz package of cream cheese
1 pint whipping cream
1/4 tsp garlic salt
2 garlic cloves, minced
4 Tbsp parsley
Dash cayenne pepper
1 Tbsp rice vinegar
1/2 tsp sale
1/4 tsp pepper
1/2 cup Parmesan cheese

- *Melt butter and stir in cream cheese.*
- *Add all ingredients except the Parmesan cheese.*
- *Simmer until thickened.*
- *Add Parmesan cheese.*
- *Serve over hot, cooked fettuccini pasta.*
- *As an option, add grilled chicken on top.*

151

CHILI SAUCE

My brother, Richard Stuessi, from Kansas City, Kansas gave this recipe to me. He learned it from our Aunt Edie. It involves a two-step process so you need to plan an all day event but it will be worth it.

Step One:

7 large yellow onions, chopped
7 to 8 bell peppers (red and green) with seeds
removed and quartered
Dried red peppers, allow one per pint

- *Process in a food processor to desired consistency.*

Step Two:

8 lbs tomatoes

- *Peel tomatoes by putting them in boiling water just long enough for skins to loosen, then quickly put into ice cold water. The skins will easily slip off.*
- *After skins are removed, core and quarter tomatoes.*
- *Put tomatoes in a large stock pot.*

Add the following:

1/4 cup kosher salt (not table or salt with iodine)
1 lb light brown sugar
1 pint cider vinegar
1 tsp ground cloves
2 heaping Tbsp ground cinnamon
2 Tbsp dry mustard

- *Cook over medium low heat, stirring frequently, until it reaches the consistency you want.*
- *Spoon excess water off early in the cooking process. Later on it becomes a part of the tomato juice and you don't want to discard that. It will cook down.*
- *Put in pint jars and process in a water bath as directed in canning instructions.*
- *Makes about 7 pints.*

BROCCOLI CHEESE LOW-FAT SAUCE

My friend, Sandi Anderson, is the health guru in Paradise, California. She keeps in shape by running and watching her diet, which includes her fat intake. This recipe of hers works perfectly to make a dish creamed or a good sauce for any vegetable you want to have a sauce.

1 packet of Butter Buds (Diet food section)
3 Tbsp flour
2 cups non-fat milk
1 cup cheddar cheese
Salt and pepper to taste

- *Combine Butter Buds, flour and milk in a small saucepan.*
- *Heat on medium, stirring constantly, until thickened.*
- *When ready to use, add cheddar cheese.*

NOTE

If you don't add the cheese, the sauce can be used as a low-fat white sauce.

MARINARA SAUCE

This is just a good pasta sauce, an original recipe. In this case, less is better with the seasoning.

Olive oil
1 small onion, chopped
2 carrots finely chopped
6 to 8 fresh basil leaves
1 to 2 garlic cloves minced, or dehydrated garlic
3 large cans of whole Italian tomatoes
including the juice, mashed with potato masher
1 small can tomato paste
Salt to taste
1/4 to 1/2 tsp red pepper flakes, optional
1/2 tsp Italian seasoning
1 Tbsp parsley

- *Put oil in a large, heavy pot with onion, carrots and garlic.*
- *Add remaining ingredients and bring to a boil; reduce to simmer.*
- *Continue to cook for 15 minutes.*
- *Serve over any type of cooked pasta.*
- *As an option, add black olives and chopped celery.*

SALSA

I was making salsa before I got married, now my husband and I have been making it together for over 30 years. You can imagine how long it was before prepared salsa became available in grocers. I should have bottled it 35 years ago. My original recipe took me four years to get the way I wanted and was not available to the public. John and I were known for our salsa which we would give as gifts to special people from "The Miles." Now I offer it to the world.

3 gallons peeled tomatoes, fresh or canned,
use juice
8 large white onions
3 quarts of tomato juice (Campbell's is the best)
1/4 cup salt
17 to 19 Anaheim California Chilies
15 yellow chilies
8 Serrano green chilies
15 Jalapeno peppers (more, if you want it hotter)
2 small bunches of cilantro
3 cup white vinegar

- *Chop tomatoes, onions, chilies and cilantro in a food processor (you decide if chunky or fine).*
- *Put in a large canning kettle and add remaining ingredients.*
- *Simmer 1 to 3 hours until it is the consistency you want.*
- *Put in canning jars and label when cool.*
- *Makes about 2 dozen jars.*

NOTE

Use gloves to keep your hands from burning from the peppers. Also, take most of the seeds out of the peppers. If you want it spicier, leave some of them in.

BLACK BEAN SALSA

One 15 oz can black beans, drained and rinsed
2 Roma tomatoes, seeded and chopped
1/4 red onion, finely chopped
1 jalapeno pepper, seeded and finely chopped
1 clove garlic, finely chopped
1 lime, juiced
Salt
A few dashes hot sauce, to your taste
Chopped cilantro leaves

- *Mix all ingredients together and chill.*

CINNAMON ROLL ICING

Use this icing on any type of sweet roll.

1/4 cup maple syrup
One 8 oz package of cream cheese, softened

153

- *Gradually add maple syrup to soften cream cheese.*
- *Whisk until well blended.*
- *Spread over hot, baked cinnamon rolls.*

ENGLISH MUFFIN SPREAD

This spread comes from Linda Sue Forrister of Chico, California. She brought this into work once in awhile for a breakfast or an appetizer treat.

1 lb uncooked bacon
1/2 lb sharp cheddar cheese
1 small onion
1/2 tsp dry mustard

- *Put all ingredients in a food processor and grind until very well blended.*
- *Spread on English muffins.*
- *Broil until cooked and browned.*

CHOCOLATE SAUCE

I got this recipe from Joan Thomsen who was living in Bedford, New Hampshire at the time. It's very good over ice cream.

1/2 cup butter or margarine
1/2 cup cocoa powder
1 large can evaporated milk
3 cups powdered sugar, sifted

- *Melt butter in a medium saucepan.*
- *Stir in cocoa powder.*
- *Add milk all at once and mix well.*
- *Stir in powdered sugar.*
- *Stir and cook over medium heat until sauce thickens.*
- *Put in a canning jar and store in refrigerator.*

154

HOT VANILLA SAUCE

Use this delicious sauce over Fruit Cocktail Cake, Pumpkin Bars, Bread Puddings, some fruits or ice cream (see the index for these recipes).

1/2 cup butter
1 cup sugar
1/2 cup evaporated milk
1/2 tsp vanilla
Dash of nutmeg

- *Mix butter, sugar and evaporated milk together in a small saucepan on low heat.*
- *Cook for 15 to 20 minutes until thickened.*
- *Do not boil.*
- *Add vanilla and nutmeg.*

HONEY CINNAMON SPREAD

1 8 oz package of regular or light cream cheese, softened at room temperature. Do not use fat-free.
2 Tbsp honey
1/4 tsp cinnamon

- *Combine all ingredients together and mix well.*
- *Spread on toasted bagels, bread, cinnamon rolls, buns, etc.*
- *Store in refrigerator.*

CRANBERRY SPREAD

One 8 oz package of cream cheese
1/2 cup Craisins
1/3 cup maple syrup
1/4 cup chopped pecans, optional

- *Add ingredients to mixing bowl and beat well.*
- *Cover and refrigerate for several hours or overnight.*
- *Serve on crackers, deli breads or bagels.*

HOT PEPPER JELLY

1½ cups cider vinegar
1 medium sweet red bell pepper, seeded and cut into wedges
2/3 cup chopped Habanera peppers (use rubber gloves or you will burn your hands)
6 cups sugar, divided.
Two 3 oz pouches of liquid fruit pectin
1 tsp red food coloring (optional)

- *Puree vinegar and peppers in food processor.*
- *Add 2 cups sugar.*
- *Put in large pan and bring to a boil.*
- *Strain mixture in cheese cloth, return juice to pan and discard the pulp.*
- *Stir in pectin, remaining sugar, food coloring and return to a rolling boil over high heat.*
- *Boil for 2 minutes, stirring constantly.*
- *Remove from heat and skim off foam.*
- *Pour into hot canning jars.*
- *Process for 5 minutes in boiling water bath.*
- *Makes 5 pints.*

HOT FUDGE

This quick, easy recipe is better than any you can buy.

1 can Eagle Brand sweetened condensed milk
2 squares semi-sweet chocolate
2 Tbsp butter
1 tsp vanilla

- Put all ingredients in a small saucepan.
- Heat over medium low heat until thickened.
- Serve over ice cream.
- Refrigerate left over sauce.

FRUIT DIP

1 small can frozen orange juice
1¼ cups cold milk
One 3 oz package of instant vanilla pudding
1/4 cup sour cream

- Beat orange juice and milk together.
- Add pudding and beat for 2 minutes on low speed.
- Stir in sour cream.
- Chill for several hours.
- Serve with fresh fruit in season.

LEMON HOT CAKE SAUCE

This can be used over Fruit Cocktail Cake, Applesauce Cake or any fruit-type cake you like.

4 Tbsp cornstarch
1/2 cup cold water
4 Tbsp butter
1/2 tsp nutmeg
2½ cups boiling water
2 Tbsp lemon juice
1 cup brown sugar
1/8 tsp salt
2 Tbsp vanilla

- Dissolve cornstarch in ½ cup cold water.
- In a large saucepan, bring to a boil the brown sugar, salt, water, nutmeg and lemon juice.
- Thicken with cornstarch mixture.
- Remove from heat and add butter and vanilla.
- Serve hot over cake with a dollop of whipped cream or ice cream.

CRANBERRY-APPLE-ORANGE SAUCE

This is a great cranberry sauce for the holidays. I use a Kuhn pressure cooker to make it.

One 12 oz package or 3 cups fresh cranberries
1 cup white sugar
1 Granny Smith apple, cored, peeled, cut in pieces
1/2 tsp cinnamon
Juice of one orange and the zest

- Mix ingredients well and put them in a 4 quart pressure cooker.
- Bring to a boil to the first ring on the lid.
- Cook at first ring for 5 minutes.
- Remove from heat and let cool naturally.
- Serve at room temperature, not chilled.

155

PEANUT BUTTER HONEY CREAM

Combine the following in any amounts that fit your taste but make honey the major component.

Honey
Peanut butter
Light Karo syrup
Sugar

- Blend well and to the consistency you want.
- Put in a squeeze bottle or a container with a lid.
- Keep refrigerated.

CHOCOLATE GLAZE

3 Tbsp butter
3 squares of unsweetened chocolate
3 Tbsp hot water
2 to 2 1/2 cups sifted powdered sugar

- Melt butter, chocolate and water in a double boiler.
- Add the powdered sugar and blend.
- Beat with a wooden spoon until smooth

CARAMEL TOPPING

1 cup sugar
1 cup boiling water

- Cook sugar only over low heat until lightly brown, stirring constantly.
- Slowly add boiling water and cook until thickened.
- Refrigerate.

ORANGE GLAZE

1/4 cup orange juice
1 Tbsp butter
1/2 cup powdered sugar

- Heat orange juice and butter until butter melts.
- Remove from heat.
- Add powdered sugar, stir until smooth.
- Brush on warm scones, cinnamon rolls, muffins or pastry of your choice.

MAPLE SYRUP

Tastes remarkably good and makes a great gift.

1 cup sugar or honey
1½ rounded Tbsp Ultra Gel (It's like corn starch but much better and is available in some grocers or check online)
1½ to 2 cups water
1 tsp Mapleine or other maple flavoring

- Mix sugar and Ultra Gel in a small pan. Stir in water.
- Cook and stir over medium heat until it boils and slightly thickens.
- Stir in maple flavoring.
- Serve hot and refrigerate the leftovers.

NOTE

Make fruit syrup by substituting juice for the water. This makes a fruit-flavored maple syrup and a very unusual and delicious gift.

BLUEBERRY MAPLE SYRUP

1 cup blueberries, fresh or frozen
1/2 cup pure maple syrup
1 tsp lemon juice

- Heat 1 cup fresh or frozen blueberries and ½ cup pure maple syrup.
- Heat for a few minutes until berries open.
- Strain through cheesecloth.
- Add 1 tsp lemon juice to strained juice.
- Serve warm.

FRUIT SYRUP FOR FRENCH TOAST

This is also excellent for pancakes, waffles or ice cream.

1 small package of frozen blackberries
1 small package of frozen raspberries
1 small package of frozen strawberries
2 Tbsp lemon juice
1/4 cup water
1/8 cup sugar
1/2 cup maple syrup

- In a large saucepan combine all but the maple syrup.
- Cook until the berries breakdown.
- Take berries out with a slotted spoon and set aside.
- Add maple syrup to juices.
- Continue to cook until the syrup thickens.
- Add berries back to the syrup and mix well.
- Serve over French toast, pancakes, waffles or ice cream.

SWEETENED CONDENSED MILK

If you run out of sweetened condensed milk you may have the ingredients to make your own.

1/2 cup warm water
1 cup plus 2 Tbsp powdered milk
3/4 cup sugar

- Put all ingredients in a mixing bowl and beat until smooth.

Sides

HONEY-GLAZED PINEAPPLE

Summer grilling is at least a weekly experience for our family. It is a fun way to invite neighbors and friends to share an evening together.

1 small ripe pineapple
1/4 cup honey
1/4 cup fresh lime juice
1 Tbsp light brown sugar

- *Peel and remove the core and slice pineapple ¾ inch thick.*
- *Put in a shallow dish.*
- *Combine the honey and lime juice in a small bowl.*
- *Brush pineapple slices with honey and lime mix, making sure to get it on all sides.*
- *Marinate 2 hours and up to 8 hours.*
- *Preheat the grill to medium.*
- *Sprinkle the brown sugar over the slices.*
- *Grill until golden brown, about 1 to 2 minutes per side.*
- *Serve hot or at room temperature.*
- *Serves 4.*

Note: You can make this a dessert by putting a scoop of ice cream in the center.

REFRIED BEANS

2 small cans of refried beans with seasoning
1/4 cup salsa
1 Tbsp dehydrated onions
Cheddar Cheese

- *Heat all ingredients until hot.*
- *Put into a baking dish and top with cheese.*
- *Bake at 375° until cheese has melted.*

HOMEMADE NOODLES

These noodles are a family tradition for the Miles' family. The recipe originated in Germany and was brought to America by my grandmother. Usually you would make these noodles for Thanksgiving but they are perfect for soups, too. And the younger generation loves them!

- *Heat a large pot of water to boiling with 1 Tbsp of salt.*

In the meantime, make the dough as follows:

1 cup flour
2 eggs
1 tsp milk
1/4 tsp salt

- *Mix flour and salt and form a well in the middle to put the eggs in.*
- *Lightly beat eggs and milk with a fork and pour into the well in the flour.*
- *Slowly, mix the egg and flour together, trying not to have the egg go outside the flour well as it just becomes harder to mix. Be careful not to over mix as it will make the noodles tough.*
- *Roll out into thin strips on a floured surface.*
- *Cut into long strips.*
- *Put in boiling salt water and cook until mostly done if you use them for soup.*
- *If you want the noodles as a dish, cook them until tender. Put them in a baking dish and top with 1 package of soda crackers crushed with a rolling pin and browned in ½ cup of butter. This is the Thanksgiving dish.*

NOTE

If you want more noodles than this will make, increase the recipe by using this formula: 2 eggs to 1 cup of flour, a touch of milk and a pinch of salt. That's how it's done the German way.

RICE PILAF

2½ cups brown rice, washed (Lundberg rice)
1/2 cup butter
2 small onions, chopped
2 Tbsp parsley flakes
1/4 tsp minced garlic
2 cans beef bouillon soup
1 tsp beef bouillon base and enough water to
    equal 5 cups liquid
Good shake of garlic salt
1½ tsp salt

- *Brown onions in butter, add parsley and garlic.*
- *Mix remaining ingredients and put in a 3 quart casserole.*
- *Cover and cook at 350° for 1½ hours.*
- *As an option add mushrooms and frozen peas.*

SPANISH RICE

1 cup of uncooked long grain fancy rice (not "sticky" rice
1 medium yellow onion, chopped
1 chicken and tomato flavor bouillon cube
(make sure it is "chicken and tomato")
4 oz can of tomato sauce or salsa
Salt and pepper to taste

- *Cover the bottom of a medium size skillet with olive oil and heat on medium heat.*
- *Put rice in skillet and cook until golden brown, stirring to prevent burning.*
- *Add remaining ingredients except the salt and pepper and stir to mix ingredients.*
- *Add enough water to cover the rice by one inch.*
- *Cook with the lid on until the rice is done, about 15 minutes. Do not stir the rice.*
- *When the rice is tender, remove the lid and fluff with a fork. Do not use a spoon or stir.*
- *Salt and pepper to taste.*

NOTE

Only use 4 ounces of the tomato sauce or salsa. You do not want it to turn really red, just a touch of color. Also, stirring the rice makes it mushy.

POTATO TACO DISH

This can be used as an appetizer or a side dish.

2 large baking potatoes
Olive oil
Salt and pepper

- *Slice the potatoes into ½ inch thick slices, toss with olive oil and salt and pepper.*
- *Arrange on a cookie sheet.*
- *Bake at 450° for 20 minutes.*

1 lb ground beef

- *Cook 1 pound of ground beef, drain.*
- *Add the following ingredients.*

1 small onion, chopped
2 Tbsp of taco seasoning
1 tsp chili powder
Garlic salt, to taste

- *Add the following.*

One 15 oz can of black beans, drained and rinsed
Cheddar cheese

- *Sprinkle the tops of the potatoes with shredded cheddar cheese.*
- *Spread half of the meat mixture over the cheese.*
- *Repeat layers, ending with cheese.*
- *Keep in the oven and only cook until the cheese is melted.*
- *Serve with the following.*

Shredded lettuce
Chopped tomatoes
Sliced green onions
Sour cream
Salsa

159

VERA'S RICE PILAF

This recipe has been going around for decades and is from Vera Larsen, formerly of Paradise, California, now living in Utah.

1 small onion, chopped
1 Tbsp dry parsley
1 cup brown rice
1/4 cup butter
Dash of garlic salt
1/2 cup fresh mushrooms, sliced
1 can beef broth, add enough water to make
   2 cups of liquid
1 tsp salt

- *Sauté onion, parsley and garlic in butter.*
- *Wash rice and put into a bowl.*
- *Add parsley mixture and mushrooms and mix well.*
- *Add beef broth and mix.*
- *Put all ingredients in a 1½ quart casserole dish.*
- *Bake covered at 350° for 40 to 45 minutes.*
- *Sprinkle with Parmesan cheese lightly over the top just before serving.*
- *As an option, use half brown rice and half wild rice.*
- *If you triple this recipe, it will fill a 3 quart casserole and feed about 20 people.*

160

GINGER CARROTS

15 to 20 carrots, peeled and cut in ½ inch slices
3/4 cup butter
3/4 cup honey
1 tsp salt
1/2 tsp fresh ginger
1/2 tsp cinnamon
Parsley

- *Cook carrots in 1 cup water until half tender.*
- *Mix all but the carrots and parsley in a medium saucepan and cook until slightly thickened.*
- *Add carrots and continue to simmer, adding water if necessary, until carrots are tender.*
- *Put in serving bowl and top with parsley.*
- *Serves 10 to 15.*

MEATBALLS

This recipe was given to me by a fellow worker who was Italian. He also taught me to make truly authentic spaghetti sauce like I had never had before. (recipe on page 99) If you want the secret of great-tasting, tender meatballs and spaghetti sauce, read these instructions. There is a secret to making these and I'm happy to share it with you.

2 lbs ground beef
1 package crushed crackers
1/2 cup Parmesan cheese
1/2 cup parsley
4 eggs
Salt and pepper to taste
1 clove of garlic, finely minced
1/2 yellow onion, finely chopped

- *Mix all ingredients with two forks until just blended. Do not use your hands. This is the secret to making the meatballs tender. Never knead the meat as you would bread. When you over mix them, they are tough and dense.*
- *Roll into medium-sized balls and put on a greased jelly roll pan.*
- *Bake at 450° for 25 minutes.*

NOTE

If you are going to make the spaghetti sauce, don't cook the meatballs in the oven. See the recipe for Spaghetti Sauce on page 150.

RICE A-LA-CAROL

I had this unnamed dish at my sister's home when they lived in Lancaster, California. Since she served it and I liked it, I named it after her.

2½ cups cooked and cooled rice (Calrose brand)
1½ cups cooked, de-boned chicken
1 small can creamy chicken mushroom soup
1/2 cup corn
1/2 cup frozen peas
1/4 cup bread crumbs
1/2 cup cheese

- *Mix all ingredients except the bread crumbs and cheese.*
- *Put in a baking dish, top with bread crumbs and cheese.*
- *Bake at 350° for 25 to 30 minutes.*

WEDDING POTATOES

This is also known as "Funeral Potatoes," but I don't like what that name implies, so I re-named them. It is easy to double this recipe.

Frozen (16 oz) package of hash browns
1/3 cup green onions, sliced
1 small can Cream of Chicken Soup
1 cup sour cream
1/4 cup melted butter
1/2 cup grated cheddar cheese
Salt and pepper, to taste
Garlic salt, to taste
Diced ham, optional

- *Mix all ingredients together in a large bowl and pour into an 8 x 8 pan.*

Top with the following mixed together:

1 cup crushed corn flakes or potato chips
1 Tbsp melted butter

- *Bake at 350° for 40 to 45 minutes until bubbling.*

GARLIC SPAGHETTI

This is a nice change from red pasta sauce.

1 lb spaghetti
1/2 cup butter
1/2 cup olive oil
4 cloves of garlic, minced (2 tsp from jar)
1/2 tsp dried basil
1/2 tsp dried oregano
1/2 tsp salt
1/2 cup dried parsley
1/8 tsp white pepper
Dash of cayenne pepper
Parmesan cheese

- *Cook spaghetti as directed on package.*
- *Melt butter and oil in a large saucepan.*
- *Sauté all but the Parmesan cheese.*
- *Drain spaghetti and return to the pan.*
- *Add sauce and heat well.*
- *Transfer to a serving dish or platter.*
- *Top with Parmesan cheese and paprika.*

BOZ'S STEAK & BEANS

This is one of the few recipes I have from a man. Bruce (Boz) and I shared some dishes at break time when we worked together in Chico, California.

Sirloin steaks cut into bite-sized pieces
1 small can tomato paste
1 large can stewed tomatoes
1 package French's Chili Seasoning
1/2 tsp bay leaves, crushed
1 large onion, diced
1/2 tsp sage
Salt and pepper, to taste
2 cloves of garlic, minced
1 celery stick, sliced
Pinto beans, canned or prepared from scratch

- *Fry sirloin meat in oil.*
- *Put all ingredients together in a large crock pot. Use as many pinto beans as you like.*
- *Cook on low heat for 3 to 4 hours.*

CRUSTY BAKED POTATOES

This looks very nice on a serving platter.

Large baking potatoes
Butter
Salt and pepper, to taste
Seasoned bread crumbs
Parmesan cheese
Paprika

- *Slice as many potatoes as you want lengthwise, about ¼ inch apart, being careful not to cut all the way through the potato.*
- *Spread butter between the slices.*
- *Salt and pepper each slice.*
- *Bake for 30 minutes at 450°.*
- *Sprinkle with seasoned bread crumbs and Parmesan cheese.*
- *Bake an additional 10 to 15 minutes.*
- *Dust with paprika.*

Yams & Apples

Another dish we use with Thanksgiving dinner.

6 to 8 yams
5 Jonathan apples, peeled, cored and sliced
1 cup water
1 cup sugar
1/2 cup butter, melted
4 Tbsp cornstarch
1 tsp salt

- *Boil yams with skins on for about 15 minutes, let cool and peel.*
- *While yams boil, whisk together the water, sugar, melted butter, cornstarch and salt.*
- *Starting with the apples, layer in a buttered casserole dish, ending with yams on top.*
- *Pour the liquid mix over the yams and apples.*
- *Bake uncovered for 50 to 60 minutes at 350°.*

> **NOTE**
> If you use canned yams, reduce the cooking time by half.

Sweet & Sour Carrots

This is a cold salad dish.

- *Marinate these ingredients together overnight.*

4 cups carrots, diced or cut on the diagonal
1 small bell pepper, chopped
1/2 cup canola oil
1/3 cup vinegar
1 cup sugar
1 small can tomato soup
1/2 tsp salt
1 small onion, chopped
1 tsp Worcestershire sauce

- *Cook carrots, but do not overcook.*
- *Mix all ingredients together and refrigerate overnight.*
- *Serve cold.*

Yorkshire Pudding

This is really old-fashioned but I still make it with a prime rib roast and it is appreciated because no one knows what it is or how to make it. You will have to have roast drippings to make this.

- *When the sirloin roast is almost done, remove from oven and take ½ cup of beef drippings out of roaster.*
- *In the meantime, mix together the batter below.*

1 cup flour
1/2 tsp salt
2 eggs
1 cup milk
1 Tbsp melted butter

- *Combine all ingredients in a food processor and beat 1 minute.*
- *Cover the bottom of a 9 x 9 pan with ½ cup of roast drippings.*
- *Gently pour the batter into the pan with drippings.*
- *Bake pudding at 450° for 10 minutes.*
- *Reduce oven to 375° and continue cooking pudding for an additional 15 minutes.*
- *After it has risen well, baste with more drippings.*
- *Cut into squares and place on a large serving platter around the roast.*

163

CAULIFLOWER DELIGHT

1 large head cauliflower, cleaned and cored
Mayonnaise
Prepared mustard
Cheddar cheese

- *Put cauliflower in a microwave-safe glass dish.*
- *Spread cauliflower with mayonnaise.*
- *Spread mustard over mayonnaise.*
- *Cover with cheddar cheese.*
- *Put just enough water to cover the bottom of the dish.*
- *Cook on high until tender.*
- *Slice as you would a pie.*

164

ZUCCHINI PANCAKES

You can put this together in ten minutes. Another good things about these pancakes is that even people who don't like zucchini like them. Yes, even children. And it's a great way to use the fresh zucchini out of your own garden. Use it as a vegetable side dish.

1/3 cup Bisquick
1/4 cup grated Parmesan cheese
1/8 tsp black pepper
1/8 tsp salt
2 large eggs, slightly beaten
2 cups coarsely grated zucchini
2 Tbsp butter, melted

- *Mix Bisquick, cheese, salt and pepper together.*
- *Stir in eggs until just moist.*
- *Fold in zucchini and melted butter.*
- *Use 2 Tbsp batter per pancake.*
- *Fry 2 to 3 minutes per side until golden brown.*
- *Makes 8 to 10 pancakes.*

NOTE
Whenever you see 1/8 tsp of any seasoning, you are safe to just eyeball it.

ORTEGA CORN

3 eggs, beaten
One 16 oz can cream-style corn
2 Tbsp butter, melted
2 Tbsp sugar
2 Tbsp cornmeal
1/2 cup buttermilk
1 tsp baking soda
One 4 oz can Ortega Chilies, diced
1 cup shredded cheddar cheese, divided

- *Mix all ingredients, reserving ¼ cup cheese for the topping.*
- *Put in a 9 x 9 baking dish.*
- *Top with remaining cheese.*
- *Bake at 350° for 35 to 40 minutes.*

STIR-FRIED ASPARAGUS

This is from my sister, Janet Gillespie. I wasn't a fan of asparagus but this recipe cured me. The sauce is also good on fresh green beans or any vegetable of your choice.

2 lbs fresh asparagus
1 Tbsp cornstarch
1 cup chicken broth
1/2 tsp minced garlic, from a jar
2½ Tbsp Lite Soy Sauce
Water chestnuts, optional
Sliced almonds, optional

- *Trim ends from asparagus and discard.*
- *Cut asparagus into 2 inch diagonal pieces.*
- *Heat 2 Tbsp oil in a wok or large skillet.*
- *Add vegetables and stir-fry until coated with oil.*
- *Pour sauce over vegetables and continue to stir-fry until sauce is thickened.*
- *Serve immediately.*

NOTE
If you bend the asparagus, it will break where it needs to. Discard the bottom ends.

SWEET & SOUR GREEN BEANS

Use a crock pot for these beans. The recipe is from Lori Kelly of Paradise, California.

1 lb fresh green beans
4 slices bacon, cut into small pieces
1 medium onion, chopped
1 Tbsp flour
1/4 cup cider vinegar
1/4 cup water
2 Tbsp sugar
1/2 tsp salt
1/4 tsp pepper

- *Break ends off green beans, wash and set aside.*
- *Fry bacon and drain, reserving 2 Tbsp drippings in the skillet.*
- *Add onions to the skillet, sauté until soft and stir in the flour.*
- *Add water and vinegar and simmer a minute.*
- *Add sugar, salt and pepper and cook until thickened.*
- *Add beans and stir to coat.*
- *Put all ingredients in a crock pot and cook on low for 4 to 5 hours.*

BAKED ONIONS

If you want a wonderful aroma in your home, have these baking when company arrives.

Several large yellow onions

- *Remove outer skin of onions.*
- *Rub with butter.*
- *Sprinkle with salt and pepper.*
- *Wrap individually in foil.*
- *Bake at 350° for 40 minutes.*
- *Remove from oven, remove the foil and place on a serving plate.*

GNOCCHI

This recipe was shared by Josette Rogers Davis. We have been to her home when all of her family get together and make a big day of making gnocchi. Then we have a grand pasta dinner. Gnocchi is a small dumpling. In Italian it means "lump." Gnocchi is served in much the same manner as pasta, with sauce or some butter and sage or Parmesan cheese.

4 lbs of potatoes, peeled and cut into quarters
1¼ tsp salt
1 large egg
2/3 cup flour (add more as needed)

- *Boil the potatoes in salted water until they are soft.*
- *Mash them evenly and smoothly.*
- *When they are tepid, beat in the egg.*
- *Slowly add the flour by sifting and mixing well after each addition.*
- *Since the quality of the potatoes will dictate the amount of flour that you use, you may use a little more or less than is called for.*
- *Knead in the flour until you achieve smooth and elastic dough.*
- *Cut off pieces of the dough about the size of a tennis ball and roll into the shape of a bread stick.*
- *Cut the dough into 1 or 1½ inch long pieces.*
- *Roll in additional flour then roll each piece on the back of a fork making an indentation on one side only.*
- *Drop in to boiling water a few at a time.*
- *When they rise to the top they are done.*
- *Drain and serve with a pasta sauce or pesto or butter and Parmesan cheese.*

165

NOTE

These can be frozen before cooking but do not let them sit as they will absorb the moisture from the air and become gooey.

PASTA WITH FRIED GREEN BEANS

You don't need to know the amounts for this recipe.

Penne pasta
Fresh green beans, julienne strip, partially cooked
Sliced red onions
Frozen peas
Fresh minced garlic
Parmesan cheese

- *Cook as much penne pasta as you desire and set aside.*
- *In a small amount of olive oil, quick fry the rest of the ingredients.*
- *Add salt and pepper.*
- *Sprinkle with Parmesan cheese and serve warm.*

166

PASTA WITH GREENS AND BEANS

6 cloves of garlic, chopped
4 cups broccoli flowerets or fresh green beans, cooked
1 small can cannellini beans, drained and rinsed
2 cups vegetable broth
6 oz uncooked pasta, cooked al dente (I use angel hair pasta)

- *Cook garlic in a small amount of olive oil.*
- *Add greens and cook 2 minutes.*
- *Add broth, bring to a boil and simmer 3 minutes.*
- *Sprinkle with Parmesan cheese.*
- *Add cooked pasta and heat through.*
- *Serves 4.*

BAKED FRUIT COMPOTE

This can be served slightly warm.

1 large can sliced peaches, including ½ of the juice
1 large can slices pears, including juice
1 large can pineapple chunks, including juice
1 large can Bing cherries, drained
1 Tbsp lemon juice

- *Combine all ingredients and pour into an oblong pan.*
- *Bake at 350° until warm.*

PENNE WITH VODKA CREAM SAUCE

This takes about 10 minutes to make.

1 Tbsp olive oil
1 Tbsp butter
2 cloves of garlic, minced
2 green onions, thinly sliced
1 cup vodka (the alcohol cooks out)
1 cup vegetable stock
One 32 oz can crushed tomatoes
1/2 cup heavy cream
20 leaves fresh basil, shredded (stack in layers, roll them up and slice them)
Kosher salt and pepper to taste
Parmesan cheese
16 oz penne pasta, cooked

- *Melt butter in a large skillet.*
- *Add olive oil, garlic and onions and sauté 3 to 5 minutes.*
- *Add vodka and cook until vodka is reduced by half.*
- *Add vegetable stock, tomatoes and salt and pepper.*
- *Bring to a boil, reduce heat and simmer for 15 minutes.*
- *In the meantime cook pasta according to package directions.*
- *Put cream into sauce and continue to cook until it comes to a boil.*
- *Put penne in a large bowl and add sauce, basil and Parmesan cheese.*
- *Toss and serve.*
- *Serves 4 to 6.*
- *As an option, you might add Italian sausage and Parmesan cheese.*

PENNE PESTO DISH

Penne pasta
Olive oil
Carrots
Cauliflower
Broccoli
Onions
3 garlic cloves, minced

- *Cook desired amount of penne pasta to al dente stage. Do not overcook.*
- *Chop vegetables into very small diced pieces.*
- *Sauté vegetables in olive oil.*
- *Add either to prepared pesto sauce or use the recipe below.*

Pesto sauce:

1½ cup fresh basil leaves
1 cup fresh Parmesan cheese (grated)
1/4 cup pine nuts
6 cloves fresh garlic
Olive oil

- *Combine all but the oil in a food processor and process until blended.*
- *While the blender is still running, add olive oil until the mixture is a good consistency.*
- *Add additional Parmesan cheese and salt and pepper to taste.*
- *Makes about ½ cup.*

167

NOTES

Soups and Stews

CHICKEN SOUP BASE

Use this base and then add what you want to make soup.

2 quarts water
One 49½ oz can of chicken broth
2 to 3 stalks of celery, sliced
1 large onion, chopped
2 cloves of garlic (or bottled minced garlic)
4 Tbsp chicken base (paste type, not dry)
2 to 3 Tbsp Mrs. Dash Seasoning, Original Blend
Two 15.5 oz cans of chunk chicken breast in water
2 Tbsp parsley
Salt and pepper, to taste

- *Combine all ingredients in a large pot and heat.*

To make this into a creamed soup:

- *After you make the above soup, thicken the base with 2 Tbsp cornstarch mixed with 1/8 cup water.*
- *Stir until thickened.*
- *Then put 1 quart of half and half in a double boiler (Use a large pan filled ¾ full with water and a smaller pan that will fit on the top).*
- *When the half and half is hot add 2 Tbsp cornstarch mixed with 1/8 cup of water.*
- *Stir until thickened and then add to the soup mixture. Stir well to mix.*
- *As an option, add noodles, frozen peas, corn, green beans, ham or cheese, as desired.*

BEEF STEW TOMATO STYLE

2½ lbs stew meat, cubed (may use canned beef)
1 can cream of celery soup
8 potatoes, quartered
8 large carrots cut into chunks
1 package dry onion soup mix
1 can cream of mushroom soup
Two 8 oz cans tomato sauce
3 cups water
2 bay leaves
1 package brown gravy mix

- *In a large pan with a tight lid, brown beef. If you're using canned beef, you do not need to brown it.*
- *Add remaining ingredients.*
- *Cook on low heat until vegetables are done.*
- *Thicken with a mixture of flour and water if necessary.*

BROCCOLI CHEESE SOUP

Substitute vegetables with dehydrated food storage items for this recipe if you want.

2 quarts water
6 to 8 chicken or vegetable bouillon cubes
1 small bag frozen hash browns
1 small bag shredded carrots
1 large onion, diced
1 large jar of Cheez Whiz (add up to another 1/4 jar, depending on your taste)
1 to 2 heads of broccoli
Diced ham, optional
1 Tbsp minced garlic
1/2 cup butter
1/3 to 1/2 cup flour

- *Boil 2 cups water with bouillon cubes.*
- *Add hash browns, carrots and onion and simmer 5 minutes.*
- *Add broccoli and boil an additional 5 minutes.*
- *Melt butter in a small pan and add flour.*
- *Cook, stirring constantly, for 3 to 4 minutes.*
- *Slowly add remaining 2 cups of water to mixture.*
- *Pour flour mixture into the vegetables.*
- *Add Cheez Whiz and mix well.*
- *Add salt and pepper to taste.*

CAULIFLOWER SOUP

3 stalks celery, chopped, include the green leafy tops
2 small white onions, chopped
1 head of cauliflower, cut into small pieces
2 Tbsp fresh thyme, pulled off the stem
3 Tbsp butter
2 Tbsp flour
1 quart canned chicken stock
1 cup half and half
Salt and pepper to taste

- *Sauté celery and onion in olive oil in a large pot.*
- *Add cauliflower and thyme.*
- *Add butter and sprinkle with flour. Let butter melt.*
- *Stir until bubbly and add canned chicken stock*
- *Add half and half and salt and pepper to taste.*
- *Put in food processor to puree.*
- *Return to pot and simmer until hot.*

CREAM SOUP

Use this technique to cream any soup.

1 quart of half and half
2 Tbsp cornstarch
1/8 cup water

- *After you make the soup of your choice, do the following.*
- *Put 1 quart of half and half in a double boiler, use a large pan filled ¾ full with water and a smaller pan that will fit on the top.*
- *When the half and half gets hot, add 2 Tbsp cornstarch mixed with 1/8 cup of water.*
- *Stir until thickened.*
- *Add to the soup mixture.*

CREAMED VEGETABLE CHEESE SOUP

16 oz frozen broccoli, cauliflower and carrot mix
1 small cans of chicken or vegetable broth
1/4 tsp Mrs. Dash Seasoning, Original Blend
Black pepper to taste
8 to 10 oz Velveeta cheese

- *Combine all but the cheese in a large saucepan and bring to a boil.*
- *Reduce heat and simmer for 15 minutes.*
- *Using an electric hand mixer or a hand potato masher, mash the vegetables to desired texture.*
- *Stir in cheese until it melts and soup is hot.*

OPTION

Put all the vegetables in your food processor and puree them to make a smooth cream soup. This is a very nice addition for a formal dinner.

CHICKEN & HOMEMADE NOODLE SOUP

2 quarts water
One 49.5 oz can of chicken broth
3 stalks of celery, sliced
1 large onion, chopped
2 cloves of garlic (or bottled minced garlic)
3 Tbsp chicken base (paste, not dry)
2 Tbsp Mrs. Dash Seasoning, Original Blend
Two 12.5 oz cans of chunk chicken breasts in water
1 cup frozen vegetables or canned corn and green beans
As many homemade noodles as you wish (recipe page 158) or package egg noodles
Salt and pepper
Cornstarch
1 quart half and half

171

- *Bring 2 quarts of water to a boil in a stock pot. Add all ingredients but the half and half.*
- *While simmering, put a round stainless steel bowl on top of stock pot and put half and half in bowl, stirring occasionally.*
- *When it gets hot, add a mixture of 2 Tbsp of cornstarch mixed with 1/8 cup water to thicken the half and half.*
- *To the stock pot add a mixture of 2 Tbsp of cornstarch with 1/8 cup water and stir into the chicken broth to thicken.*
- *Pour half and half into the stock pot, combining both mixtures and stir well.*
- *Simmer ½ to 1 hour, stirring to be sure it does not stick on the bottom.*
- *This soup is also good over mashed potatoes.*

NOTE

You must thicken both mixtures separately and then put them together. As an option, add black beans (drained and rinsed), white potatoes (cut into bite-sizes) or anything else you wish.

CHICKEN SOUP STEW

You can call this soup or stew. Either way, it's great.

2 cups of cooked, cubed chicken (use canned
     or leftovers)
I medium onion, sliced in narrow slivers
I tsp minced garlic (from a jar)
1/2 tsp olive oil
I tsp chili powder
I tsp cumin
I tsp cinnamon
7 cups, or I large can, of chicken broth
One 14.5 oz can of Mexican-style stewed
     tomatoes, including the juice
3 zucchinis, diced (optional)
I½ cups frozen corn
I½ Tbsp minced pickled jalapeno chilies
     (Escabeche brand)
1/2 tsp oregano

- *In a large pot, sauté onion, garlic and oil about five minutes.*
- *Add all dry seasoning, mixing well.*
- *Add chicken broth, tomatoes and juice, zucchini, corn and Jalapenos.*
- *Simmer 5 minutes.*
- *Add chicken, cover and simmer for 5 to 10 minutes.*

ITALIAN PEASANT SOUP

2 lbs Italian sausage, cooked and drained
I onion, chopped
4 cloves of garlic, crushed
3 carrots, peeled and shredded
3 quarts of chicken broth
2 small cans diced tomatoes
2 cans white beans, drained and rinsed
I Tbsp dried basil
2 cups penne pasta, cooked and drained
Salt and pepper to taste
2 cups chopped, cooked chicken (optional)

- *Sauté onion and garlic with the sausage.*
- *Mix remaining ingredients, but pasta, in a large pot.*
- *Bring to a boil and let simmer for 15 minutes.*
- *Just before serving, add pasta.*

CREAMED CHICKEN & CELERY SOUP

This is made with dried soup mix.

I package of dehydrated noodle soup mix
I small can of cream of celery soup (puree the
     soup, to make it creamier)
1/2 tsp dehydrated onions
I tsp chicken paste broth or I bouillon cube
4 cups water (You may need to add more, according
to what you put in the soup)
1/4 tsp Mrs. Dash Seasoning, Original Blend
Salt and pepper to taste

- *Mix dry soup mix as directed on the package but use hot water and do not bring to a boil.*
- *Add remaining ingredients.*
- *Bring to a boil and simmer for 5 minutes.*
- *Add any of the optional ingredients below.*

Precooked carrots
Sliced celery
Frozen corn
Leftover cooked chicken
Leftover baked potatoes
Broccoli
Cauliflower

LESLIE'S NAVY BEAN SOUP

Leslie Tall shares a lot of great meals with us and this is one of them.

I½ lbs white Navy beans, soaked overnight
1/4 lb butter
Salt and pepper

- *Drain beans and put in large heavy pot.*
- *Cover with 2½ quarts water.*
- *Add butter, salt and pepper.*
- *Cover and cook over medium heat for 1½ hours, stirring occasionally.*
- *Add: the following ingredients.*

I onion, chopped
I cup carrots cut up
4 Tbsp parsley
1/4 lb ham hock

- *Simmer until beans are tender.*

172

HAM STEW

This is my own creation and great for a cold winter night.

2 cups ham
1 medium onion, chopped
Olive oil

- *Cut up leftover ham, about 2 cups, and set aside.*
- *Sauté onion in 3 Tbsp olive oil until they are clear.*
- *Add the following ingredients.*

1/2 tsp kosher salt
Black pepper to taste
1 tsp chili powder
1 small can tomato soup
1 can corn
1 can Italian tomatoes, pureed
1 can small black beans, drained
1 small can Bush Baked Beans
1 cup precooked potatoes, diced
2 precooked carrots, diced
2 stalks celery, diced

- *Simmer all ingredients together for 20 minutes.*

POTATO ORTEGA SOUP

This recipe comes from the grandmother of Cassandra Mata of Rockland, California.

5 to 6 medium size red potatoes unpeeled, sliced in rounds, cover with water
2 to 3 whole garlic cloves (or minced)
Canned Ortega chilies cut into strips
One whole boiling onion
1 bay leaf
Shredded roast beef (optional)
Monterey Jack cheese

- *Combine all ingredients and let potatoes cook until tender.*
- *When tender remove garlic cloves, onion and bay leaf. If you use whole garlic cloves, they may be smashed and added back into the soup.*
- *Cool slightly and grate ½ to 1 cup Monterey Jack Cheese.*

CREAMY CHICKEN & WILD RICE SOUP

This is from Erica Williams who shares great recipes.

4 cups chicken broth
2 cups water
2 cooked, boneless chicken breast halves, shredded
One 4.5 ounce package quick cooking long grain and wild rice with seasoning packet
1/2 tsp salt
1/2 tsp ground black pepper
3/4 cup all to purpose flour
1/2 cup butter
2 cups heavy cream

- *In a large pot over medium heat combine broth, water and chicken.*
- *Bring just to boiling, then stir in rice, reserving seasoning packet.*
- *Cover and remove from heat.*
- *In a small bowl, combine salt, pepper and flour.*
- *In a medium saucepan over medium heat, melt butter.*
- *Stir in contents of seasoning packet until mixture is bubbly.*
- *Reduce heat to low, then stir in flour mixture by tablespoons to form a roux.*
- *Whisk in cream, a little at a time, until fully incorporated and smooth.*
- *Cook until thickened, 5 minutes.*
- *Stir cream mixture into broth and rice.*
- *Cook over medium heat until heated through, 10 to 15 minutes.*

173

NOTE

Uncle Ben's quick-cooking long grain and wild rice mix works well in this recipe.

PASTA E FAGIOLI SOUP

1 lb ground beef
One 15 oz can tomato sauce
One 15 oz can red kidney beans with liquid
1 cup onions, diced
One 12 oz can V-8 Juice
1 cup carrots, julienne style
One 15 oz can Great Northern beans with liquid
1 Tbsp white vinegar
1 cup celery, chopped
1½ tsp salt
1 tsp basil
1/2 tsp thyme
1/2 tsp pepper
2 cloves garlic, minced
1 tsp oregano
1 cup Ditali pasta, cooked el dente and set aside
Two 14.5 oz cans diced tomatoes

174

- *Brown beef in a large pot over medium heat, then drain.*
- *Add onion, carrots, celery, and garlic and sauté for 10 minutes.*
- *Add remaining ingredients except pasta and simmer for 1 hour.*
- *Add pasta when ready to serve.*

NOTE

If you don't plan on using all the soup at one serving, add the pasta only as you serve it, as it will swell up and get mushy.

CREAMED TOMATO GARLIC SOUP

This is quick, easy and great.

4 small cans of tomato soup, undiluted
1 soup can of whole milk
1 quart half and half
2 to 4 cloves of garlic, minced
1 tsp dry Italian seasoning

- *Mix all ingredients together and cook over medium heat until almost to the boiling stage.*

ITALIAN TOMATO SOUP

If you can get fresh herbs, use them instead of the dried.

One 16 oz package frozen stir-fry mix
One 14.5 oz can of diced tomatoes, including juice
One 15 oz can chicken broth
One 8 oz can navy beans, rinsed and drained
1 garlic clove, minced
2 Tbsp dried basil
2 Tbsp dried parsley
1/2 tsp dried oregano
1 Tbsp balsamic vinegar
1/4 tsp crushed red pepper flakes
1 Tbsp olive oil
1/4 tsp salt

- *Process all ingredients except oil and salt in a food processor, just until chunky.*
- *Put in large pot and bring to a boil.*
- *Reduce heat and simmer covered for 20 minutes.*
- *Stir in oil and salt and serve.*

LENTILS WITH VEGETABLES SOUP

2 lbs stew meat
1 small onion, chopped
2 carrots, diced
3 celery stalks, sliced
6 garlic cloves, chopped (use fresh)
2 cups dried lentils

- *In a large pot, brown 2 lbs stew meat.*
- *Remove from pan; set aside.*
- *In same pot, sauté together the onion, carrots, celery and garlic.*
- *Add the following ingredients.*

1 large can diced tomatoes
1 tsp fresh rosemary (removed from stem)
1 tsp dried oregano
4 cups beef broth
Parsley

- *Add meat to pot and simmer for 1 hour.*
- *Add the 2 cups dried lentils.*
- *Cook 30 minutes, covered.*
- *When ready to serve, add parsley.*

OVEN STEW

1 lb stew meat, cut into small pieces
3 large potatoes, peeled and cut
6 carrots, peeled and sliced
1/2 onion, chopped
One 26 oz can of cream of chicken or
    cream of mushroom soup
2 cups water
Salt and pepper to taste

- *Brown meat in a large Dutch oven or oven-proof roasting pan.*
- *Add salt and pepper and remove from the pan.*
- *Add the onions, carrots, soup and water.*
- *Add salt, pepper and garlic salt.*
- *Put a lid on the pan and bake in the oven 2 to 3 hours at 350°.*
- *When finished cooking, thicken with a mixture of 2 Tbsp flour and ¼ cup cold water and cook another 20 minutes.*

CHICKEN SOUP

This is the fastest soup I have ever made.

2 quarts water
1 medium yellow onion, chopped
2 stalks of celery, sliced
2 cloves of garlic, minced
1/4 cup chicken base (paste type) or ½ cup dry
    bouillon
2 tsp Mrs. Dash Seasoning (no salt)

- *Combine all of the ingredients and heat through.*

To make a cream soup:

- *Put 1 quart of half and half in a double boiler or use a large pan filled ¾ full with water and a smaller pan that will fit on the top.*
- *When the half and half is hot, add 2 Tbsp cornstarch mixed with 1/8 cup of water.*
- *Stir until thickened and add to the soup mixture.*

NOTE

Add any other ingredients you want to this soup. Use this recipe to cream other types of soup.

POTATO CHEESE SOUP

This version is lower in fat.

1 medium onion, chopped
2 medium carrots, coarsely grated
3/4 tsp Mrs. Dash Seasoning, Original Blend
1/2 tsp white pepper
1/2 tsp paprika
1/2 tsp dry mustard
1 lb potatoes cut into ½ inch cubes
One 29 oz can vegetable or chicken broth
1/2 cup low to fat half and half
8 oz reduced fat cheddar cheese

- *Cook onions with a small amount of olive oil until they begin to color.*

Add the following ingredients:

Carrots
Mrs. Dash Seasoning, Original Blend
Pepper
Paprika
Mustard

- *Cook until carrots begin to soften, about 3 minutes.*
- *Add potatoes, broth, and half and half, increase the heat and bring to a boil. Then reduce heat to simmer.*
- *Cook until potatoes are tender, about 20 minutes.*
- *Add cheese and stir to melt.*
- *For a different texture, puree in a blender, leaving some of it in pieces, not completely smooth.*

175

TOMATO BEAN SOUP

This turns out great with canned and frozen foods.

One 19 to 20 oz can condensed tomato soup
1 soup can of water
1½ cup frozen mixed vegetables
**One 15 oz can Great Northern beans, drained
   and rinsed**
Mrs. Dash Seasoning, Original Blend to taste
Black pepper, to taste
Pinch of red pepper flakes, optional

- *Mix all ingredients in a medium pot.*
- *Simmer until vegetables are tender.*

QUICK BEEF STEW

1 to 2 lbs round steak, cut into squares
Olive oil
Beef broth or bouillon paste

- *Brown beef in olive oil using an 8 to 12 quart pot.*
- *Put 3 cups beef broth or bouillon paste mixed in 3 cups of water in, cover with lid and simmer for 2 hours.*
- *Add the following ingredients.*

1 medium onion, chopped
2 stalks of celery, diced
Salt and pepper to taste
1/4 tsp ground clove
One 14.5 oz can of diced tomatoes with Jalapenos
2 Tbsp lime juice
1/3 cup fresh cilantro
1/2 tsp minced garlic or use minced in a jar
4 cups of white potatoes, peeled and cubed
2 carrots, sliced
1 cup frozen or canned corn
1 cup frozen or canned green beans

- *Sprinkle with flour; stir well to thicken.*
- *Continue to simmer until carrots and potatoes are tender.*

NOTE

Cook the meat for 25 minutes in a pressure cooker to speed the process up or use canned beef.

SPLIT PEA SOUP

2 ham hocks
1/8 tsp thyme
1 tsp salt
1 bay leaf
1/8 tsp white pepper
1 tsp sugar
3 whole cloves
1/2 cup celery, chopped
1/2 cup carrots, chopped
1 large onion, coarsely chopped
2 cups chicken broth
1½ quarts water
3 cups dried peas

- *Soak the peas overnight or for several hours.*
- *Separate the bad peas, some may be small rocks, and rinse.*
- *In a stock pot, cover peas with 1½ quarts of water and chicken broth.*
- *Add the carrots, celery, ham hocks, onion, cloves, bay leaf, and thyme and cook until the peas are mushy and thick.*
- *If the soup is not as thick as you would like, lift the lid and let it boil down.*
- *Add seasonings to taste.*

TOMATO BASIL SOUP

**One 16 oz can of tomatoes with garlic,
   oregano and basil, chopped in food processor**
One 10.75 oz can tomato soup
3 Italian Roma tomatoes, chopped, seeds removed
1/2 onion, chopped
1 stalk celery, chopped
1 small carrot, shredded
1 beef or chicken bouillon cube
1 tsp sugar
1/2 cup small shell pasta, cooked
2 cups water
Salt and pepper to taste
Fresh or dried basil, to taste
Spinach, shredded (optional)

- *Even though the canned tomatoes are diced, chop or mince them in a food processor. The tomatoes should be very small in size.*
- *Mix all ingredients together except the cooked pasta and simmer until vegetables are done.*
- *Just before serving, add pasta.*

177

BEEF STEW GRAVY STYLE

This is the brown gravy-type, crock pot style. Save cooking time by using ground beef instead of stew meat. Cut all ingredients equally into small sizes.

1½ lbs stew meat or round steak, cut in small
    pieces, browned in oil
3 potatoes, peeled and cubed into small pieces
4 carrots, peeled and diced in small pieces
1/2 cup frozen peas, optional
1/2 cup corn, optional
3 small onions, cubed
1 stalk celery, diced
1 clove of garlic, crushed and chopped
1 tsp paprika
Salt and pepper to taste
1 bay leaf
1 Tbsp beef base (bouillon)
2 cups water
1/4 cup flour

- *Mix water, beef base and flour together.*
- *Put all ingredients in crock pot and cook on high for 6 to 8 hours.*

CHICKEN SOUP FOR ONE

I guess I should do a cookbook for just one! Well, this could actually be for two.

One 12 oz can of chicken broth
1 Tbsp long grain rice
1/8 tsp dried dill weed
1/2 tsp dried chopped onions
Salt and pepper to taste
1/3 cup frozen mixed vegetables
Leftover cooked chicken, chopped

- *Put all ingredients except the frozen vegetables and chicken in a medium saucepan.*
- *Cook for 10 minutes, stirring occasionally.*
- *Add the vegetables and chicken.*
- *Simmer 5 more minutes.*

TACO SOUP

You may want to double this recipe. It could be called a chili dish.

1 lb ground beef
1 onion, chopped
1/2 package taco seasoning (prepared or
    see recipe on page 149)
1 Tbsp chili powder
1/4 cup salsa
Grated carrots
Canned chilies, optional
1 cup frozen or canned corn
Black olives, sliced
One 10 oz can vegetable beef soup (undiluted)
One 10 oz can tomato soup (undiluted)
One 10 oz can kidney beans (not drained)
One 10 oz can pinto beans, drained
One 16 oz can diced Mexican-style tomatoes,
    pureed
1¾ cup water

- *Brown ground beef with seasonings and onions. Drain.*
- *Mix all ingredients and bring to a boil.*
- *Crush tortilla chips in a bowl and pour soup over chips.*
- *Top with shredded cheese and sour cream.*

COUNTRY-STYLE POTATO SOUP

6 to 10 slices of bacon
1 cup onion, chopped
4 to 5 cups potatoes, cubed
2 cups water
2 small cans cream of chicken soup, undiluted
2 cups whole milk
1 tsp salt
2 Tbsp fresh parsley, chopped
1 package Smoky Links, cut diagonally

- *Sauté bacon and onions in a large pot.*
- *Discard all but about 3 Tbsp of drippings.*
- *Add potatoes, water and sausage to the drippings.*
- *Cook covered for 15 minutes or until potatoes are tender.*
- *Add remaining ingredients and heat thoroughly. Do not boil.*
- *Serve with freshly baked bread and crisp salad.*

178

VEGETABLE BARLEY SOUP

I cloned this from a Mexican restaurant in California.

1 cup barley
1 quart of canned chicken, beef or vegetarian
   soup stock
1 quart of water
4 carrots cut into bite sizes
4 white potatoes, cubed
2 stalks of celery, sliced
1 medium onion, chopped
One 12 oz can of diced tomatoes in herbs
1 cup cooked barley
1/4 cup salsa
1/3 tsp white pepper
Salt and pepper to taste
1 cup sliced cabbage
1 cup cauliflower, cut into chunks

- *In a medium saucepan, put barley and enough water to cover it. Simmer for 1 hour.*
- *In a large pot, bring the broth and water to a boil.*
- *Add carrots and cook on high for 10 minutes.*
- *Add all but the cabbage and cauliflower.*
- *Simmer for 15 minutes.*
- *Make sure all vegetables are tender before serving.*
- *20 minutes before serving add the cabbage and cauliflower.*

CREAM OF BROCCOLI SOUP

Easily make this Broccoli Cheese soup by adding Cheez Whiz after the soup has cooked. Don't add salt to this as there is enough in the soup mix.

3½ cups whole milk
One 10 oz package of frozen chopped broccoli
1 envelope of Lipton Chicken Noodle Soup mix
1 Tbsp flour

- *Bring 3 cups of the milk and broccoli to a boil and simmer for 5 minutes.*
- *Stir in soup mix and flour.*
- *Pepper to taste. You may want to do this after the soup is made.*
- *Blend with the remaining ½ cup milk.*
- *Bring to a boil, stirring constantly.*
- *Simmer for 10 minutes.*
- *As an option, if you have leftover chicken, cut it up and add to the soup. Excellent!*
- *Serves 2 to 4.*

POTATO ONION CHEESE SOUP

Jeanette Van Alfen of Provo, Utah, gave me this recipe at least 25 years ago, before it became so popular. We all lived in Anaheim, California at the time. It is incredibly good.

4 Tbsp chicken bouillon
3 cups hot water
3/4 cup butter
3/4 cup flour
5 cups potatoes, diced
1 cup celery, diced
1 cup carrots, diced
1/2 cup onions, chopped
One 8 oz jar of Cheez Whiz
2 cups whole milk
2 cups half and half

- *Dissolve bouillon in hot water.*
- *Add potatoes, celery, onion and carrots and cook for 10 minutes.*
- *Melt butter and add flour, stirring until well mixed.*
- *Add to potato mix.*
- *Continue stirring and slowly add milk and half and half.*
- *Add Cheez Whiz.*
- *Simmer until carrots are tender.*

179

> **NOTE**
> This keeps well so you may want to double the recipe.

Hamburger Soup

During the winter this is still one of my very favorite soups.

2 lbs ground beef, cooked and drained
4 carrots, chopped
1 cup celery, diced
1 large onion, chopped
1 small can diced tomatoes
1 cup ketchup
One 8 oz can tomato juice
1 Tbsp chicken broth base
1 tsp Mrs. Dash Seasoning

- *Put all ingredients in a large stock pot.*
- *Cook until carrots are tender*
- *Add the following ingredients.*

1/2 cup frozen peas
1/2 cup frozen green beans
1/2 cup frozen corn
1/2 cup uncooked pasta
3 to 4 potatoes or turnips, cubed
1 cup cabbage, cut up
3 Tbsp sugar
Dash of Worcestershire sauce
Salt and pepper to taste

- *Simmer until all vegetables and pasta are tender.*

180

Harvest Soup Gift Jar

Make the instructions the gift card.

1/3 cup beef bouillon granules
1/4 cup dried minced onion
1/2 cup dried split peas
1/2 cup dry macaroni
1/4 cup barley
1/2 cup lentils
1/3 cup long grain white rice
1 cup tri-colored dry spiral pasta

- *Layer ingredients in the order given into a 1 quart canning jar.*
- *Pack each layer in place before adding the next ingredient.*
- *Use a ribbon to attach a gift tag with the following cooking instructions.*

Harvest Soup Instructions:

1 jar Harvest Soup Mix
1 lb ground beef, browned and drained

Remove the tri-colored pasta from the Harvest Soup Mix and set aside. Place the balance of the mix in a large soup pot. Add 12 cups of water and bring to a boil. Lower heat and simmer 45 minutes. Add tri-colored pasta. Continue to simmer until pasta is done.

Vegetables

BAKED BEETS

2 cans of sliced beets, drained
1 small shallot, chopped
Sprinkle with olive oil
Salt and pepper

- *Mix all ingredients and bake at 325° until heated.*

BAKED BRUSSELS SPROUTS

Crisp on the outside and soft on the inside, these will have a very different texture.

- *Trim the ends off sprouts and remove loose leaves.*
- *Sprinkle with olive oil, salt and pepper and mix well.*
- *Put on cookie sheet and bake at 400° for 40 minutes.*

BAKED CAULIFLOWER

1 medium head of cauliflower
1 cup sour cream
1 cup shredded cheddar cheese
1/2 cup crushed corn flakes
1/4 cup chopped green pepper
1 tsp salt
1/4 cup grated Parmesan cheese
Paprika

- *Place cauliflower in a small amount of water in a medium saucepan.*
- *Cover and cook for 5 minutes. Drain.*
- *Add cheddar cheese, corn flakes, salt and pepper to cauliflower.*
- *Transfer to a 2 quart baking dish.*
- *Sprinkle with paprika and Parmesan cheese.*
- *Bake, uncovered, at 350° for 25 to 30 minutes.*

BAKED GARLIC POTATOES

This is my own recipe and combination.

White potatoes peeled and cut into quarters or cubed (you can leave the skins on)
1 yellow onion cut into small cubes
Olive oil

- *Season as desired with the following ingredients*

McCormick's Montreal Steak Seasoning
Mrs. Dash Seasoning Salt
Garlic powder
Italian seasoning salt
Some paprika

- *Put all the ingredients in a ziplock bag with enough virgin olive oil to coat the potatoes.*
- *Spread in a single layer, cut side down, in a jelly roll pan.*
- *Bake 45 minutes at 450°, turning the potatoes halfway through.*

NOTE

The potatoes should be golden brown, but not overcooked. As an option, change the seasoning to just coarse salt and ground pepper. This will make a milder dish.

BROCCOLINI

This is a great replacement for regular broccoli. It's a cross between broccoli and cauliflower. You do not need to remove the leaves and peel the stems as you do with broccoli.

Cut ends off a large bunch of broccolini
Peel of 1 lemon
1 Tbsp olive oil
Salt

- *Put in microwave dish and cover with plastic wrap with a corner left open.*
- *Microwave 5 minutes.*

CORN COMBO

This is great with fresh garden vegetables.

Red bell peppers
Yellow bell peppers
Yukon potatoes peeled
Zucchini
Yellow onion
Fresh corn on the cob; cut the corn off the cob
McCormick Montreal Grilling Seasoning
Sugar
Salt and pepper

- *Cut all the fresh vegetables into small ½ inch cubes*
- *Add olive oil to a large skillet over medium-high heat.*
- *Put all cut vegetables in the skillet.*
- *Salt and pepper to taste.*
- *Add Montreal Grilling Seasoning to taste.*
- *Add a small amount of sugar.*
- *Heat until all vegetables are just tender.*
- *Do not overcook. The vegetables should be firm.*

CORN ON THE COB

6 ears of fresh corn on the cob
2 Tbsp sugar
Butter
Juice of one lime
Sprinkle with chili powder and coarse salt

- *Husk corn.*
- *Cook corn about 10 minutes in boiling water and sugar. Drain.*
- *Leave corn in pot.*
- *Add butter, lime juice, chili powder and coarse salt.*
- *As an option, instead of chili powder and salt, try lemon pepper*
- *Put lid on pot and shake up to coat the corn.*
- *Serve immediately.*

NOTE

Sugar in the water makes the corn sweet. If you add salt to the water, it has a tendency to make the corn tough.

CREAMED BAKED CORN

This is another traditional dish for Thanksgiving at my home. There are two version of this recipe. Decide which one you have time for.

Two 16 oz packages frozen white corn
1 cup heavy whipping cream, not whipped
1/2 tsp salt
1 tsp sugar
2 Tbsp melted butter
2 Tbsp flour

- *Boil and simmer corn and whipping cream for 5 minutes.*
- *Stir in salt and sugar.*
- *Mix together melted butter and flour and add to the corn. Stir until thickened.*
- *Transfer to a baking dish.*
- *Sprinkle with Parmesan cheese and paprika.*
- *Place under broiler and brown.*

183

Short version:

1/2 tsp salt
1 tsp sugar
1 cup heavy whipping cream
3 cans of corn, drained
2 Tbsp flour
2 Tbsp butter
Salt and pepper
Parmesan cheese

- *Melt butter and mix with flour.*
- *Add salt and sugar.*
- *Mix well and add whipping cream and canned corn.*
- *Simmer until thickened and comes to a boil.*
- *Transfer to a baking dish.*
- *Top with Parmesan cheese and paprika.*
- *Broil until browned.*

MEXICAN CORN

2 cans whole kernel corn, drained
One 8 oz package cream cheese
1/4 cup butter
5 to 10 jalapeno peppers, chopped
    (quantity depends on how hot you want this to
    be; use plastic gloves to prevent burning your
    hands)
1 tsp garlic salt

- Heat all ingredients in a medium saucepan.
- Cook over medium heat until cream cheese melts, stirring constantly.
- Serves 6 to 8.

FRIED GREEN TOMATOES

If you're not frying your green tomatoes in bacon grease, then you've lost half of the great flavor! This recipe isn't for everyone. The bacon grease shows how old it is.

184

1/2 cup bacon grease
1/3 cup flour
3/4 cup cornmeal
1/4 tsp ground black pepper
Red pepper flakes, optional
1 egg
1/4 cup milk
Green tomatoes cut into 1/4 inch slices

- Heat bacon grease in a skillet over medium heat.
- In a small bowl, mix the flour, cornmeal and pepper.
- In another bowl, whisk together the egg and milk.
- Dip the tomato slices in the egg mixture and then coat with the dry mixture.
- Place the breaded tomato slices in the hot bacon grease.
- Cook until browned on each side, about 3 to 4 minutes per side.
- Put on paper towels, to absorb excess grease.

NOTE

Bacon grease burns easily so watch your heat. Also, green tomatoes are in abundance. If you have tomatoes in your garden, just pick them at the end of the season, not at the beginning.

CUBED BUTTERNUT SQUASH

I never cared much for squash but when Leslie Tall made this dish, I fell for it. I especially like this one because it's not mushy and is better than sweet potatoes.

2 lbs butternut squash peeled and cut into
    1 inch squares
1 Tbsp olive oil
1/2 tsp pumpkin pie spice
1/3 cup maple syrup
Salt
Pinch of ground red pepper

- Line a jelly roll baking pan with foil and spray with vegetable spray.
- Put cubed squash in a bowl, drizzle with oil and sprinkle with salt and toss.
- Put in baking pan and separate cubes so they don't touch each other.
- Roast for 15 minutes at 425º.
- Combine 1/3 cup of maple syrup with the pumpkin pie spice and red pepper.
- Pour mixture over the squash and lightly toss with a spatula.
- Separate pieces again and continue to cook 15 to 20 minutes longer.
- Put in serving dish and pour remaining drippings on top and serve immediately.

CREAMED PEAS & CARROTS

2 Tbsp melted butter
2 Tbsp flour
1/2 tsp salt
1 tsp sugar
1 cup heavy whipping cream
1 cup of carrots
1 to 2 cups frozen peas
1 cup pearl onions

- In a large skillet or pan, mix butter and flour.
- Add salt and sugar
- Mix well and add whipping cream, carrots, frozen peas and onions.
- Simmer until thickened and it comes to a boil.
- Transfer to a baking dish.
- Bake at 350º for 35 minutes.

GARLIC BROCCOLI

I made this recipe up and it is now one of my most used vegetable dishes.

Broccoli
Olive oil
Minced garlic
Kosher salt
Seasoned black pepper

- *Cut and peel as much broccoli as you want. Cut into the flowerets.*
- *Cover the bottom of a skillet or wok with olive oil.*
- *Use as much fresh minced garlic as you want, at least 1 clove per 2 cups of broccoli.*
- *Add kosher salt to taste.*
- *Add seasoned black pepper to taste.*
- *Stir-fry in hot oil until the broccoli is well-coated and slightly cooked.*
- *Serve immediately.*
- *Do not overcook. The broccoli should be semi-firm.*

GARLIC ROASTED POTATOES

6 medium white or red potatoes, quartered
2 Tbsp olive oil
8 unpeeled garlic cloves
Sprig of fresh rosemary, optional
Kosher salt to taste
Ground pepper to taste

- *Preheat oven to 450º.*
- *Put all ingredients in a bowl and toss well.*
- *Spread potatoes in a single layer, cut sides down in a baking dish.*
- *Roast, turning halfway through, until golden brown (about 45 minutes).*
- *Squeeze garlic cloves out of their skins and serve with the potatoes.*

NOTE

White and red potatoes hold a firmness to them, but russets have a tendency to get too soft or even mushy.

GINGER CARROTS

5 carrots, peeled and cut into 1/2 inch slices
1/4 stick of margarine or butter
1/4 cup honey
1/4 tsp salt
1/4 tsp ground ginger (fresh is best, if available)
1/4 tsp cinnamon

- *Cook carrots in water until half tender. Drain.*
- *Mix remaining ingredients in a medium saucepan and cook until well blended.*
- *Add carrots and continue to simmer until well heated and tender.*
- *Do not overcook.*

GRILLED ASPARAGUS

This is great for the BBQ party.

185

Asparagus
Olive oil
Minced garlic
Lemon zest
Salt and pepper

- *Skewer six asparagus spears onto skewers. You'll need two skewers in order to secure them—one at the top and one at the bottom.*
- *Brush with a mixture of the olive oil, garlic, lemon zest, salt and pepper.*
- *Place on the grill and cook until tender.*
- *Allow six asparagus spears on two skewers per person.*

GRILLED VEGETABLES

Use as many vegetables and varieties as you like. Below you will find my own recipe and combinations.

Red new potatoes, sliced thin and then in halves
Sliced sweet onions
Fresh green beans, sliced diagonal
Thinly sliced carrots
Brussels sprouts, cut in half
Cauliflower, sliced

- *Put all vegetables in a large bowl.*
- *Season as desired with the following mixture; just shake and wing it. You can't mess this up.*

Seasoning:

McCormick Montreal Steak Seasoning
Garlic salt
Dry Italian Seasoning salt
Ground rosemary
Paprika
Parsley

- *Put enough virgin olive oil to coat the vegetables.*
- *Grill in a BBQ skillet. They have holes to allow them to cook and brown. Or use a George Foreman Grill or a regular skillet on medium-high heat until browned.*
- *Do not overcook.*

ITALIAN MARINADE VEGETABLES

This must chill overnight and up to two days.

1/2 cup olive oil
3/4 cup red wine vinegar
2 Tbsp sugar

- *Add the following ingredients as you desire.*

Basil
Oregano
Tarragon
Salt
Pepper
Garlic
Parsley

- *Add fresh vegetables of your choice.*
- *Chill overnight or longer.*

MIXED VEGETABLES ITALIENNE

1/4 cup olive oil
One 16 oz can stewed tomatoes
1 beef, chicken or vegetable bouillon cube
4 cups zucchini cut in 1 inch pieces
1 cup frozen peas
1 cup frozen corn
1 cup sliced carrots
1 cup diced potatoes
1 cup chopped onions
1 tsp oregano leaves
1½ tsp salt
1/8 tsp pepper

- *Put all ingredients in a 10 inch skillet.*
- *Cover and simmer only until tender, about 15 to 20 minutes.*

NEW PEAS IN CREAM SAUCE

187

4 cups of shelled, fresh or frozen green peas
2 tsp sugar
2 tsp salt
4 to 5 pea pods
2 small green onions with tops, chopped
2 Tbsp margarine or butter
1/2 tsp pepper
1 cup light cream

- *Cook peas in sugar, salt, pea pods, onion and enough water to cover.*
- *Cook 10 to 15 minutes or just until tender. The water should be almost evaporated.*
- *Add margarine, pepper and cream.*
- *Heat but do not cook any longer.*
- *Transfer to a serving bowl.*

PARMESAN MASHED POTATOES

2 to 3 lbs of red new potatoes
1½ cups of half and half
1/4 cup butter
1/2 cup sour cream
1/2 cup Parmesan cheese
Salt and pepper

- *Boil red new potatoes with skins on until tender. Drain.*
- *Put in mixer and process but leave them chunky.*
- *Heat together the half and half and butter.*
- *Add to the potatoes.*
- *Then add the sour cream, Parmesan, salt and pepper.*
- *Mix together and remove to a large bowl.*
- *Set bowl over a pot of boiling water to keep potatoes moist and warm until ready to serve.*

POTATO PANCAKES

Use as many mashed potatoes as you will need for your meal. Include some chunks of potato. Leftovers work well.

Onions, chopped
Garlic salt, pepper and salt to taste
Milk
Vegetable oil
Seasoned Italian bread crumbs with garlic salt, pepper and parsley

- *Mix all ingredients together except bread crumbs and milk.*
- *Make potatoes into round patties.*
- *Dip in milk and then the mixture of bread crumbs.*
- *Fry in vegetable oil and drain on paper towels.*
- *Serve hot.*

ROASTED POTATOES

This is my original recipe.

4 to 5 large red potatoes
1/4 package dry Italian Dressing
Just enough olive oil to cover all the pieces
2 tsp McCormick Montreal Grilling Pepper
1 tsp rosemary
1/4 tsp garlic powder (do not salt as the Italian dressing is salty)

- *Cut potatoes into large bite-size pieces or wedges and put in a large bowl.*
- *Add the Italian dressing mix, olive oil, McCormick Montreal seasoning, rosemary, and garlic powder.*
- *Mix well and spread in a single layer in a baking pan sprayed with vegetable spray.*
- *Bake at 450° for 40 to 45 minutes until browned and crisp.*

NOTE

Red potatoes have the best consistency, but you can use Yukon Gold or white. Russet potatoes do not work well as they get mushy. As an option, try pan frying them until browned but they will not be as crisp.

Alternative recipe (process the same as above):

2 Tbsp olive oil
2 tsp season salt
1½ tsp chili powder

SWEET POTATO FRITTERS

Large sweet potato
4 Tbsp butter
2 Tbsp flour
Chives, to taste
Corn, as much as you want

- *With a knife stick a few holes in a large sweet potato and microwave on a paper towel for 6 minutes.*
- *Remove the skin and mash with the butter, flour chives and corn.*
- *Cover and refrigerate overnight.*
- *Use a tablespoon to form fritter.*
- *Fry in oil and serve immediately.*

ROASTED SWEET POTATOES

2 sweet potatoes, peeled or unpeeled
1 cup carrots

Mix together:

3 Tbsp olive oil
2 tsp cumin
1 tsp hot paprika
1 tsp ground ginger
1/4 tsp cayenne pepper
1 tsp salt
1/2 tsp white pepper

- *Preheat oven to 400°.*
- *Cut sweet potatoes into wedges and toss with the spices. When well coated, put on a baking sheet and sprinkle the remaining spices on top.*
- *Bake for 15 minutes, turn and continue baking for an additional 15 minutes.*

NOTE

Try using red or white potatoes with the sweet potatoes to add variety.

VEGETABLES WITH HERB SAUCE

There are very low in fat.

Two 16 oz packages of frozen corn, thawed
2 cups small baby carrots
4 green onions, sliced
2 small red bell peppers, diced, optional
One 1.6 oz package Knorr Garlic and Herb
    Sauce mix
1½ cups fat-free half and half (or light)
3 cups broccoli flowerets
Buttered bread crumbs

- *Combine all ingredients except the broccoli in a slow cooker.*
- *Cook on high for 1 hour.*
- *Stir in broccoli and cook another hour.*
- *Transfer to a serving bowl.*
- *Sprinkle with buttered bread crumbs.*
- *Serve immediately.*

SWEET & SOUR WINTER VEGGIES

This recipe comes from Margie Wilson of Paradise, California.

1 cup sweet potato
1 cup rutabaga
1 cup turnips
1 cup parsnips
2 Tbsp extra virgin olive oil
2 Tbsp chopped fresh rosemary
Salt and freshly ground black pepper to taste
2 Tbsp maple syrup
2 Tbsp balsamic vinegar
1/4 cup chicken or vegetable broth

- *Preheat oven to 400°.*
- *Peel and dice the vegetables.*
- *Toss the vegetables with the olive oil, rosemary, salt and pepper.*
- *Spread on a cookie sheet, sprayed with vegetable spray.*
- *Bake for 40 minutes, stirring a few times.*
- *In the meantime, combine in a small saucepan the maple syrup, balsamic vinegar and broth.*
- *Simmer until reduced and thickened, about 10 minutes.*
- *Drizzle over vegetables in the oven and continue to bake another 5 minutes.*
- *Remove from pan and put in a serving bowl.*

189

NOTE

If you double the recipe, reduce the rosemary as it gets too strong.

PICKLED BEETS

Thanksgiving would not be complete without my mother's pickled beets. Can you believe a ten year-old boy would ask for these for his birthday and Christmas gifts? So, Jeff Carter got them!

3 cans of whole beets, drained
1/4 tsp salt
3 whole cloves
1 cup sugar
½ cup water
½ cup white vinegar

- *Drain canned beets and put them in hot, clean pint canning jars.*
- *Bring sugar, water and vinegar to a boil.*
- *Add the salt and the cloves.*
- *Pour boiling mixture over beets.*
- *Put canning rims and lids on and let stand at room temperature until cooled.*
- *Tighten lids and refrigerate for one week before serving.*

190

> ### NOTE
> If you happen to be shy a little liquid, use water to bring it up to 1/8 inch from the top of the jar.

Non-Edibles

BODY SCRUBS

These are fantastic gifts and as good as the most expensive name brand scrubs. Give a copy of the instructions with the gift which are: "Wet hands. Put one teaspoon of the scrub on your hands and rub together for twenty seconds. Then rinse and pat dry."

BROWN SUGAR SCRUB

1½ cups light brown sugar
1/2 cup grape seed oil
1 tsp glycerin
1/2 tsp cranberry seeds

- *Mix well and put in a tight container.*

WHITE SUGAR SCRUB

1½ cups white sugar
2/3 cup grape seed oil
1 tsp glycerin
6 drops of essential oil such as grapefruit, lavender, apricot, vanilla, etc.

- *Mix well and put in an airtight container.*
- *Optional Recipe: If you have tougher skin, you can substitute kosher salt for the sugar which will make it more abrasive. Your skin type will decide.*

193

OTHER NON-EDIBLES

PLAY DOUGH

This is much better and less expensive that the commercial Play Dough. It makes a large batch.

2 cups flour
2 cups water
1/2 cup salt
2 Tbsp oil
2 tsp cream of tartar
Food coloring, only a few drops

- *Mix all ingredients together in a large pan.*
- *Cook on medium heat, stirring until it forms into a large ball.*
- *Remove from heat and let cool.*

NOTE
This cooks up all of a sudden so watch it carefully or you won't be able to stir it all together.

FLUBBER RUBBER

Karen Christoffersen of Salt Lake City highly recommends this play putty for kids. It is safe, not messy and a lot of fun. Add a tiny bit of food coloring.

Dissolve together and mix well:

2 tsp white glue (such as Elmer's)
1 tsp water

Mix together:

7/8 cup water
2 tsp Borax

- *Add 2 tsp of the Borax mixture to the glue mixture.*
- *Stir for 5 minutes and put on a piece off wax paper to set.*
- *Squeeze and play to your heart's content!*

INDEX

202

204